THE DARKNESS

ACCURSED
VOLUME 5

WRITTEN BY:
PHIL HESTER
&
JOSHUA HALE FIALKOV

THE DARKNESS CREATED BY:
MARC SILVESTRI, GARTH ENNIS
AND DAVID WOHL

published by
Top Cow Productions, Inc.
Los Angeles

The Darkness® Accursed Volume 5

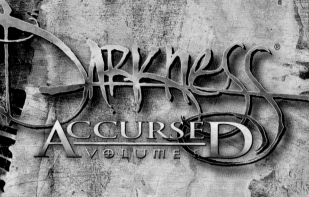

writers: **Phil Hester & Joshua Hale Fialkov**
pencilers: **Sheldon Mitchell & Romano Molenaar**
inkers: **Joe Weems, Ryan Winn, Rick Basaldua, Sal Regla, & Jason Gorder**
colors: **Arif Prianto** of IFS **& Michael Atiyeh**
letters: **Troy Peteri**

Jackie's caption font by David Lanphear

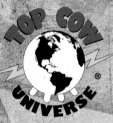

for Top Cow Productions Inc.
Marc Silvestri - CEO
Matt Hawkins - President and COO
Filip Sablik - Publisher
Bryan Rountree – Assistant to Publisher
Elena Salcedo – Sales Assistant

IMAGE COMICS, INC.
Robert Kirkman - chief operating officer
Erik Larsen - chief financial officer
Todd McFarlane - president
Marc Silvestri - chief executive officer
Jim Valentino - vice-president

Eric Stephenson - publisher
Todd Martinez - sales & licensing coordinator
Sarah deLaine - pr & marketing coordinator
Branwyn Bigglestone - accounts manager
Emily Miller - administrative assistant
Jamie Parreno - marketing assistant
Kevin Yuen - digital rights coordinator
Tyler Shainline - production manager
Drew Gill - art director
Jonathan Chan - senior production artist
Monica Garcia - production artist
Vincent Kukua - production artist
Jana Cook - production artist
www.imagecomics.com

to find the comic shop nearest you call:
1-888-COMICBOOK

Want more info? check out:
www.topcow.com and ***www.topcowstore.com***
for news and exclusive Top Cow merchandise!

For this edition Cover art by:
Michael Broussard, Steve Firchow

For this edition Book Design and Layout by:
Phil Smith

Original editions edited by:
Filip Sablik & Phil Smith

The Darkness: Accursed **Volume 5 Trade Paperback**
November 2011. FIRST PRINTING. Direct Market Edition. ISBN: 978-1-60706-080-2
Published by Image Comics Inc. Office of Publication: 2134 Allston Way, Second Floor Berkeley, CA 94704. $16.99 U.S.D. Originally published in single magazine form as **THE DARKNESS #85-89**.
Printed in the U.S.A. For information regarding the CPSIA on this printed [illegible]3-595-3636 and provide reference # EAST – 388933

TABLE OF CONTENTS

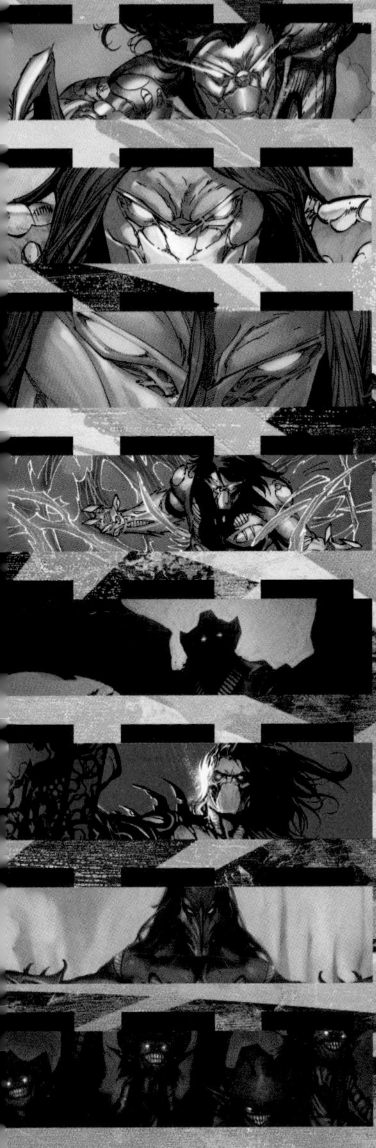

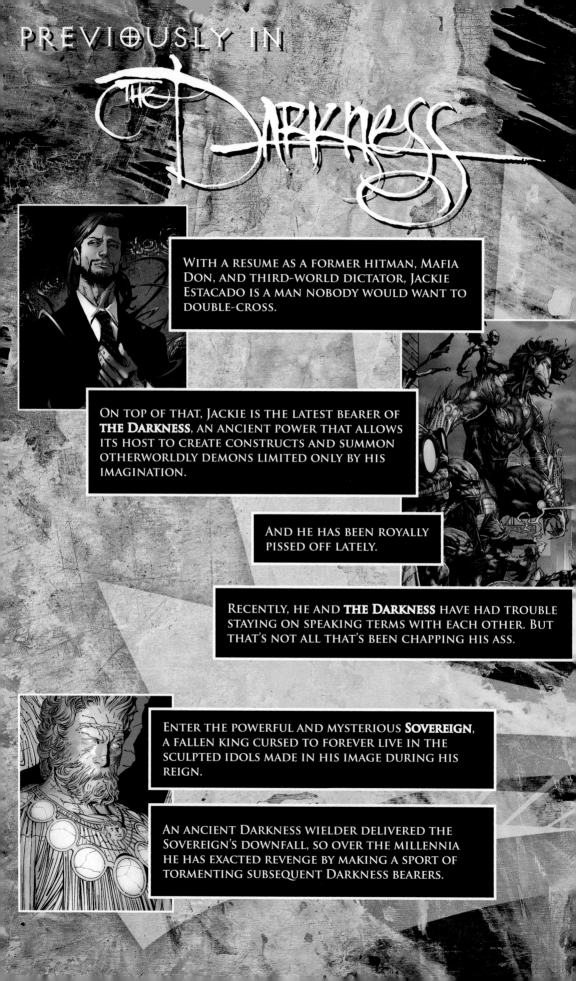

PREVIOUSLY IN THE DARKNESS

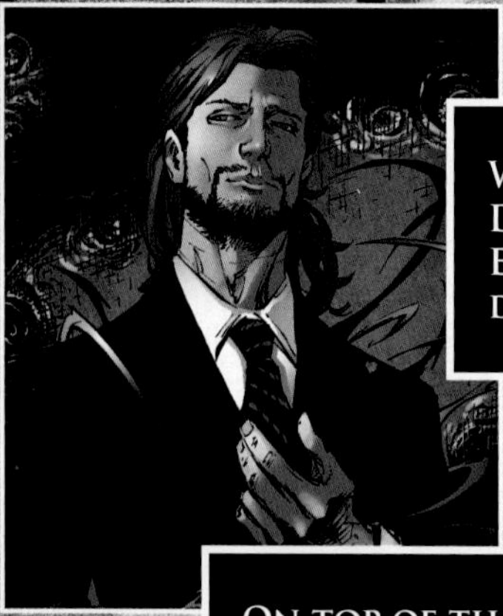

WITH A RESUME AS A FORMER HITMAN, MAFIA DON, AND THIRD-WORLD DICTATOR, JACKIE ESTACADO IS A MAN NOBODY WOULD WANT TO DOUBLE-CROSS.

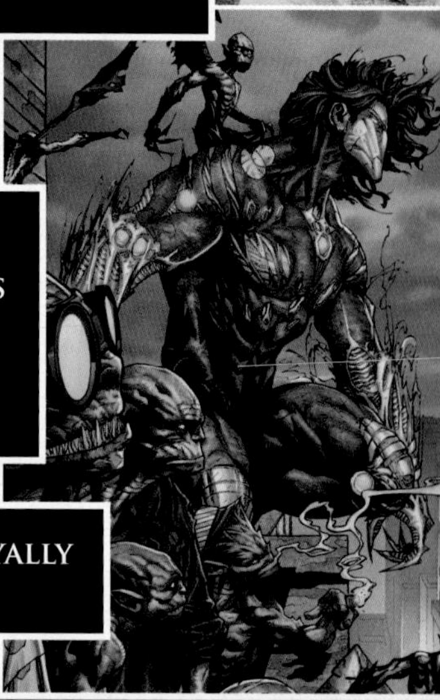

ON TOP OF THAT, JACKIE IS THE LATEST BEARER OF **THE DARKNESS**, AN ANCIENT POWER THAT ALLOWS ITS HOST TO CREATE CONSTRUCTS AND SUMMON OTHERWORLDLY DEMONS LIMITED ONLY BY HIS IMAGINATION.

AND HE HAS BEEN ROYALLY PISSED OFF LATELY.

RECENTLY, HE AND **THE DARKNESS** HAVE HAD TROUBLE STAYING ON SPEAKING TERMS WITH EACH OTHER. BUT THAT'S NOT ALL THAT'S BEEN CHAPPING HIS ASS.

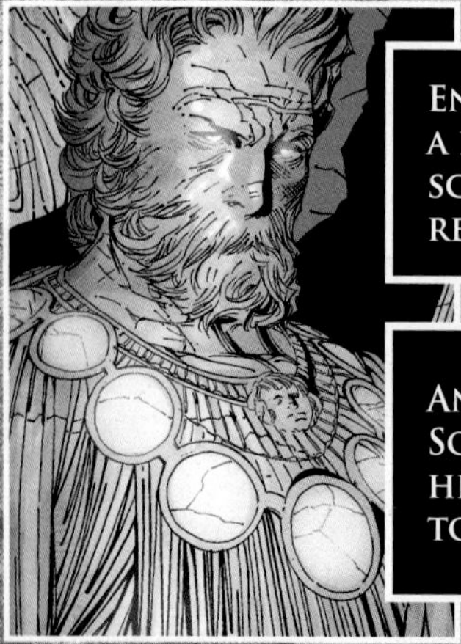

ENTER THE POWERFUL AND MYSTERIOUS **SOVEREIGN**, A FALLEN KING CURSED TO FOREVER LIVE IN THE SCULPTED IDOLS MADE IN HIS IMAGE DURING HIS REIGN.

AN ANCIENT DARKNESS WIELDER DELIVERED THE SOVEREIGN'S DOWNFALL, SO OVER THE MILLENNIA HE HAS EXACTED REVENGE BY MAKING A SPORT OF TORMENTING SUBSEQUENT DARKNESS BEARERS.

And thus Jackie found himself at the shit-end of the stick.

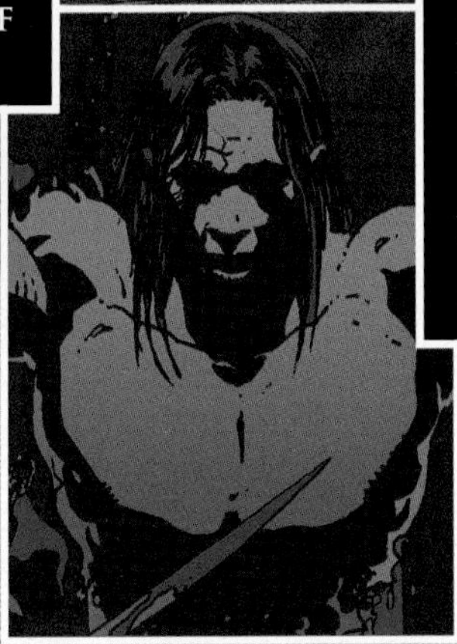

Tricked into believing his body and soul were separated, the Sovereign deployed Jackie as his "bag boy" to settle old scores and bad debts with others who had betrayed the Sovereign.

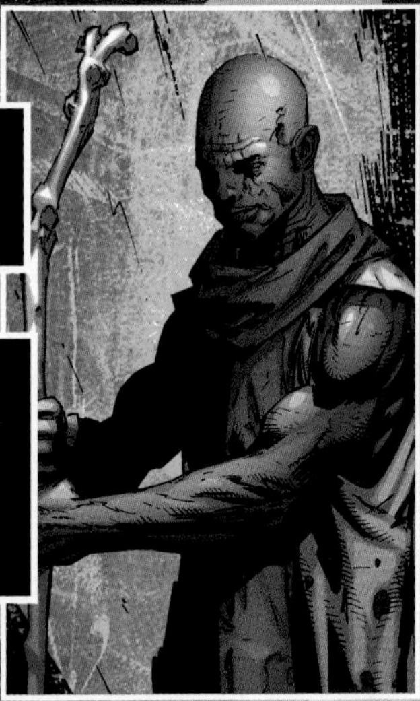

On one of these errands, a shadowy figure claiming to have been a former wielder of the Darkness approached Jackie.

Known only as **the Foreigner**, the strange man bonked Jackie on the head with his walking stick and in a wise voice spoke, ***"If you do not control the Darkness, the Darkness will control you."***

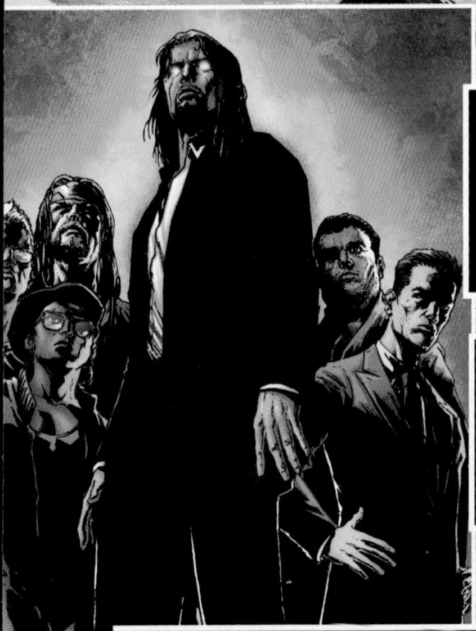

With his full powers back in order, Jackie gathered a motley crew of thieves, smugglers, and weapons specialists to track down and destroy each and every one of the Sovereign's host bodies.

And he promised each one of them two millions bucks to do it, too.

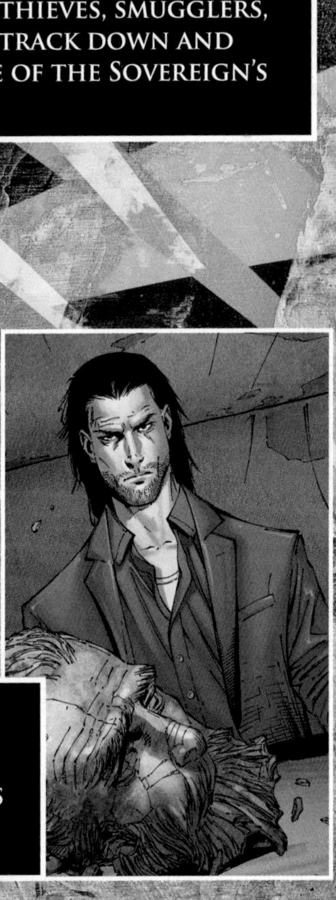

Their quest to eradicate that stony bastard has taken them all over Europe, to the Florida Everglades, and even Fort Knox.

With no end in sight to his mission and the Foreigner's words that one can conquer and rid himself of the Darkness ringing inside his head, Jackie is left to wonder, ***"What's next?"***

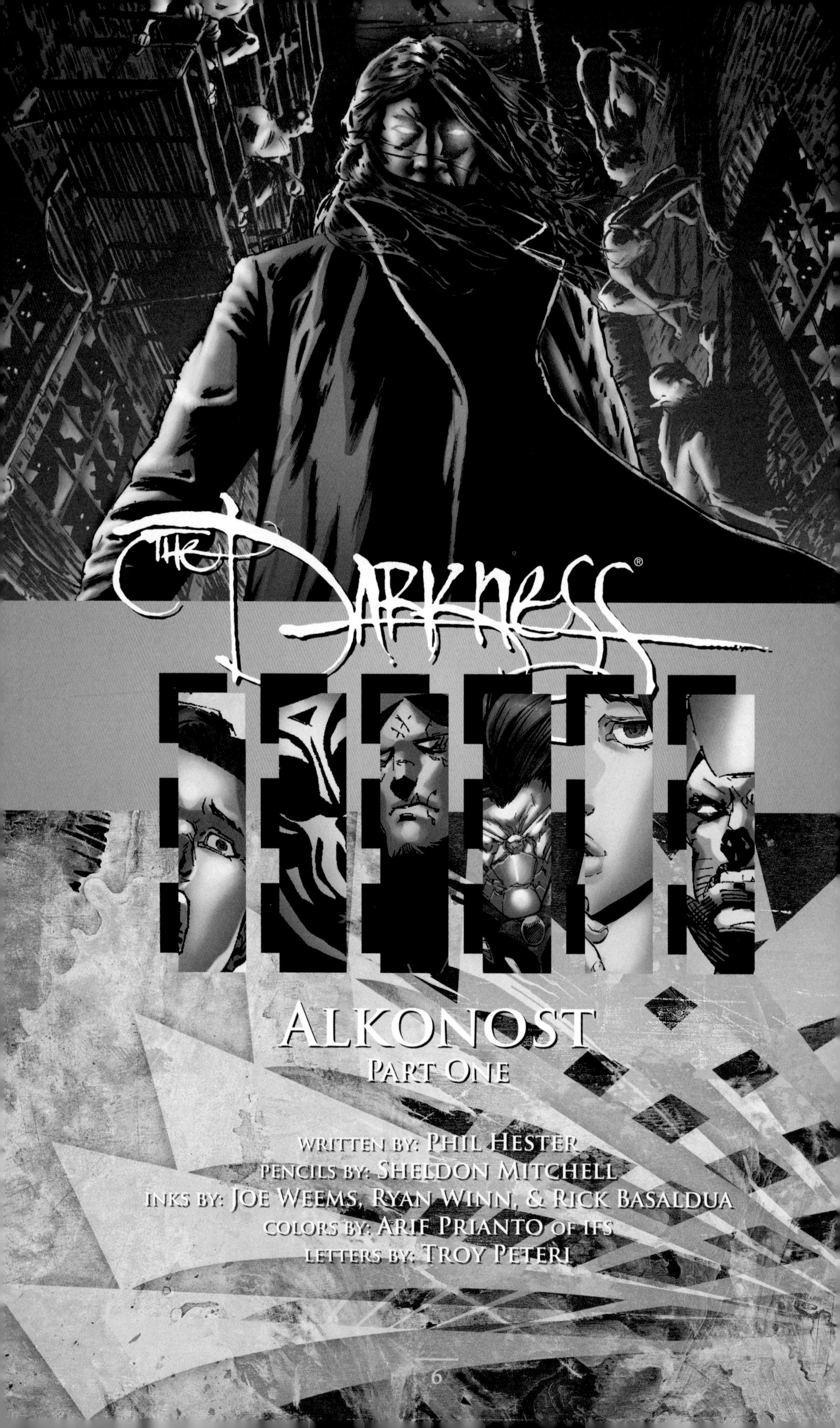

The Darkness®

Alkonost

Part One

written by: Phil Hester
pencils by: Sheldon Mitchell
inks by: Joe Weems, Ryan Winn, & Rick Basaldua
colors by: Arif Prianto of IFS
letters by: Troy Peteri

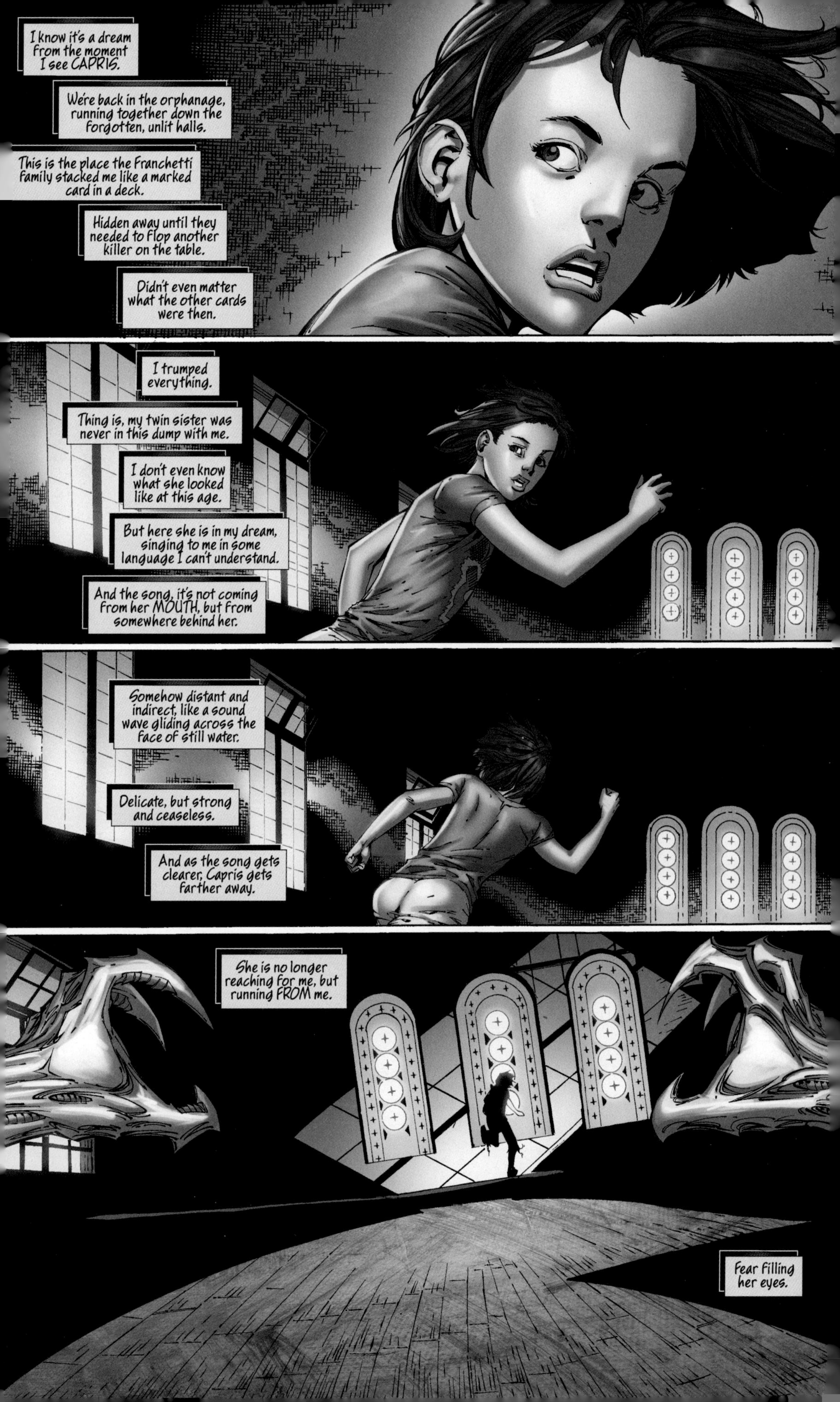
I know it's a dream from the moment I see CAPRIS.
We're back in the orphanage, running together down the forgotten, unlit halls.
This is the place the Franchetti family stacked me like a marked card in a deck.
Hidden away until they needed to flop another killer on the table.
Didn't even matter what the other cards were then.
I trumped everything.
Thing is, my twin sister was never in this dump with me.
I don't even know what she looked like at this age.
But here she is in my dream, singing to me in some language I can't understand.
And the song, it's not coming from her MOUTH, but from somewhere behind her.
Somehow distant and indirect, like a sound wave gliding across the face of still water.
Delicate, but strong and ceaseless.
And as the song gets clearer, Capris gets farther away.
She is no longer reaching for me, but running FROM me.
Fear filling her eyes.

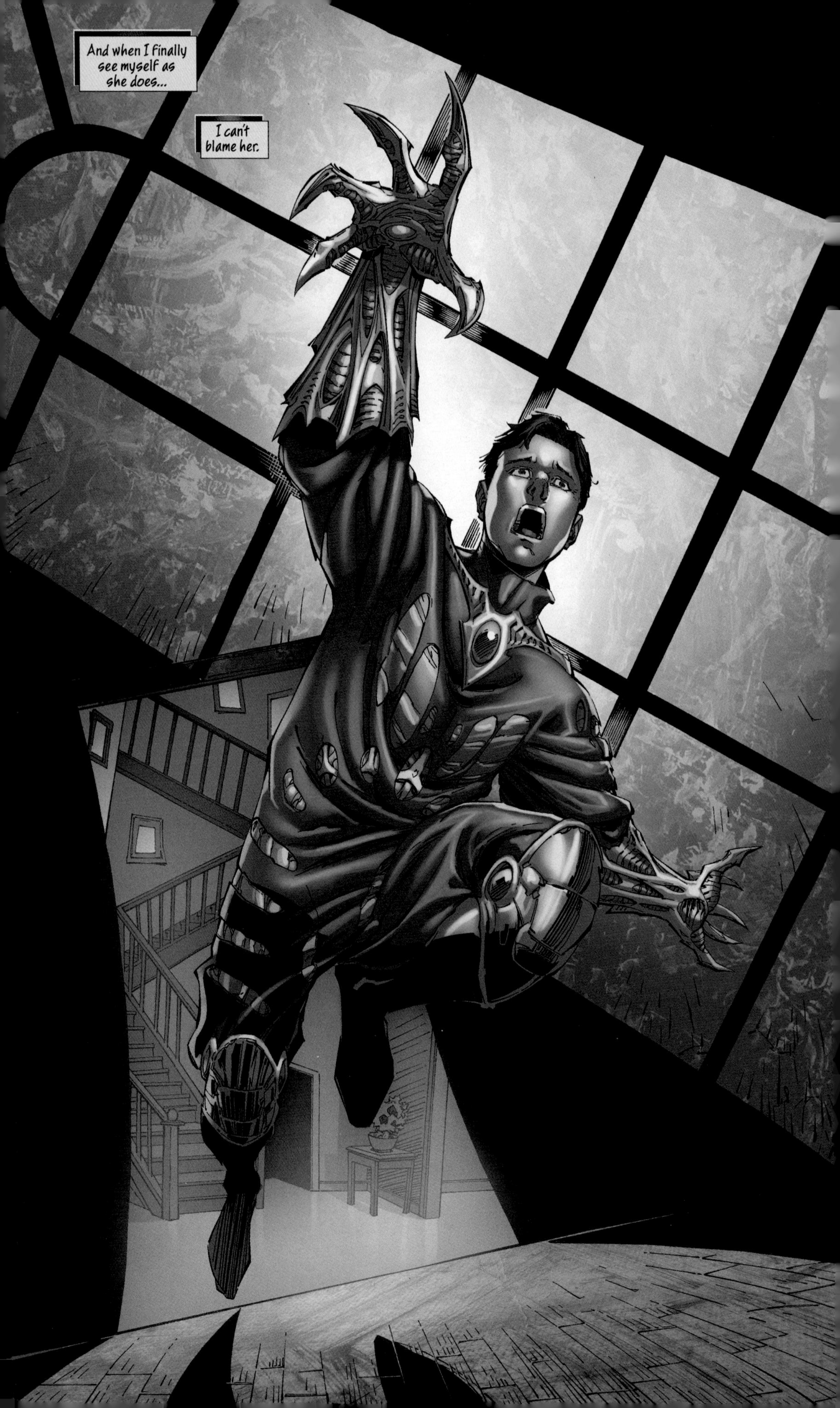
And when I finally see myself as she does...
I can't blame her.

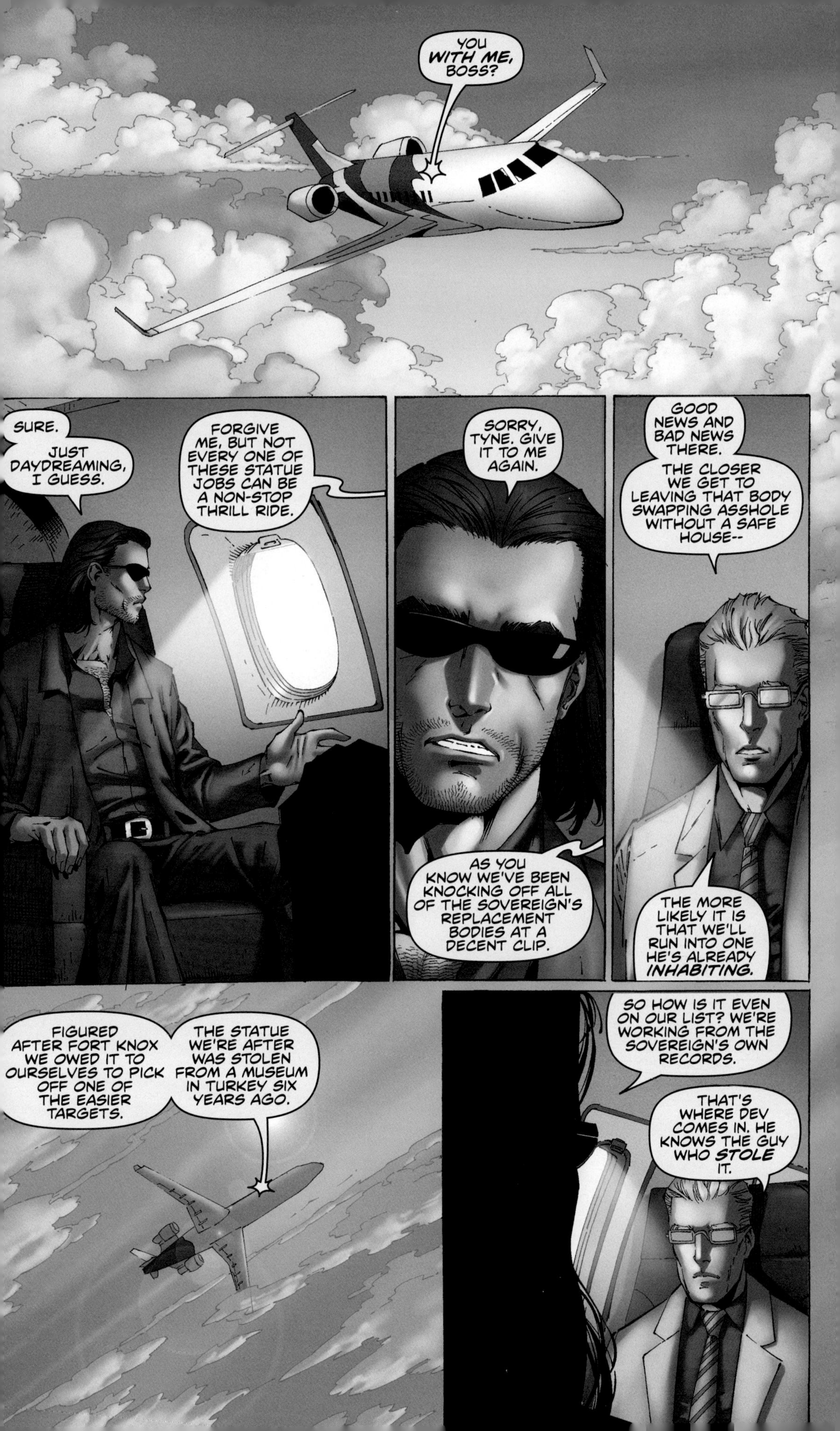
YOU WITH ME, BOSS?
SURE.
JUST DAYDREAMING, I GUESS.
FORGIVE ME, BUT NOT EVERY ONE OF THESE STATUE JOBS CAN BE A NON-STOP THRILL RIDE.
SORRY, TYNE. GIVE IT TO ME AGAIN.
AS YOU KNOW WE'VE BEEN KNOCKING OFF ALL OF THE SOVEREIGN'S REPLACEMENT BODIES AT A DECENT CLIP.
GOOD NEWS AND BAD NEWS THERE.
THE CLOSER WE GET TO LEAVING THAT BODY SWAPPING ASSHOLE WITHOUT A SAFE HOUSE--
THE MORE LIKELY IT IS THAT WE'LL RUN INTO ONE HE'S ALREADY INHABITING.
FIGURED AFTER FORT KNOX WE OWED IT TO OURSELVES TO PICK OFF ONE OF THE EASIER TARGETS.
THE STATUE WE'RE AFTER WAS STOLEN FROM A MUSEUM IN TURKEY SIX YEARS AGO.
SO HOW IS IT EVEN ON OUR LIST? WE'RE WORKING FROM THE SOVEREIGN'S OWN RECORDS.
THAT'S WHERE DEV COMES IN. HE KNOWS THE GUY WHO STOLE IT.

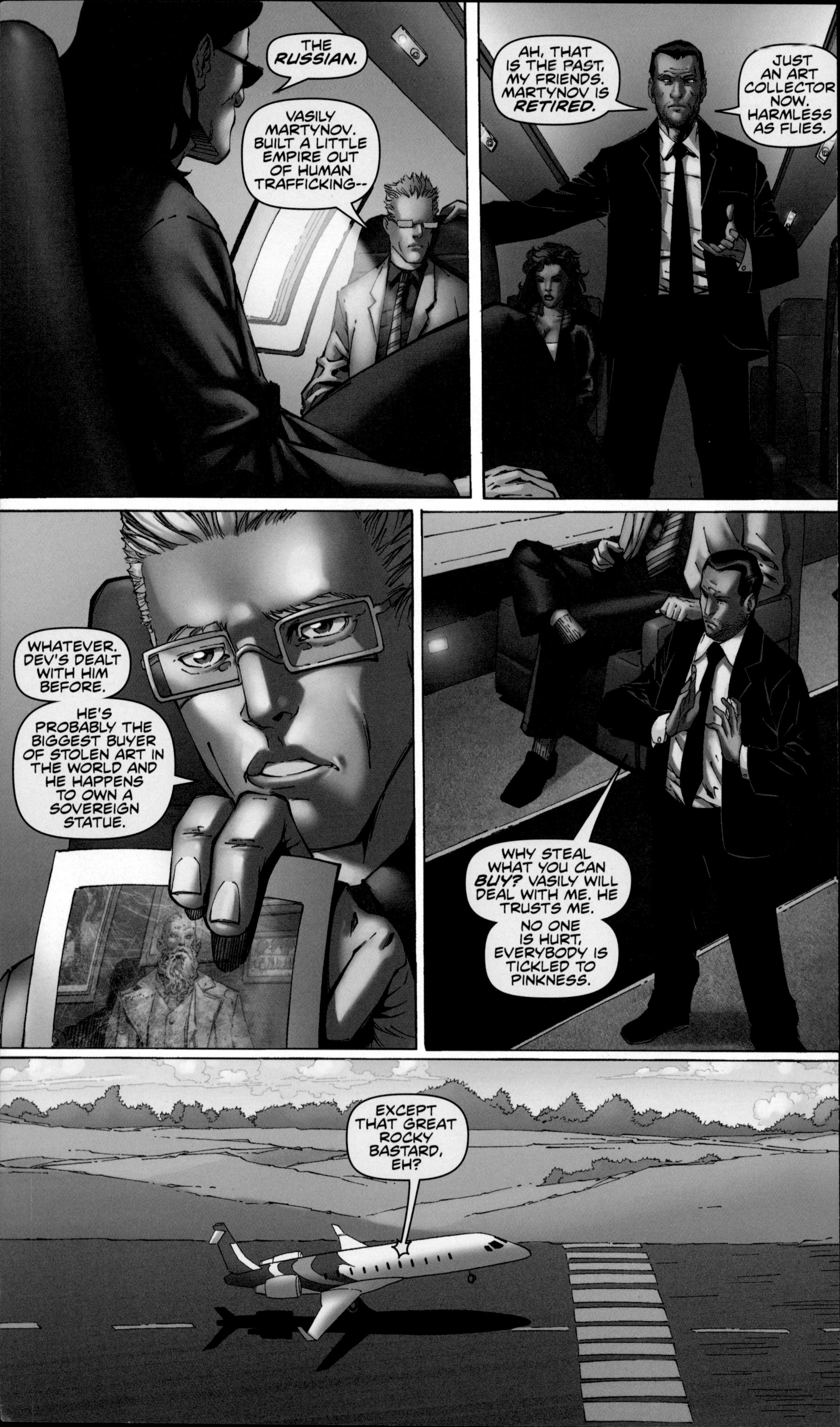
THE RUSSIAN.
VASILY MARTYNOV. BUILT A LITTLE EMPIRE OUT OF HUMAN TRAFFICKING--
AH, THAT IS THE PAST, MY FRIENDS. MARTYNOV IS RETIRED.
JUST AN ART COLLECTOR NOW. HARMLESS AS FLIES.
WHATEVER. DEV'S DEALT WITH HIM BEFORE.
HE'S PROBABLY THE BIGGEST BUYER OF STOLEN ART IN THE WORLD AND HE HAPPENS TO OWN A SOVEREIGN STATUE.
WHY STEAL WHAT YOU CAN BUY? VASILY WILL DEAL WITH ME. HE TRUSTS ME.
NO ONE IS HURT, EVERYBODY IS TICKLED TO PINKNESS.
EXCEPT THAT GREAT ROCKY BASTARD, EH?

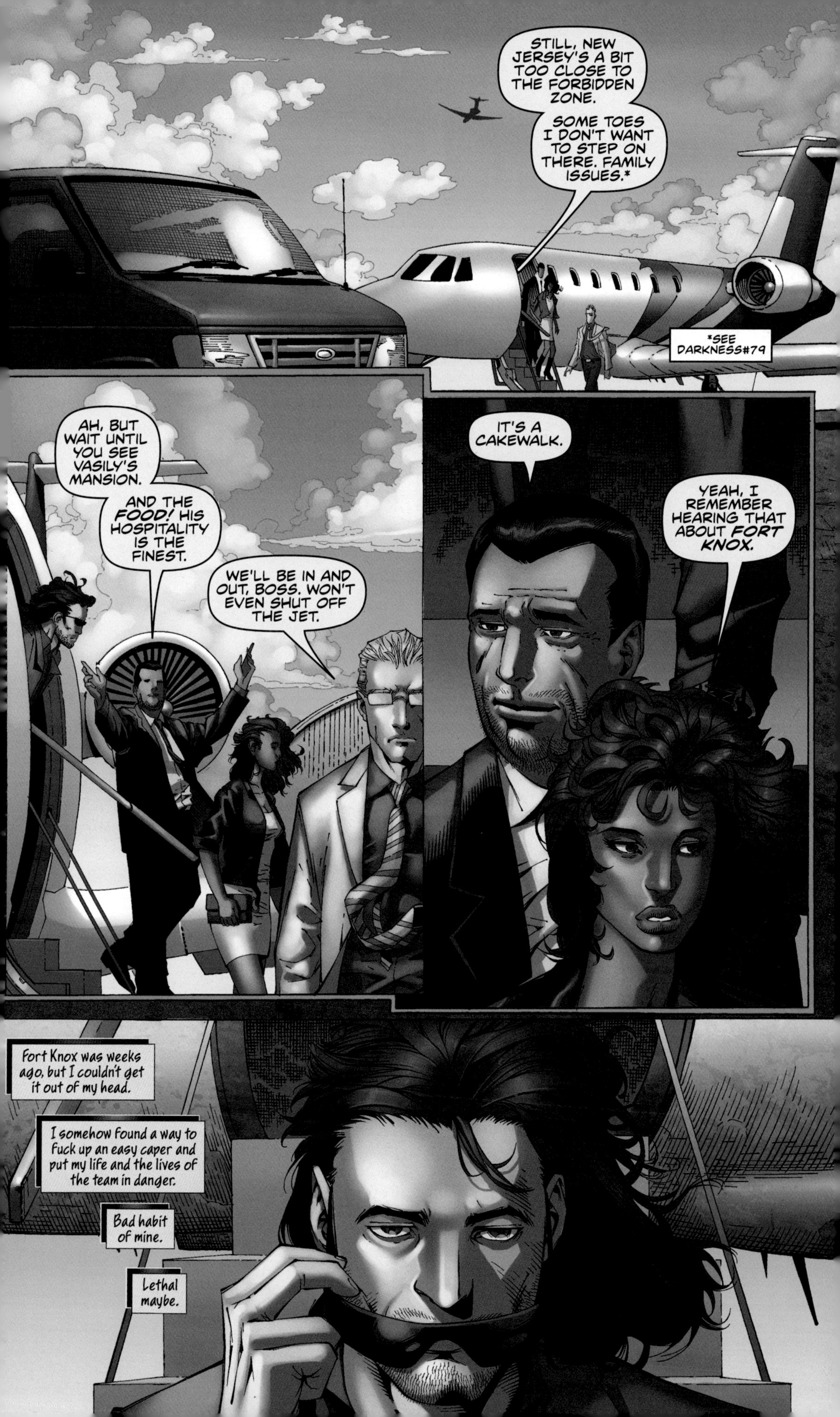
STILL, NEW JERSEY'S A BIT TOO CLOSE TO THE FORBIDDEN ZONE.
SOME TOES I DON'T WANT TO STEP ON THERE. FAMILY ISSUES.*
*SEE DARKNESS#79
AH, BUT WAIT UNTIL YOU SEE VASILY'S MANSION.
AND THE *FOOD!* HIS HOSPITALITY IS THE FINEST.
WE'LL BE IN AND OUT, BOSS. WON'T EVEN SHUT OFF THE JET.
IT'S A CAKEWALK.
YEAH, I REMEMBER HEARING THAT ABOUT *FORT KNOX.*
Fort Knox was weeks ago, but I couldn't get it out of my head.
I somehow found a way to fuck up an easy caper and put my life and the lives of the team in danger.
Bad habit of mine.
Lethal maybe.

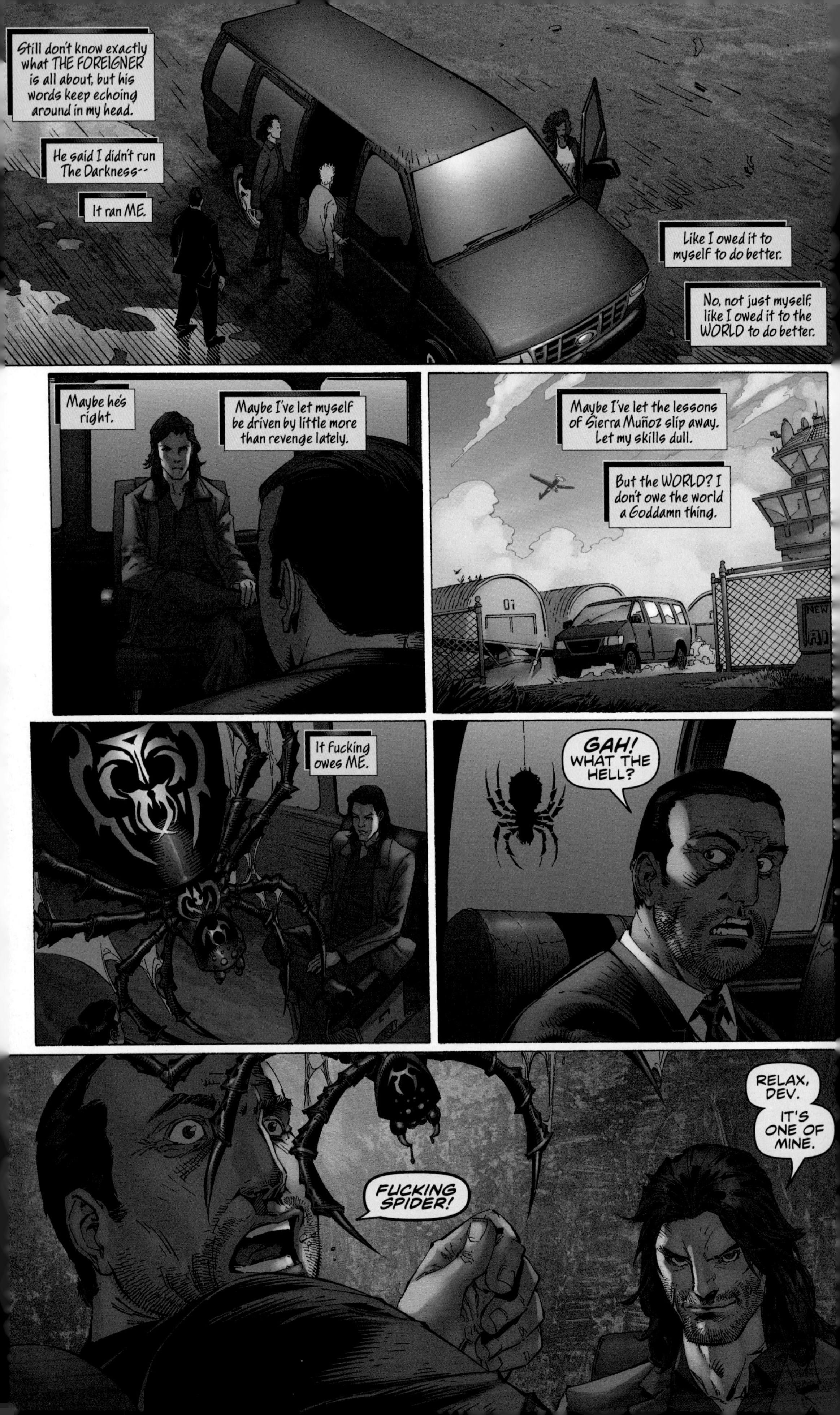

Still don't know exactly what THE FOREIGNER is all about, but his words keep echoing around in my head.
He said I didn't run The Darkness--
It ran ME.
Like I owed it to myself to do better.
No, not just myself, like I owed it to the WORLD to do better.
Maybe he's right.
Maybe I've let myself be driven by little more than revenge lately.
Maybe I've let the lessons of Sierra Muñoz slip away. Let my skills dull.
But the WORLD? I don't owe the world a Goddamn thing.
It fucking owes ME.
GAH! WHAT THE HELL?
RELAX, DEV.
IT'S ONE OF MINE.
FUCKING SPIDER!

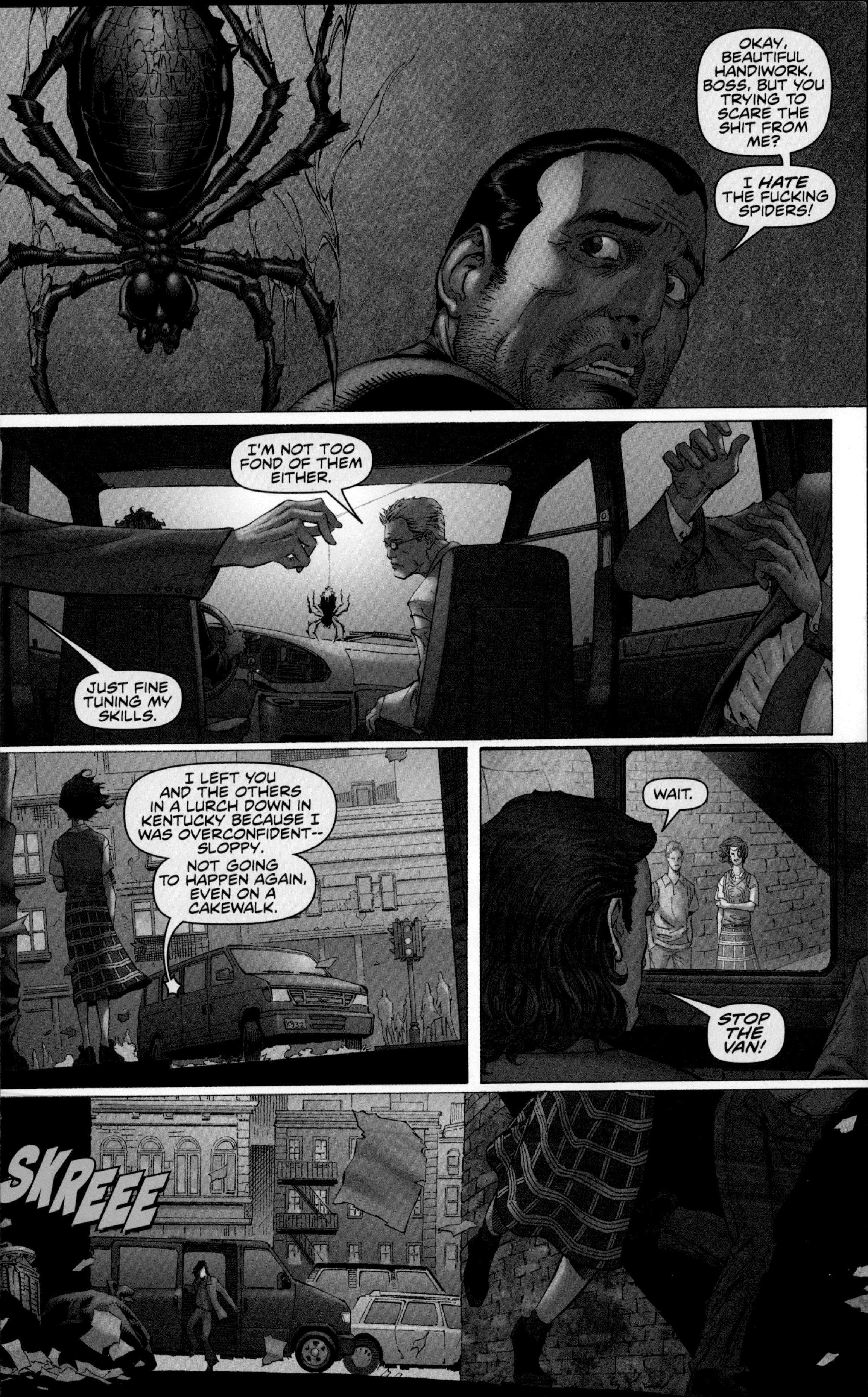
OKAY, BEAUTIFUL HANDIWORK, BOSS, BUT YOU TRYING TO SCARE THE SHIT FROM ME?
I HATE THE FUCKING SPIDERS!
I'M NOT TOO FOND OF THEM EITHER.
JUST FINE TUNING MY SKILLS.
I LEFT YOU AND THE OTHERS IN A LURCH DOWN IN KENTUCKY BECAUSE I WAS OVERCONFIDENT-- SLOPPY.
NOT GOING TO HAPPEN AGAIN, EVEN ON A CAKEWALK.
WAIT.
STOP THE VAN!
SKREEE

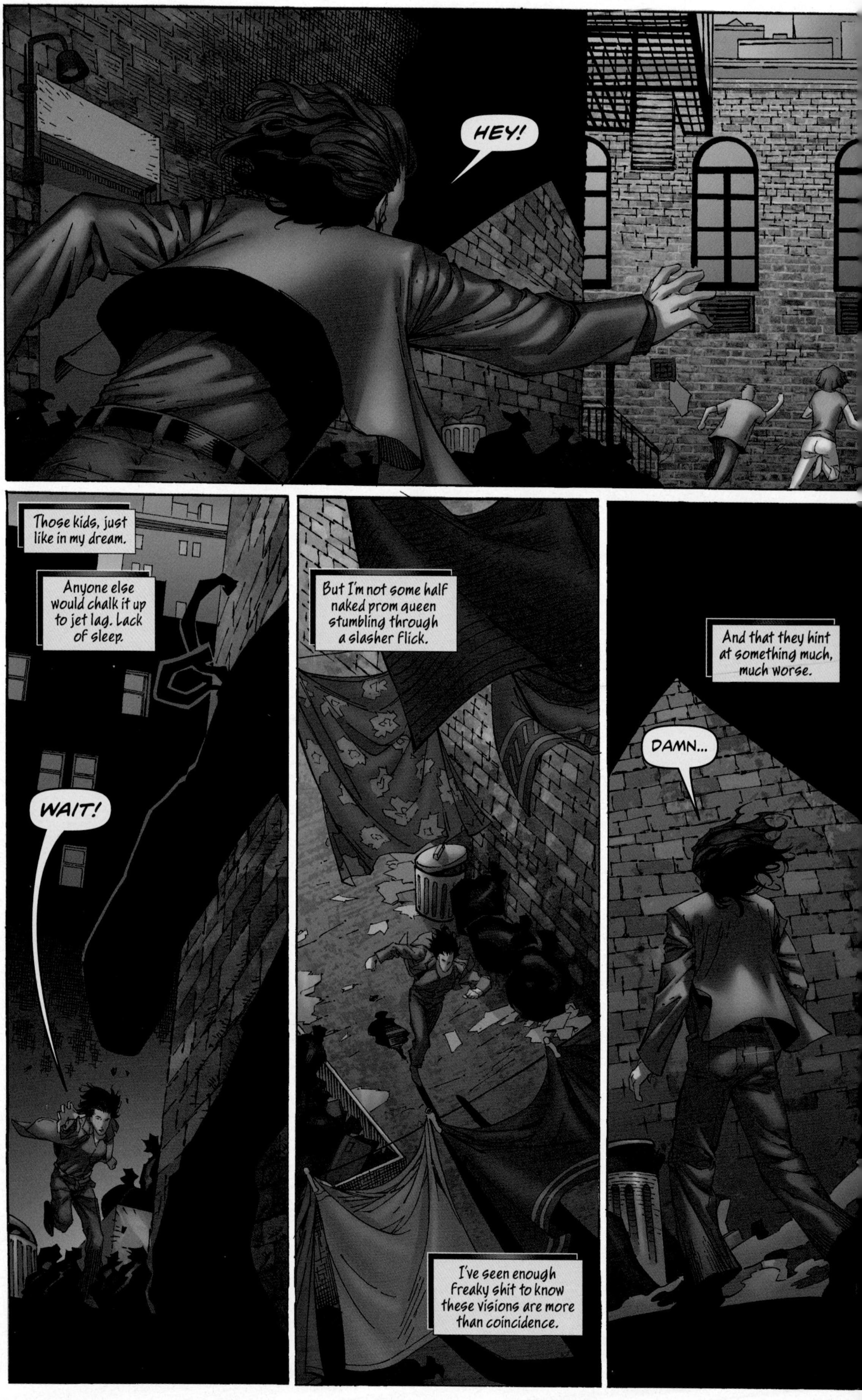
HEY!
Those kids, just like in my dream.
Anyone else would chalk it up to jet lag. Lack of sleep.
WAIT!
But I'm not some half naked prom queen stumbling through a slasher flick.
I've seen enough freaky shit to know these visions are more than coincidence.
And that they hint at something much, much worse.
DAMN...

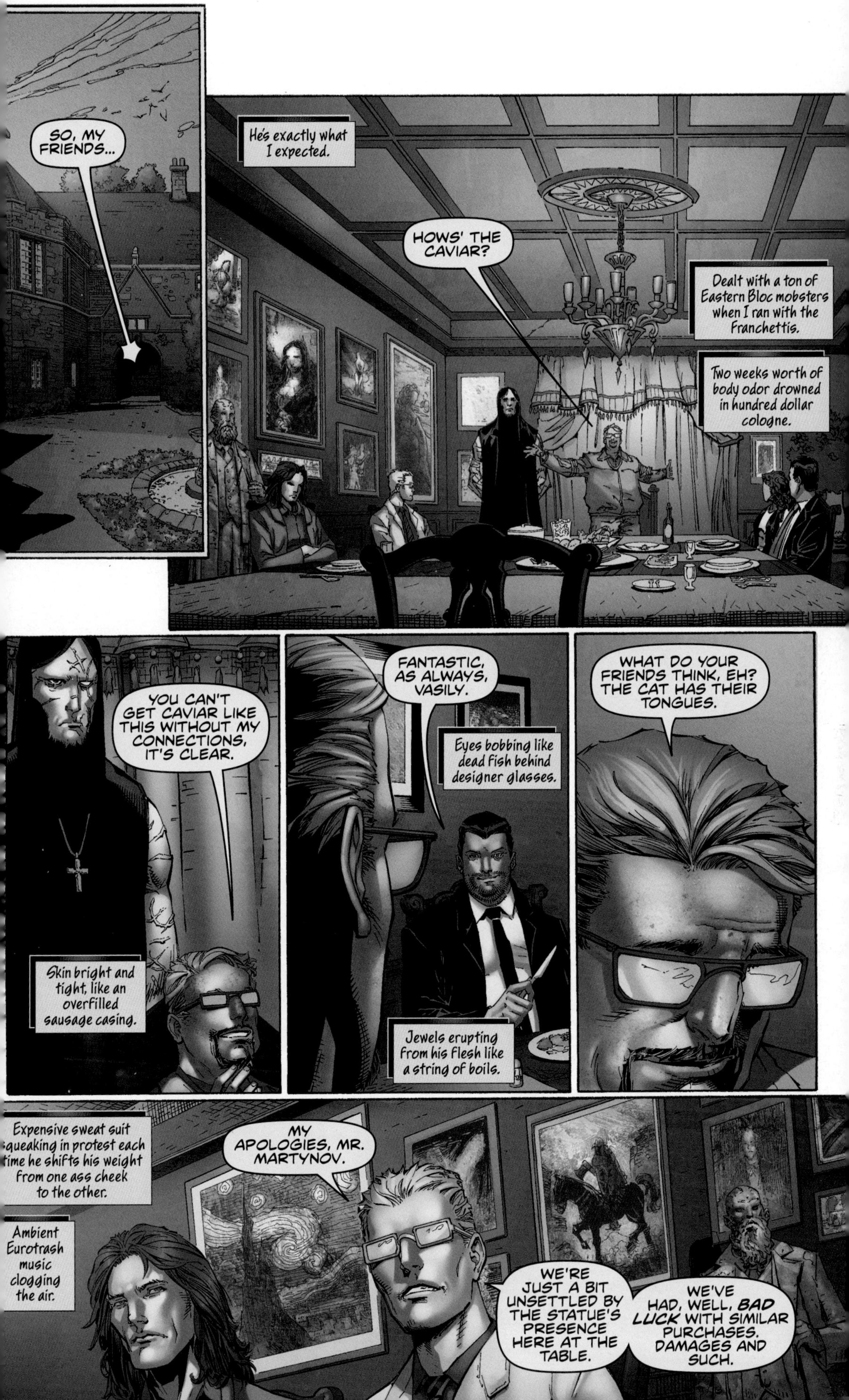
SO, MY FRIENDS...
He's exactly what I expected.
HOWS' THE CAVIAR?
Dealt with a ton of Eastern Bloc mobsters when I ran with the Franchettis.
Two weeks worth of body odor drowned in hundred dollar cologne.
YOU CAN'T GET CAVIAR LIKE THIS WITHOUT MY CONNECTIONS, IT'S CLEAR.
Skin bright and tight, like an overfilled sausage casing.
FANTASTIC, AS ALWAYS, VASILY.
Eyes bobbing like dead fish behind designer glasses.
Jewels erupting from his flesh like a string of boils.
WHAT DO YOUR FRIENDS THINK, EH? THE CAT HAS THEIR TONGUES.
Expensive sweat suit squeaking in protest each time he shifts his weight from one ass cheek to the other.
Ambient Eurotrash music clogging the air.
MY APOLOGIES, MR. MARTYNOV.
WE'RE JUST A BIT UNSETTLED BY THE STATUE'S PRESENCE HERE AT THE TABLE.
WE'VE HAD, WELL, BAD LUCK WITH SIMILAR PURCHASES. DAMAGES AND SUCH.

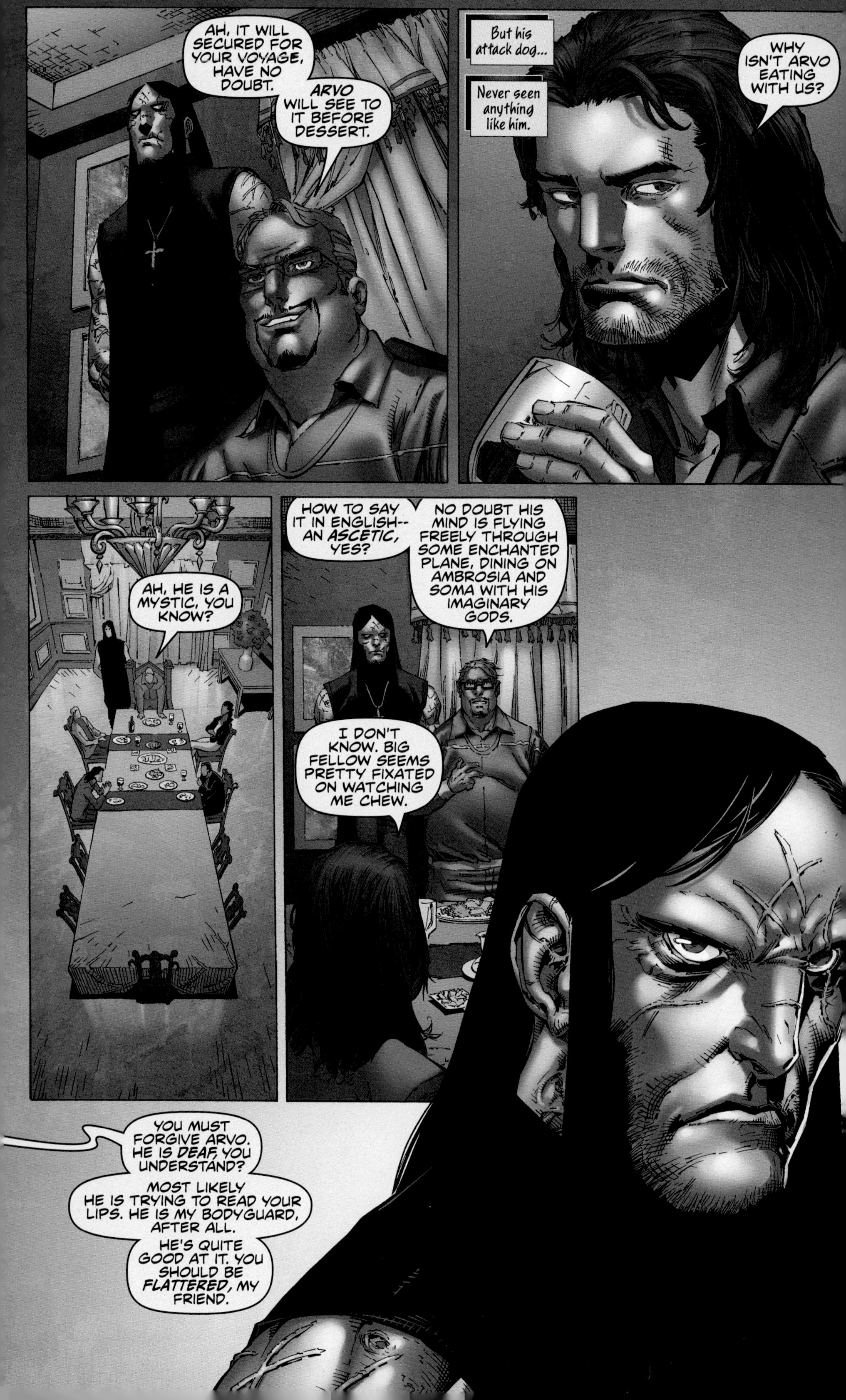
AH, IT WILL SECURED FOR YOUR VOYAGE, HAVE NO DOUBT.
ARVO WILL SEE TO IT BEFORE DESSERT.
But his attack dog...
Never seen anything like him.
WHY ISN'T ARVO EATING WITH US?
AH, HE IS A MYSTIC, YOU KNOW?
HOW TO SAY IT IN ENGLISH-- AN ASCETIC, YES?
NO DOUBT HIS MIND IS FLYING FREELY THROUGH SOME ENCHANTED PLANE, DINING ON AMBROSIA AND SOMA WITH HIS IMAGINARY GODS.
I DON'T KNOW. BIG FELLOW SEEMS PRETTY FIXATED ON WATCHING ME CHEW.
YOU MUST FORGIVE ARVO. HE IS DEAF, YOU UNDERSTAND?
MOST LIKELY HE IS TRYING TO READ YOUR LIPS. HE IS MY BODYGUARD, AFTER ALL.
HE'S QUITE GOOD AT IT. YOU SHOULD BE FLATTERED, MY FRIEND.

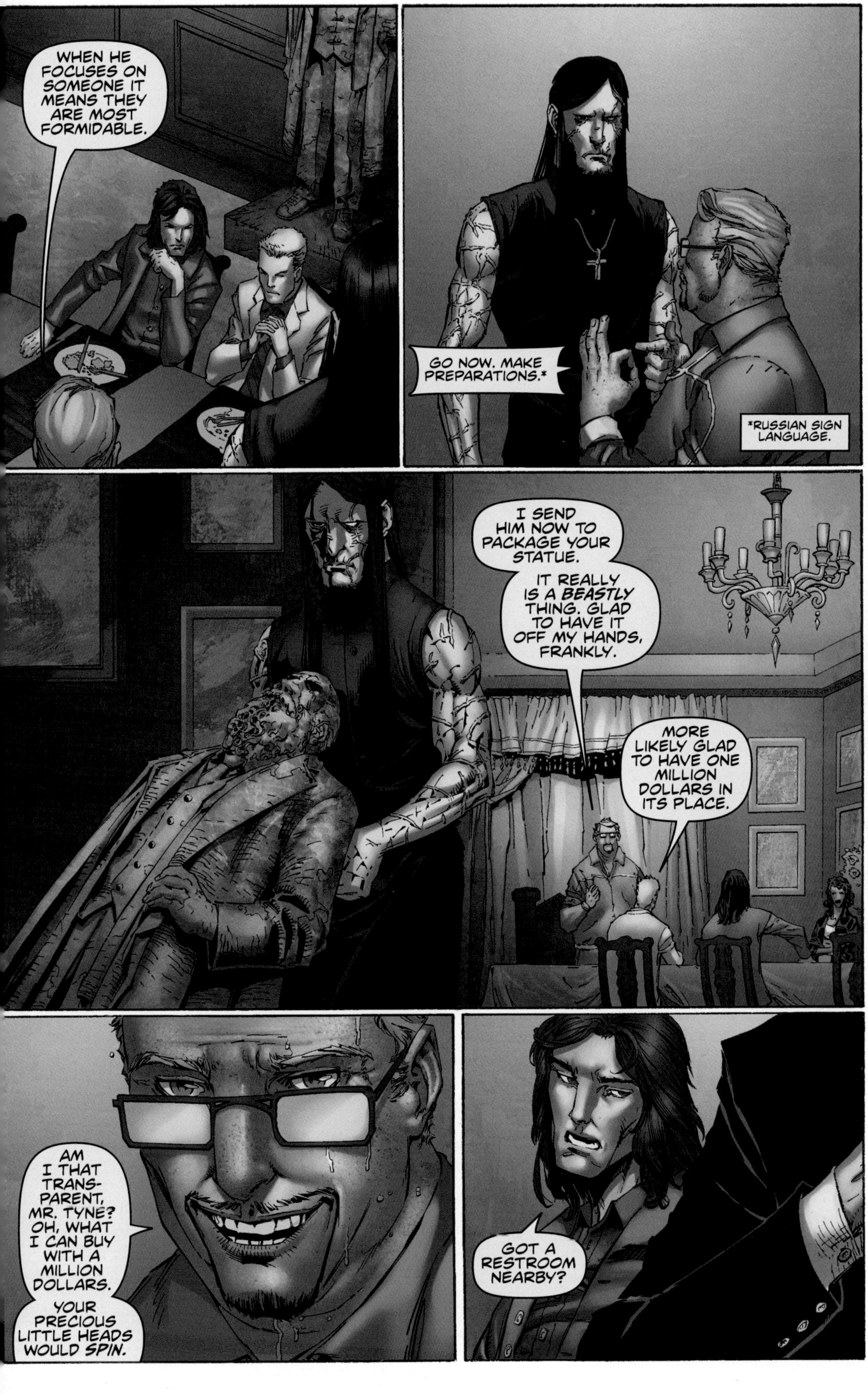
WHEN HE FOCUSES ON SOMEONE IT MEANS THEY ARE MOST FORMIDABLE.
GO NOW. MAKE PREPARATIONS.*
*RUSSIAN SIGN LANGUAGE.
I SEND HIM NOW TO PACKAGE YOUR STATUE.
IT REALLY IS A *BEASTLY* THING. GLAD TO HAVE IT OFF MY HANDS, FRANKLY.
MORE LIKELY GLAD TO HAVE ONE MILLION DOLLARS IN ITS PLACE.
AM I THAT TRANS-PARENT, MR. TYNE? OH, WHAT I CAN BUY WITH A MILLION DOLLARS.
YOUR PRECIOUS LITTLE HEADS WOULD *SPIN*.
GOT A RESTROOM NEARBY?

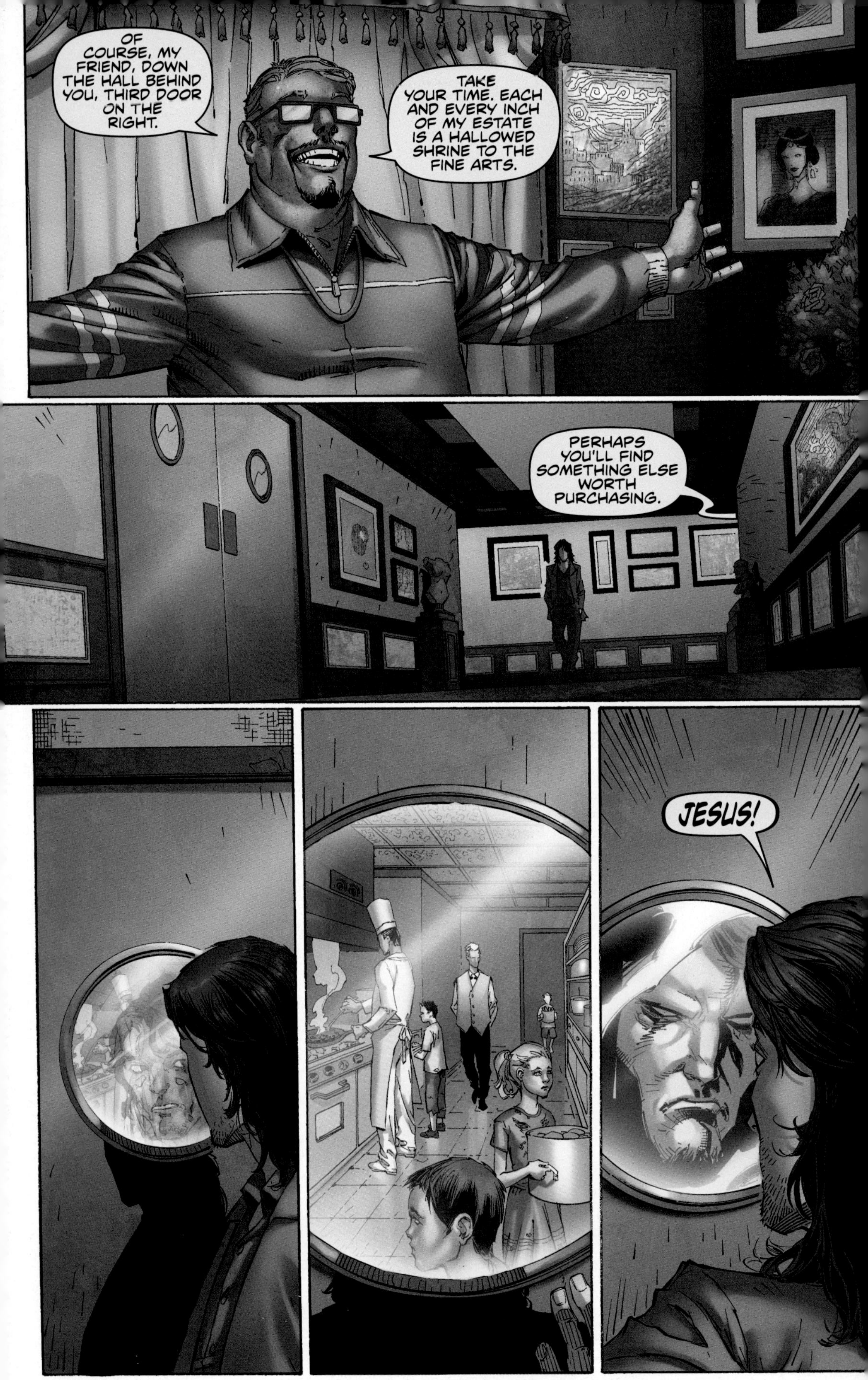
OF COURSE, MY FRIEND, DOWN THE HALL BEHIND YOU, THIRD DOOR ON THE RIGHT.
TAKE YOUR TIME. EACH AND EVERY INCH OF MY ESTATE IS A HALLOWED SHRINE TO THE FINE ARTS.
PERHAPS YOU'LL FIND SOMETHING ELSE WORTH PURCHASING.
JESUS!

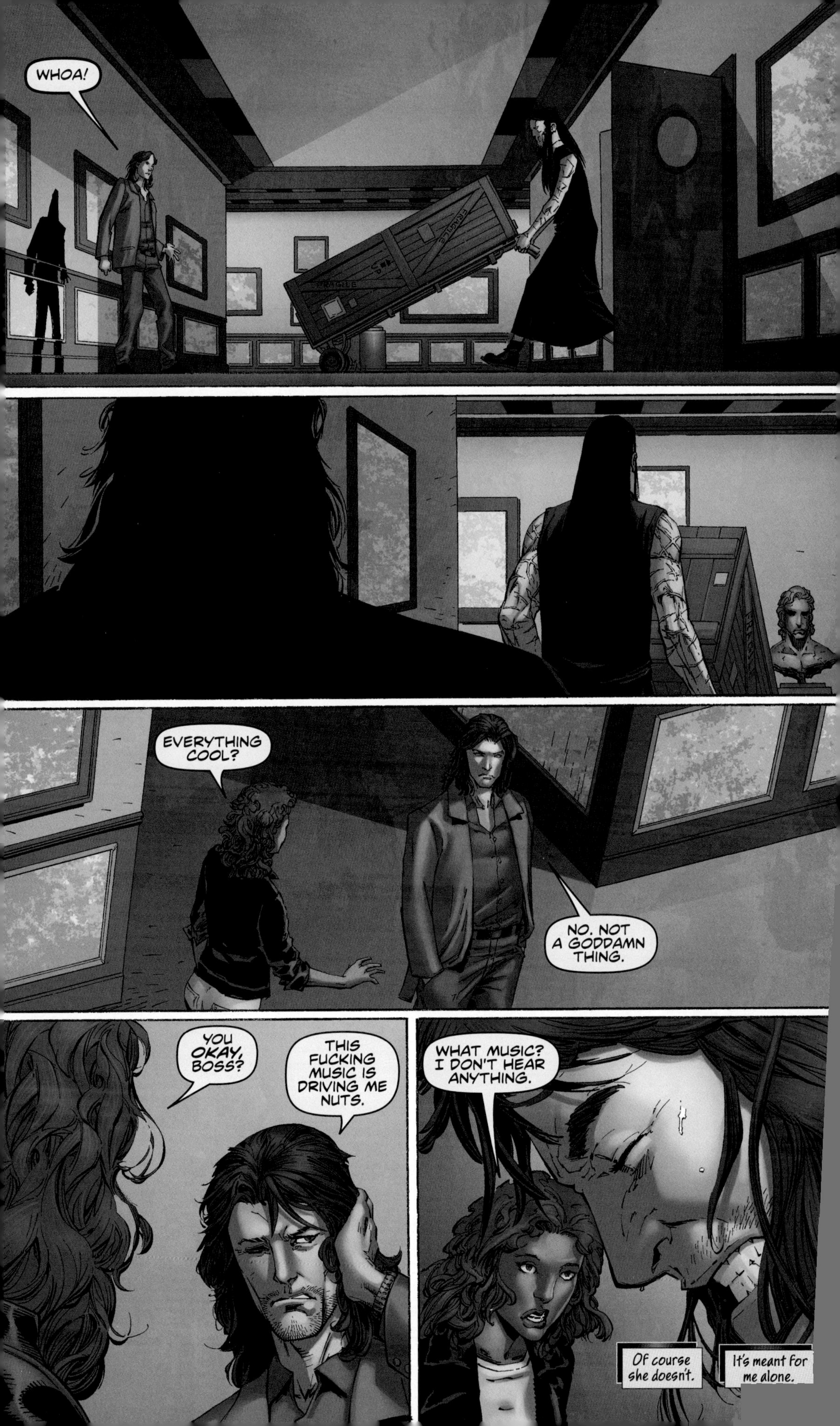
WHOA!
EVERYTHING COOL?
NO. NOT A GODDAMN THING.
YOU OKAY, BOSS?
THIS FUCKING MUSIC IS DRIVING ME NUTS.
WHAT MUSIC? I DON'T HEAR ANYTHING.
Of course she doesn't.
It's meant for me alone.

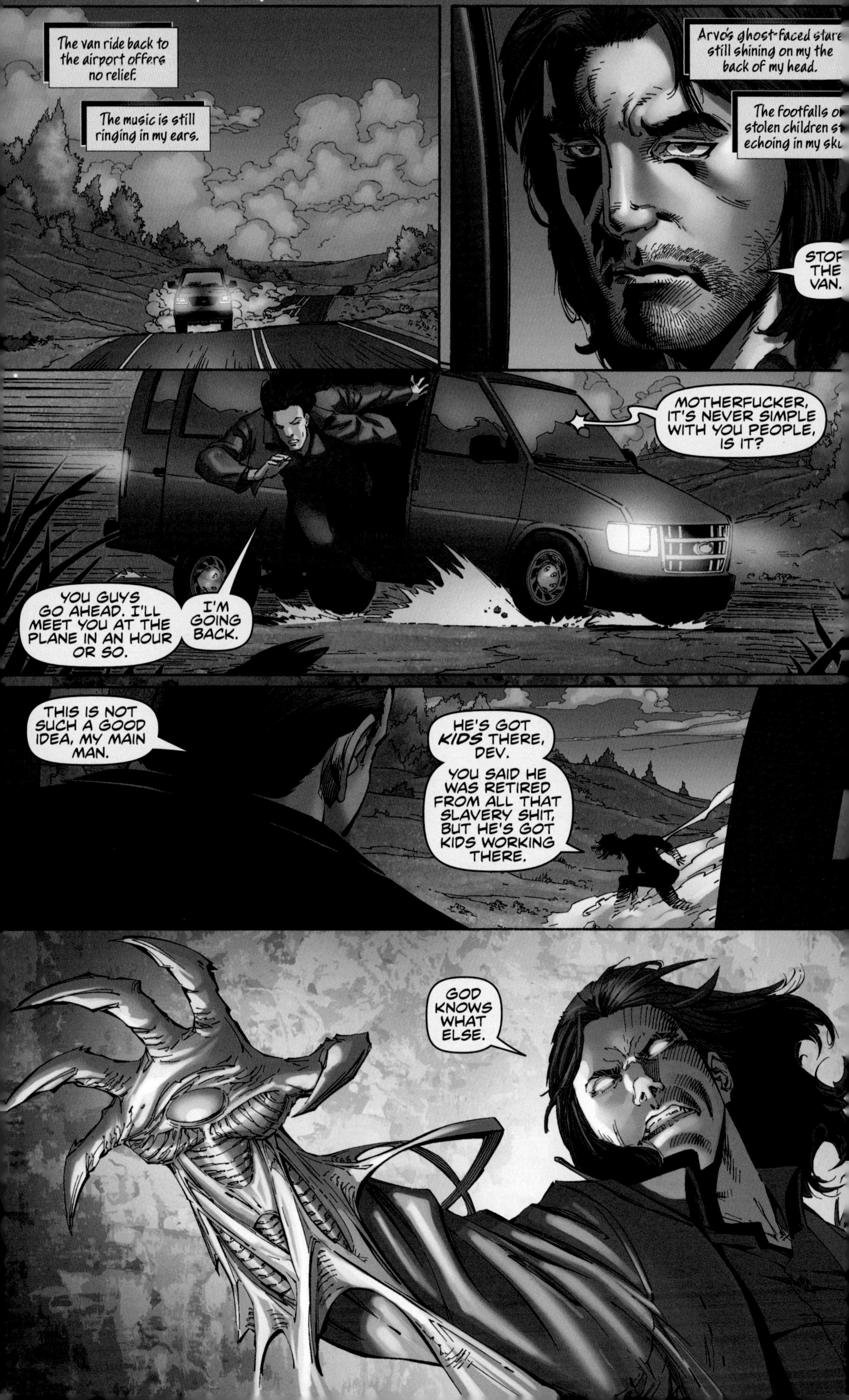

The van ride back to the airport offers no relief.
The music is still ringing in my ears.
Arvo's ghost-faced stare still shining on my the back of my head.
The footfalls o stolen children s echoing in my sk
STOP THE VAN.
MOTHERFUCKER, IT'S NEVER SIMPLE WITH YOU PEOPLE, IS IT?
YOU GUYS GO AHEAD. I'LL MEET YOU AT THE PLANE IN AN HOUR OR SO.
I'M GOING BACK.
THIS IS NOT SUCH A GOOD IDEA, MY MAIN MAN.
HE'S GOT KIDS THERE, DEV.
YOU SAID HE WAS RETIRED FROM ALL THAT SLAVERY SHIT, BUT HE'S GOT KIDS WORKING THERE.
GOD KNOWS WHAT ELSE.

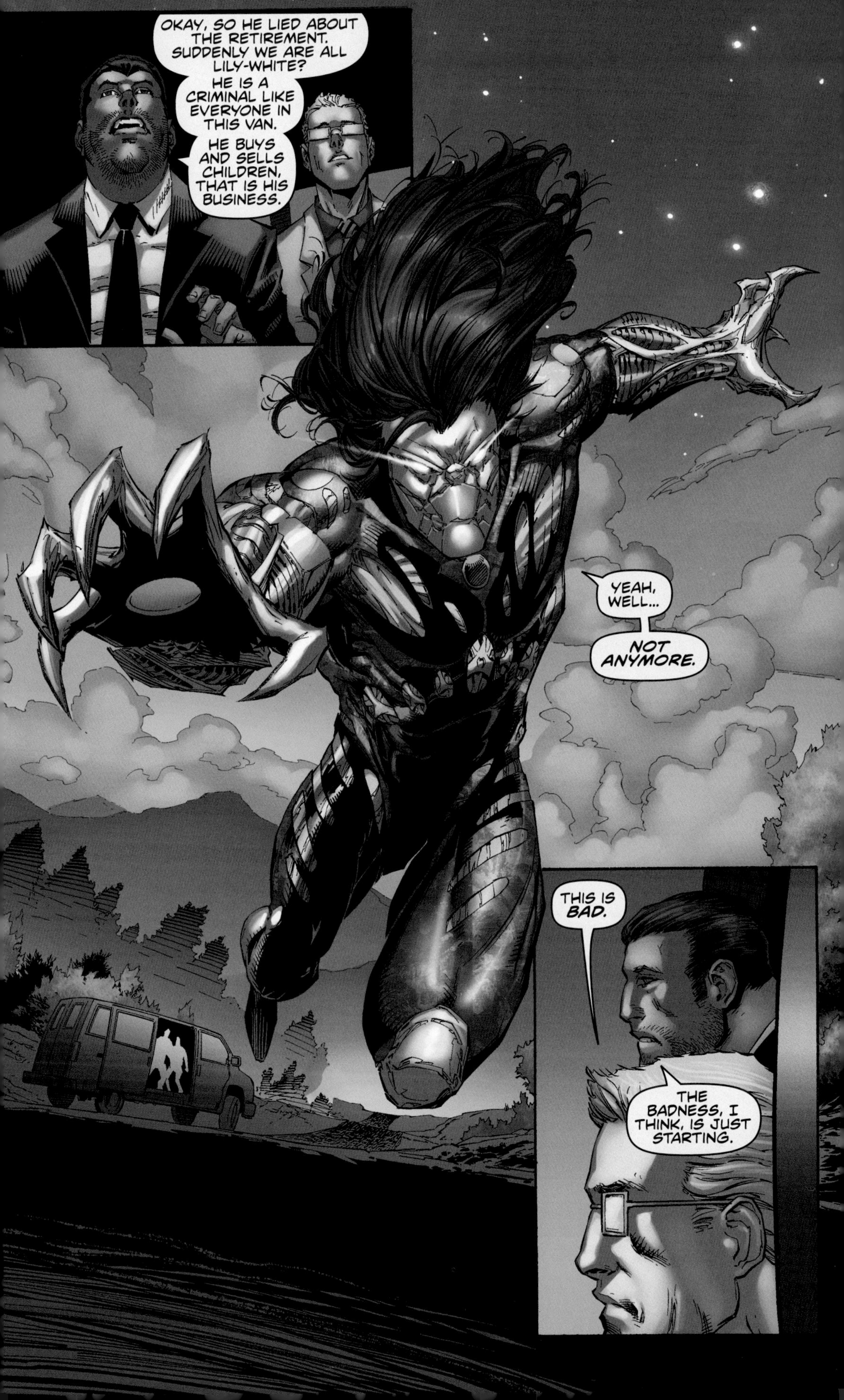
OKAY, SO HE LIED ABOUT THE RETIREMENT. SUDDENLY WE ARE ALL LILY-WHITE?
HE IS A CRIMINAL LIKE EVERYONE IN THIS VAN.
HE BUYS AND SELLS CHILDREN, THAT IS HIS BUSINESS.
YEAH, WELL...
NOT ANYMORE.
THIS IS BAD.
THE BADNESS, I THINK, IS JUST STARTING.

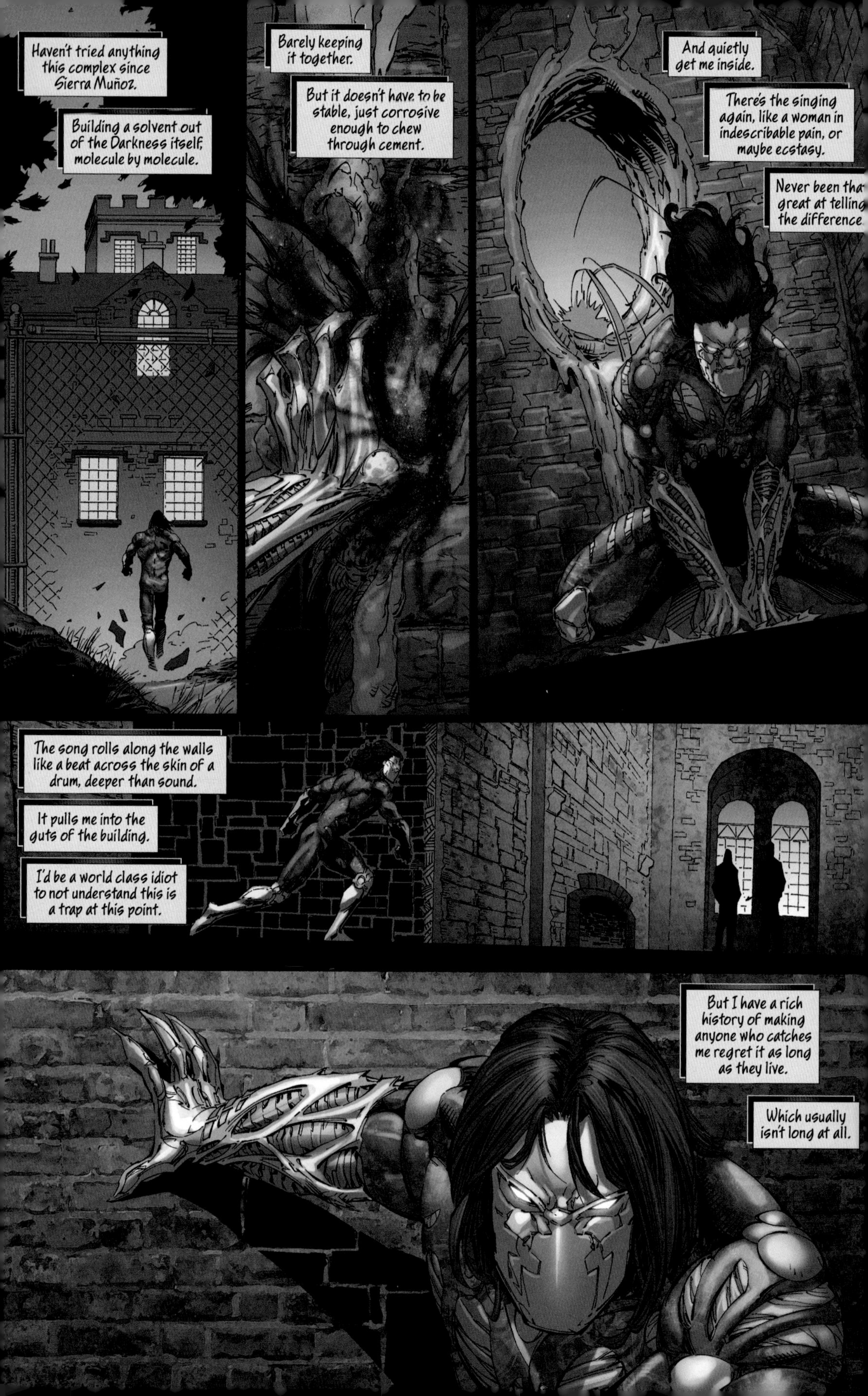

Haven't tried anything this complex since Sierra Muñoz.
Building a solvent out of the Darkness itself, molecule by molecule.
Barely keeping it together.
But it doesn't have to be stable, just corrosive enough to chew through cement.
And quietly get me inside.
There's the singing again, like a woman in indescribable pain, or maybe ecstasy.
Never been tha great at telling the difference.
The song rolls along the walls like a beat across the skin of a drum, deeper than sound.
It pulls me into the guts of the building.
I'd be a world class idiot to not understand this is a trap at this point.
But I have a rich history of making anyone who catches me regret it as long as they live.
Which usually isn't long at all.

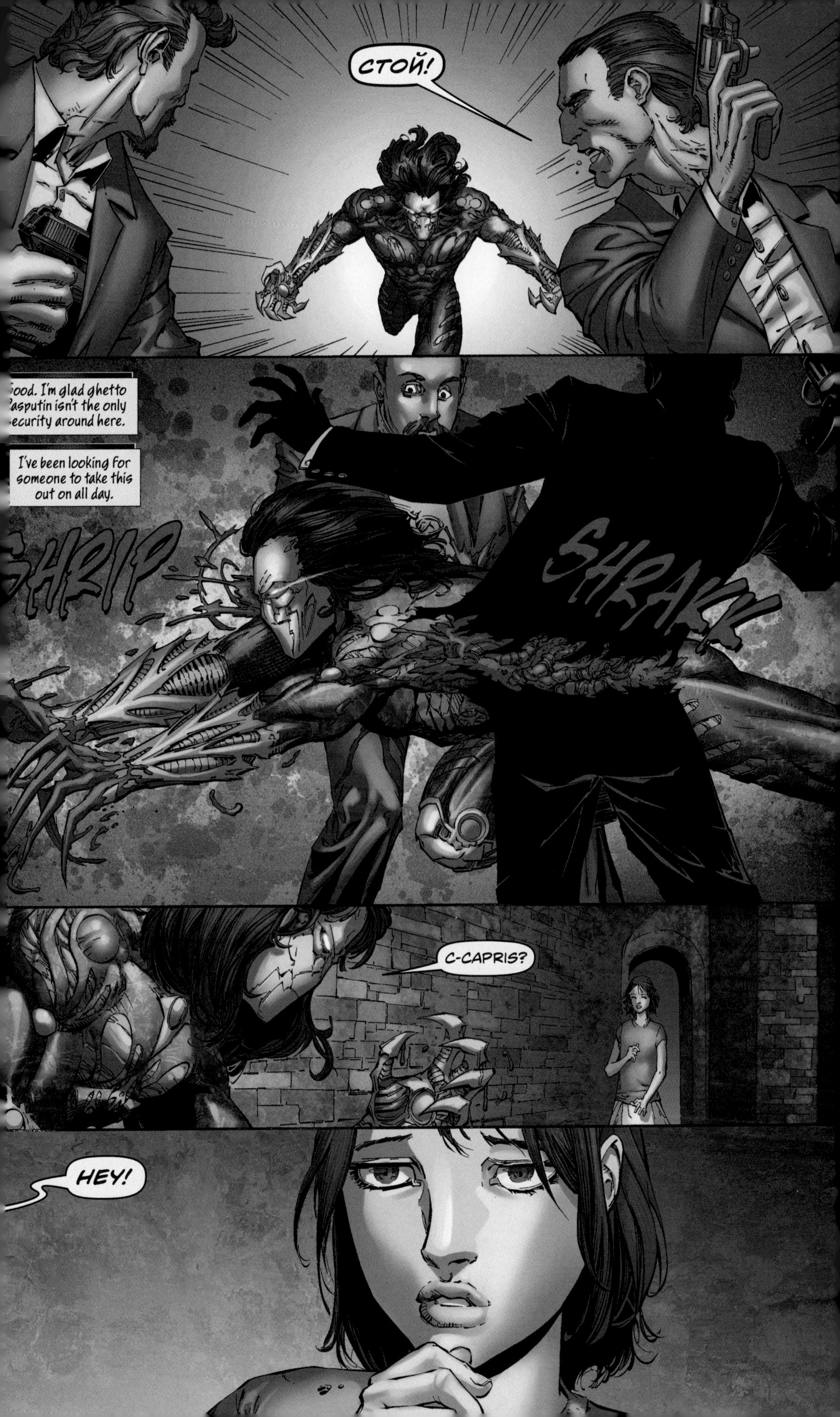
СТОЙ!
Good. I'm glad ghetto Rasputin isn't the only security around here.
I've been looking for someone to take this out on all day.
SHRIP
SHRAKK
C-CAPRIS?
HEY!

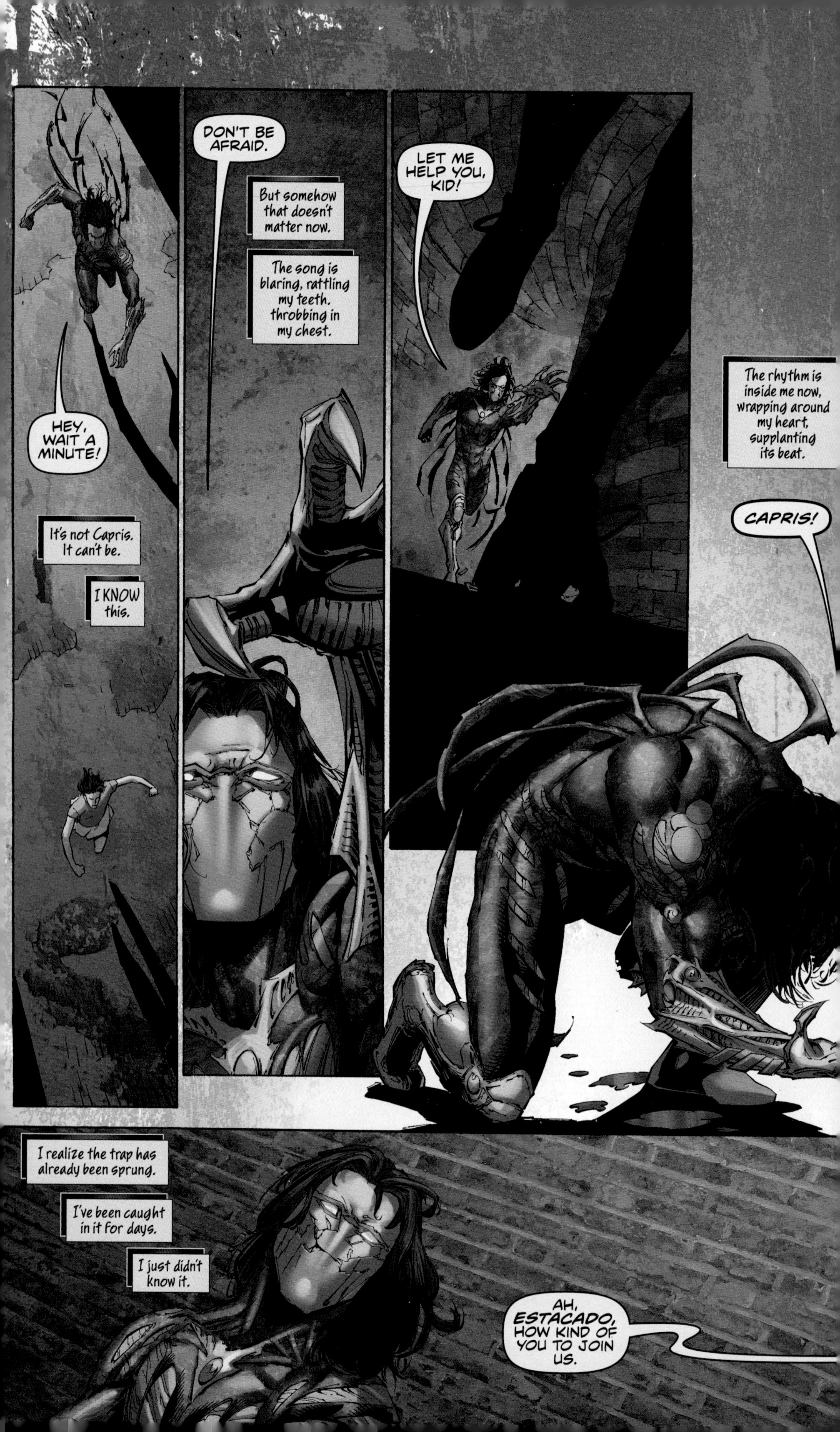
HEY, WAIT A MINUTE!
It's not Capris. It can't be.
I KNOW this.
DON'T BE AFRAID.
But somehow that doesn't matter now.
The song is blaring, rattling my teeth. throbbing in my chest.
LET ME HELP YOU, KID!
The rhythm is inside me now, wrapping around my heart, supplanting its beat.
CAPRIS!
I realize the trap has already been sprung.
I've been caught in it for days.
I just didn't know it.
AH, ESTACADO, HOW KIND OF YOU TO JOIN US.

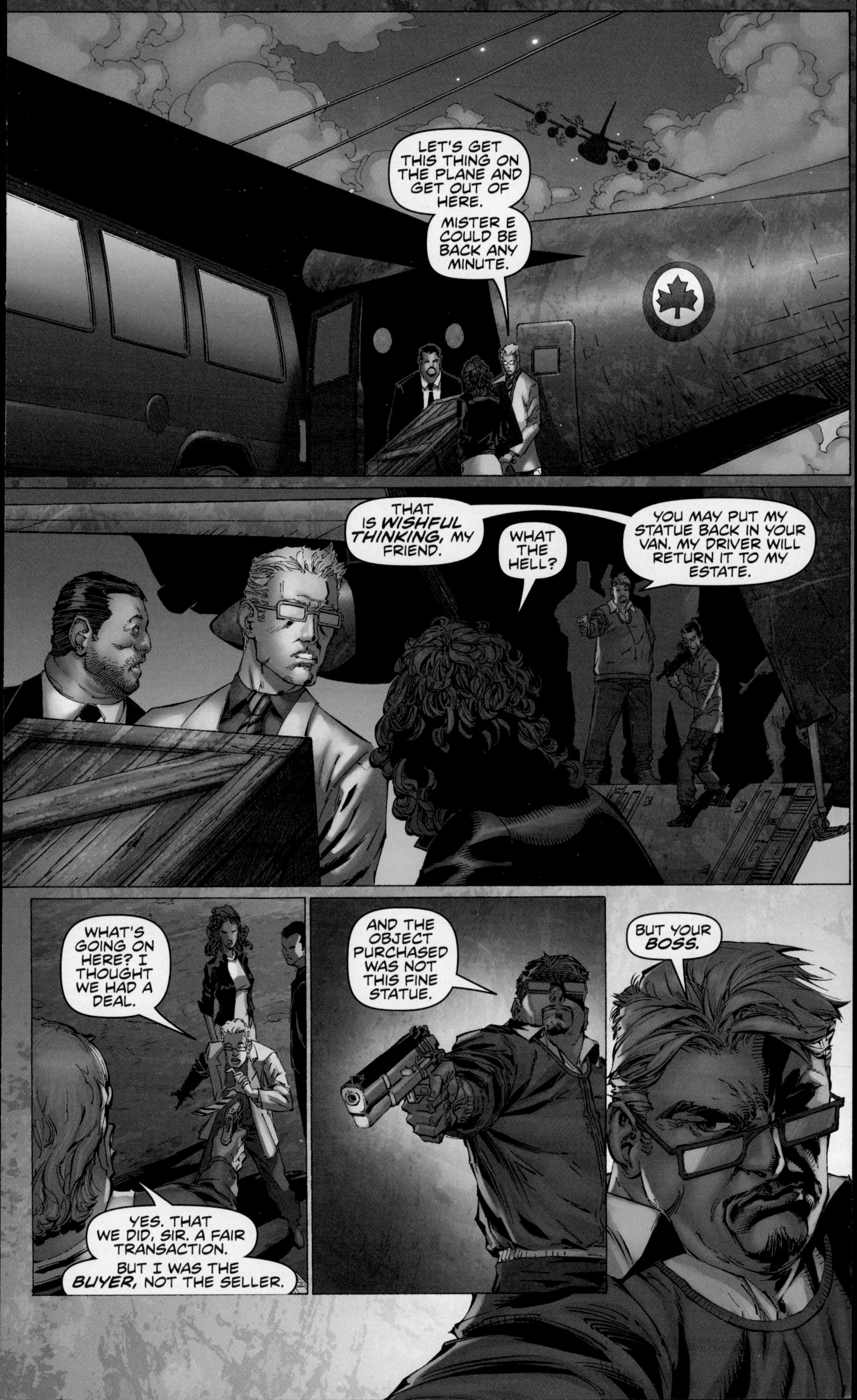
LET'S GET THIS THING ON THE PLANE AND GET OUT OF HERE.
MISTER E COULD BE BACK ANY MINUTE.
THAT IS *WISHFUL THINKING*, MY FRIEND.
WHAT THE HELL?
YOU MAY PUT MY STATUE BACK IN YOUR VAN. MY DRIVER WILL RETURN IT TO MY ESTATE.
WHAT'S GOING ON HERE? I THOUGHT WE HAD A DEAL.
YES. THAT WE DID, SIR. A FAIR TRANSACTION.
BUT I WAS THE *BUYER*, NOT THE SELLER.
AND THE OBJECT PURCHASED WAS NOT THIS FINE STATUE.
BUT YOUR *BOSS*.

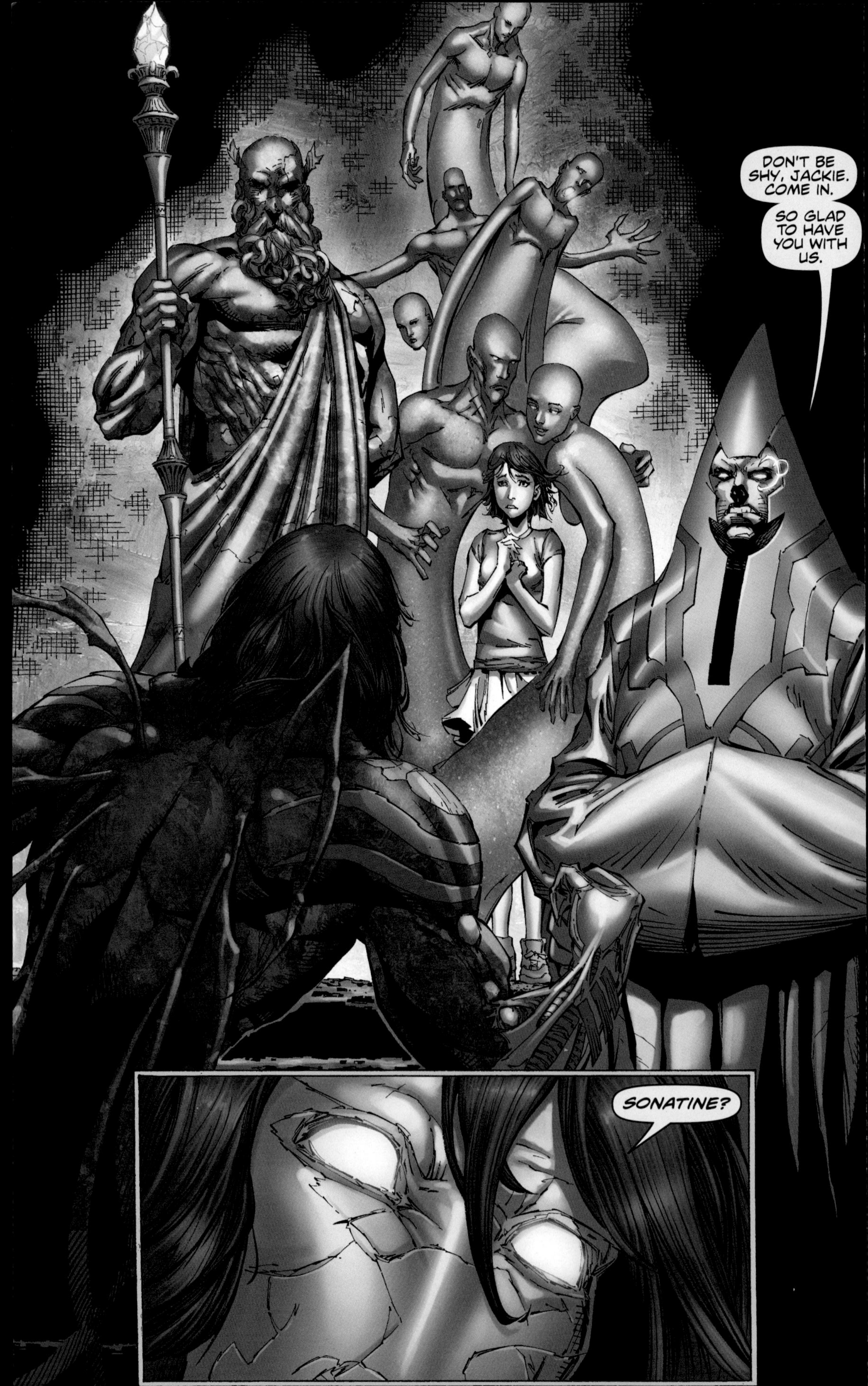
DON'T BE SHY, JACKIE. COME IN.
SO GLAD TO HAVE YOU WITH US.
SONATINE?

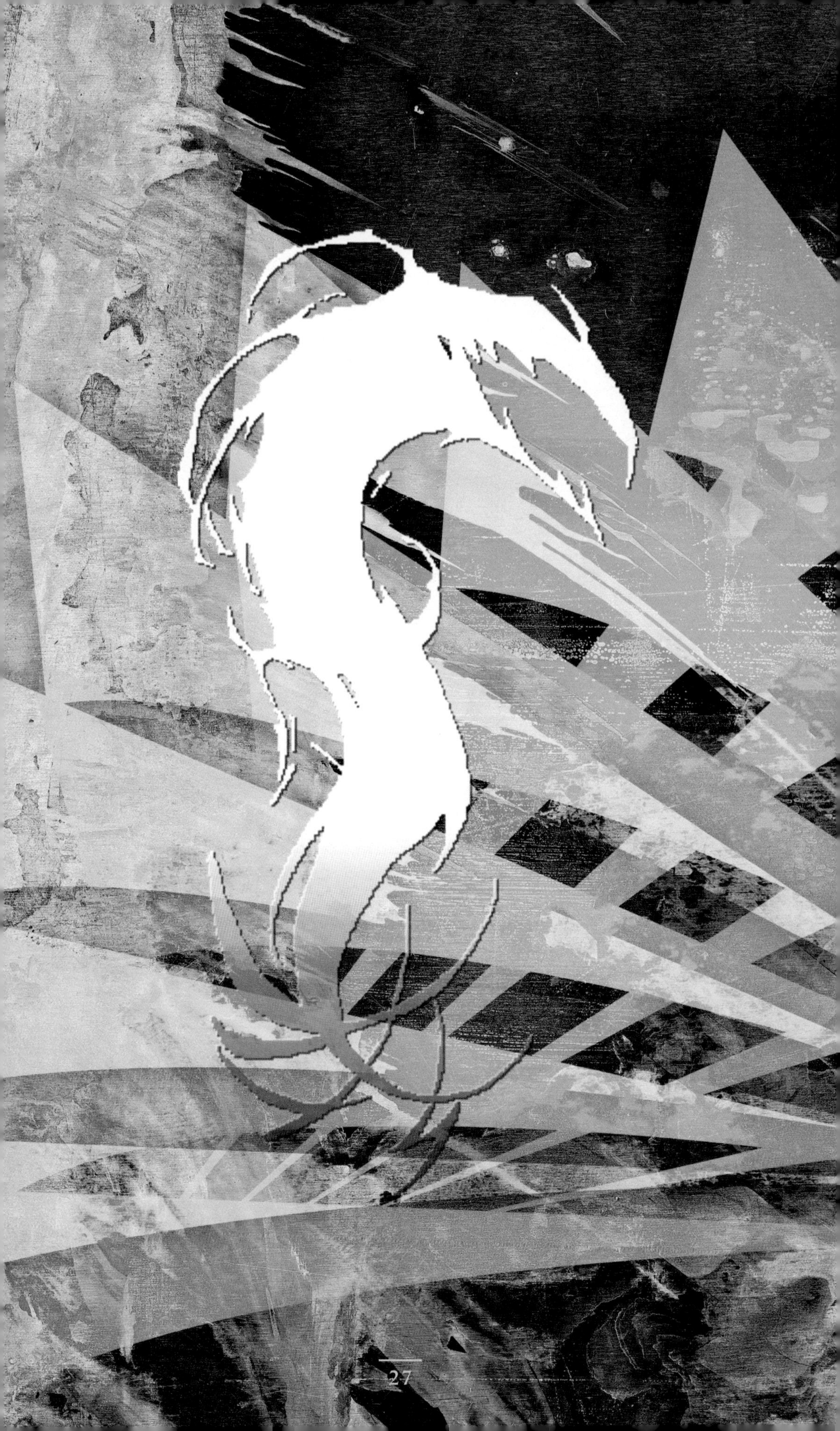

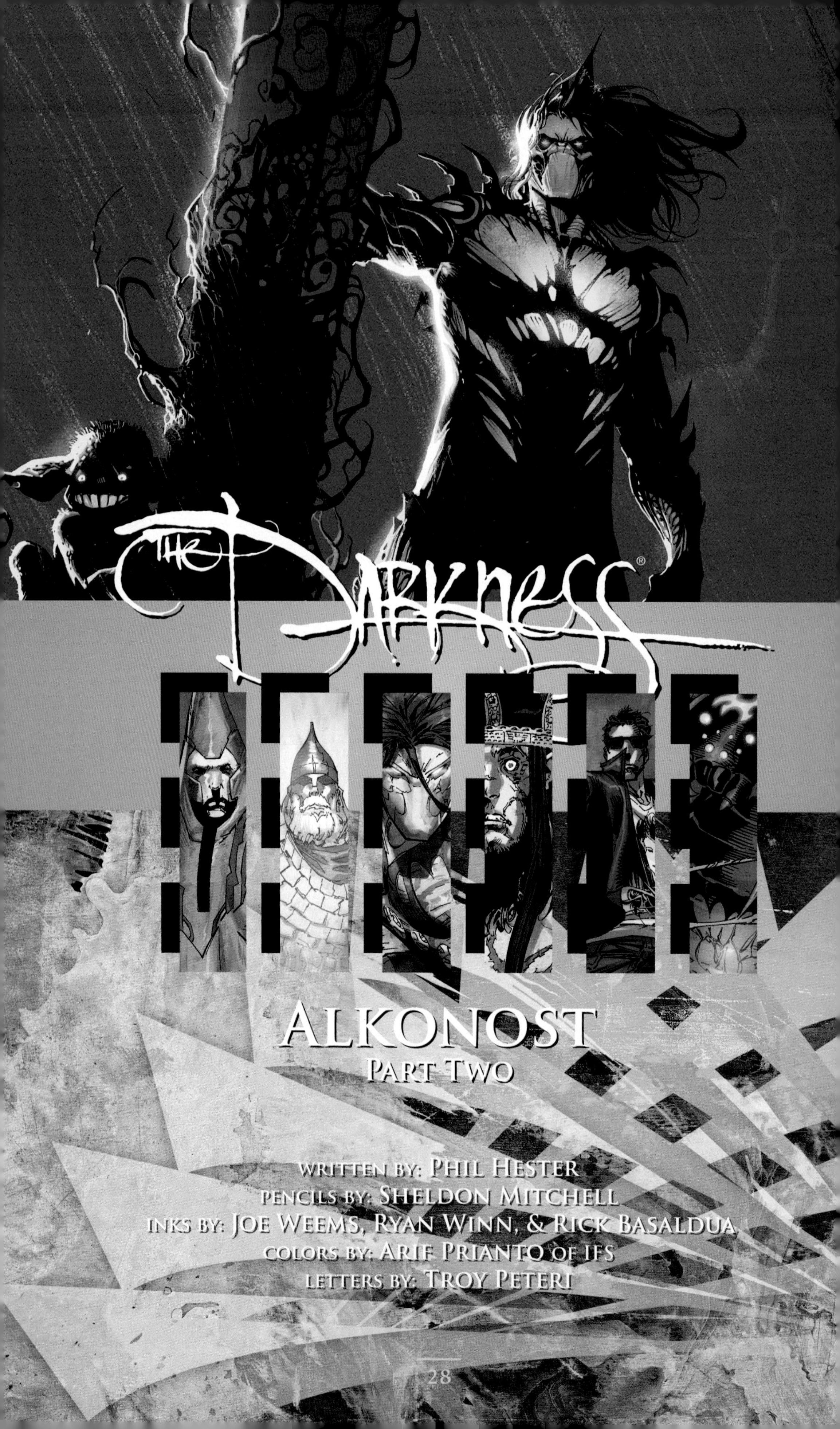

The Darkness®

Alkonost
Part Two

written by: Phil Hester
pencils by: Sheldon Mitchell
inks by: Joe Weems, Ryan Winn, & Rick Basaldua
colors by: Arif Prianto of IFS
letters by: Troy Peteri

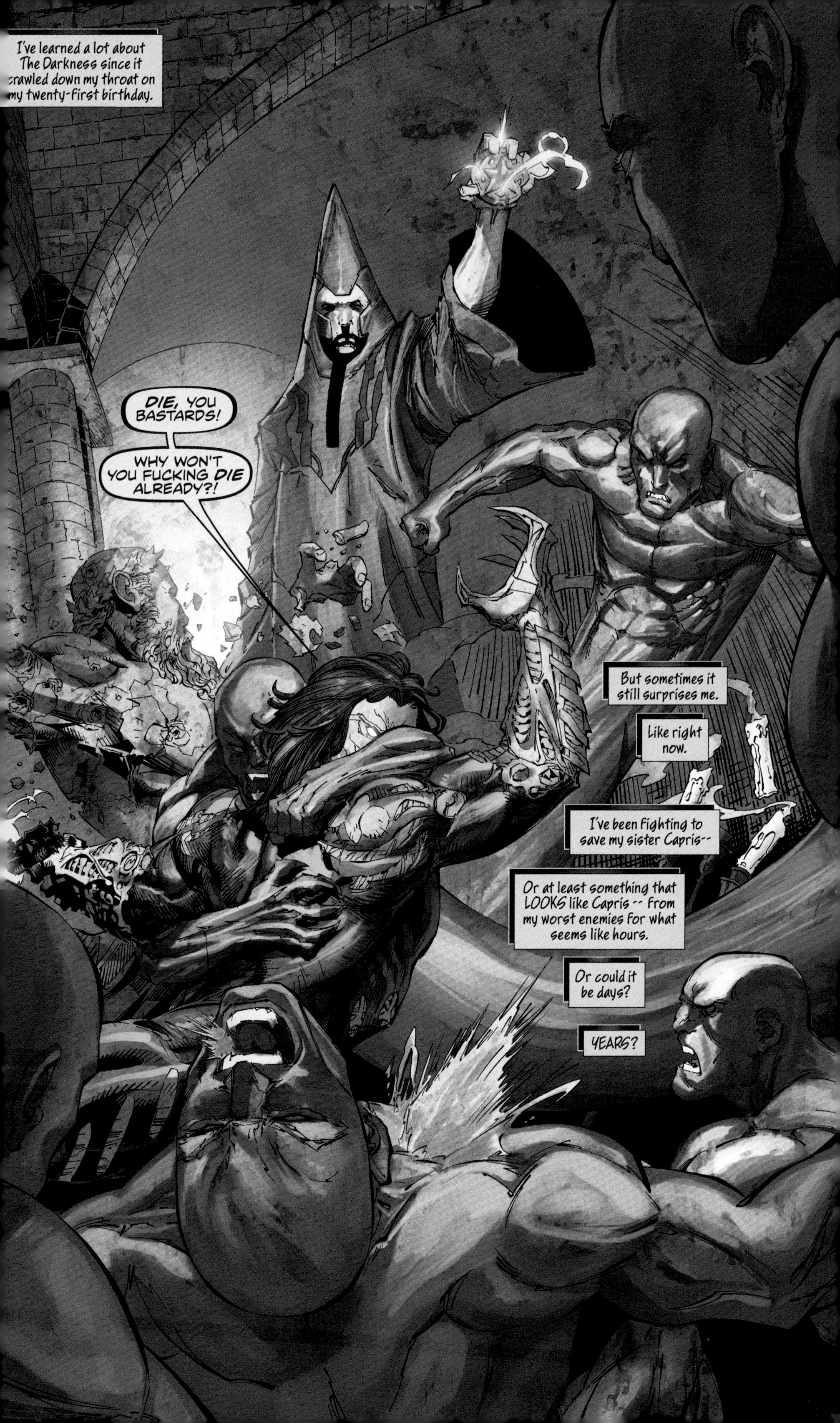
I've learned a lot about The Darkness since it crawled down my throat on my twenty-first birthday.
DIE, YOU BASTARDS!
WHY WON'T YOU FUCKING DIE ALREADY?!
But sometimes it still surprises me.
Like right now.
I've been fighting to save my sister Capris--
Or at least something that LOOKS like Capris -- from my worst enemies for what seems like hours.
Or could it be days?
YEARS?

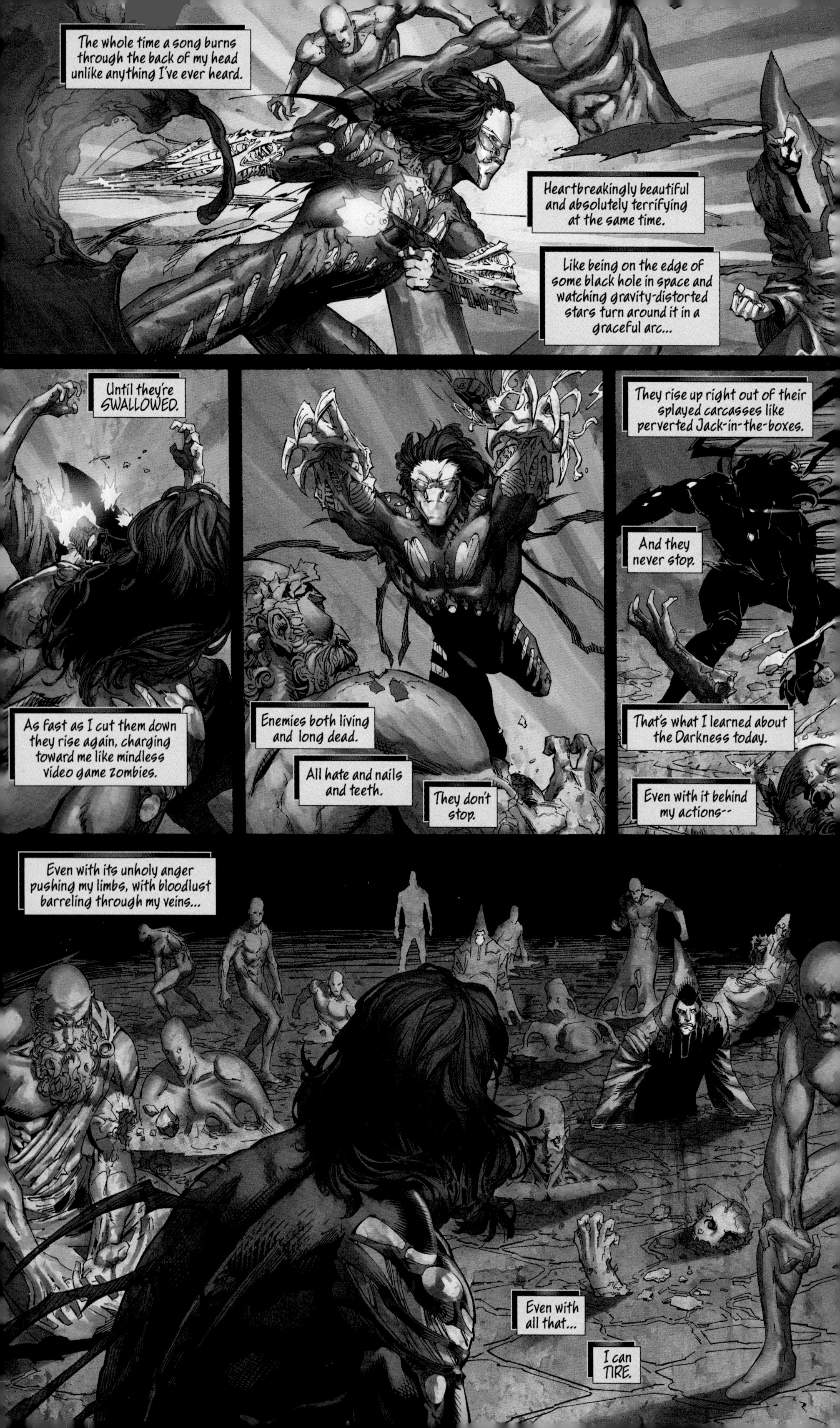
The whole time a song burns through the back of my head unlike anything I've ever heard.
Heartbreakingly beautiful and absolutely terrifying at the same time.
Like being on the edge of some black hole in space and watching gravity-distorted stars turn around it in a graceful arc...
Until they're SWALLOWED.
As fast as I cut them down they rise again, charging toward me like mindless video game zombies.
Enemies both living and long dead.
All hate and nails and teeth.
They don't stop.
They rise up right out of their splayed carcasses like perverted Jack-in-the-boxes.
And they never stop.
That's what I learned about the Darkness today.
Even with it behind my actions--
Even with its unholy anger pushing my limbs, with bloodlust barreling through my veins...
Even with all that...
I can TIRE.

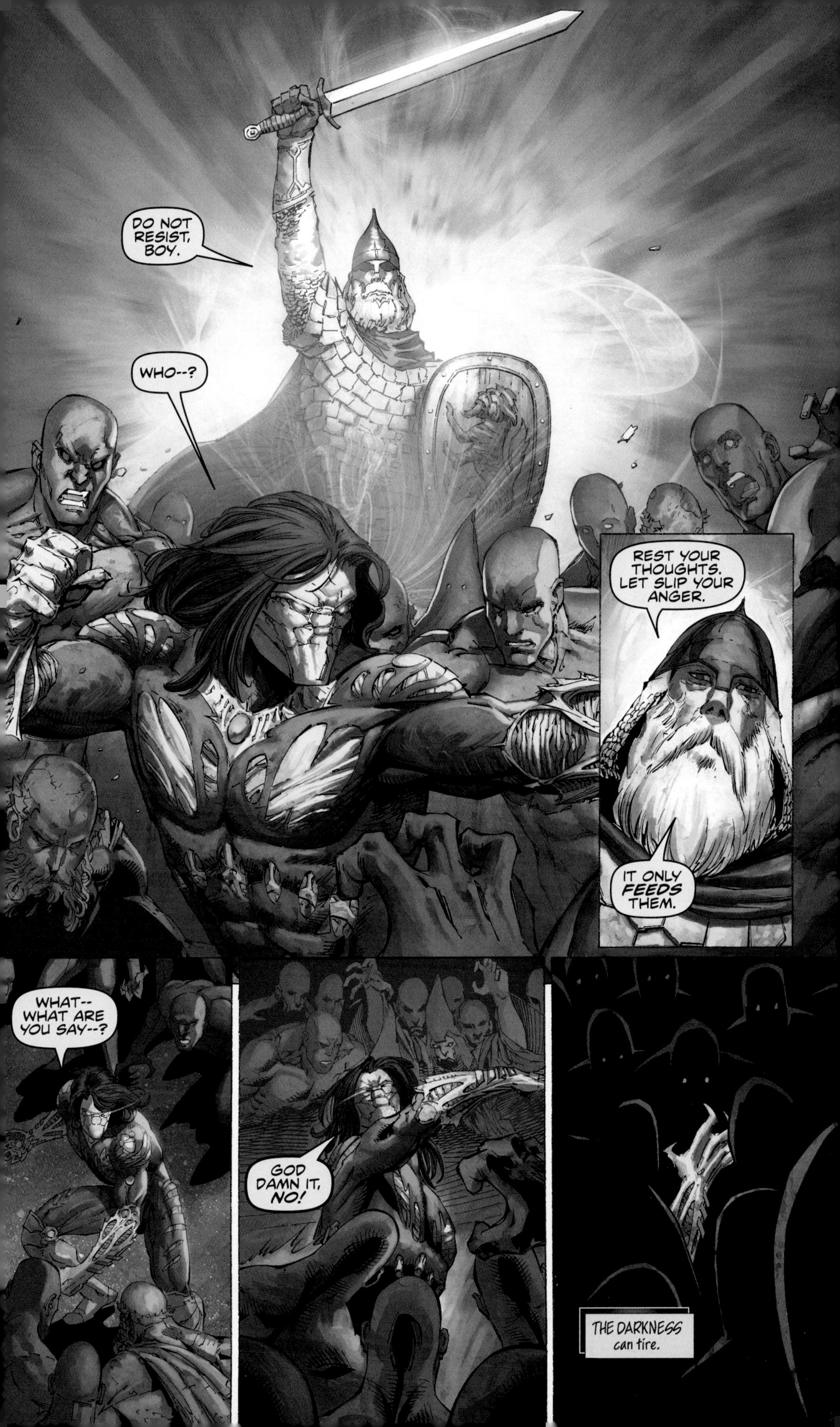
DO NOT RESIST, BOY.
WHO--?
REST YOUR THOUGHTS. LET SLIP YOUR ANGER.
IT ONLY FEEDS THEM.
WHAT-- WHAT ARE YOU SAY--?
GOD DAMN IT, NO!
THE DARKNESS can tire.

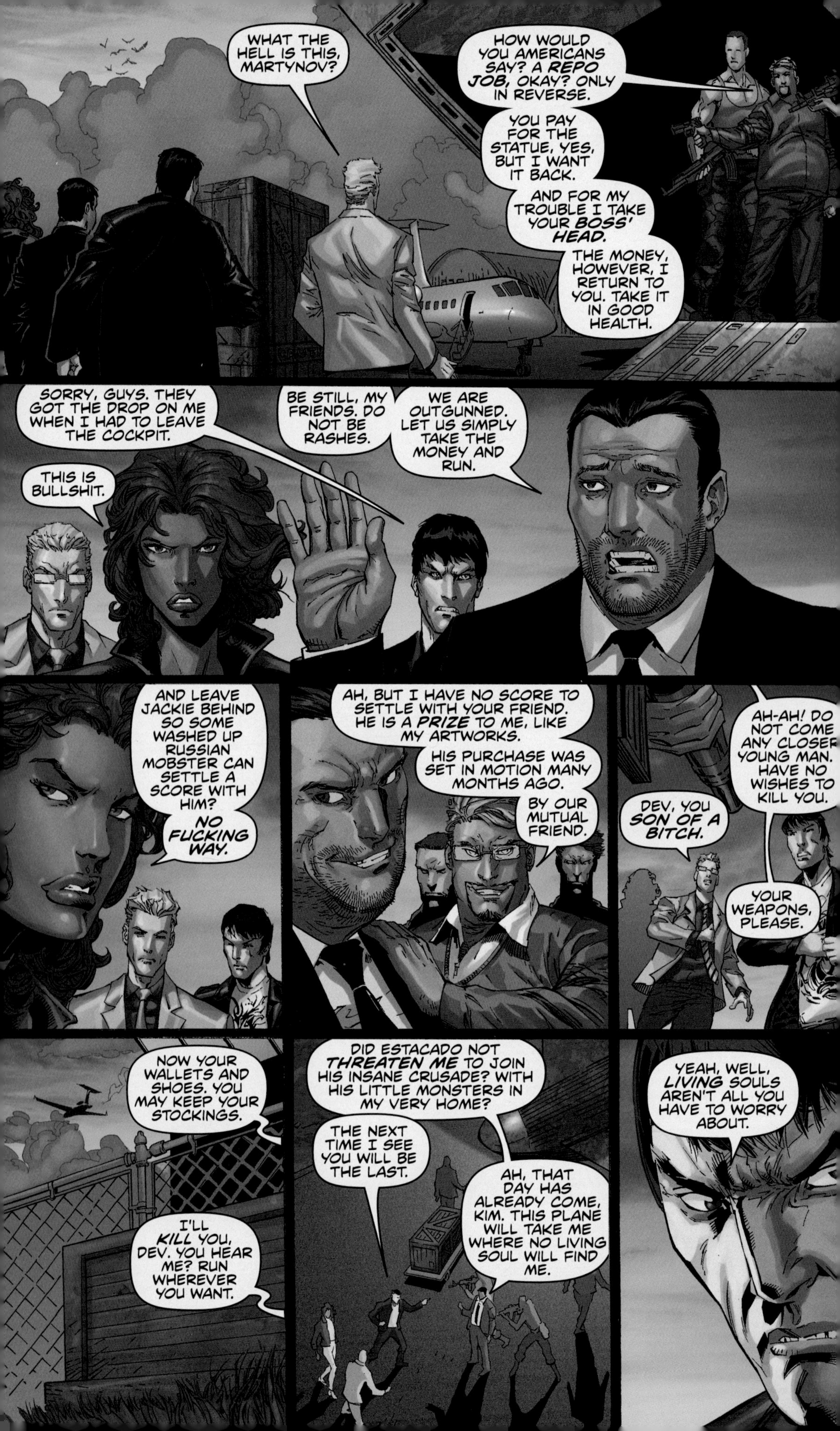
WHAT THE HELL IS THIS, MARTYNOV?
HOW WOULD YOU AMERICANS SAY? A REPO JOB, OKAY? ONLY IN REVERSE.
YOU PAY FOR THE STATUE, YES, BUT I WANT IT BACK.
AND FOR MY TROUBLE I TAKE YOUR BOSS' HEAD.
THE MONEY, HOWEVER, I RETURN TO YOU. TAKE IT IN GOOD HEALTH.
SORRY, GUYS. THEY GOT THE DROP ON ME WHEN I HAD TO LEAVE THE COCKPIT.
THIS IS BULLSHIT.
BE STILL, MY FRIENDS. DO NOT BE RASHES.
WE ARE OUTGUNNED. LET US SIMPLY TAKE THE MONEY AND RUN.
AND LEAVE JACKIE BEHIND SO SOME WASHED UP RUSSIAN MOBSTER CAN SETTLE A SCORE WITH HIM?
NO FUCKING WAY.
AH, BUT I HAVE NO SCORE TO SETTLE WITH YOUR FRIEND. HE IS A PRIZE TO ME, LIKE MY ARTWORKS.
HIS PURCHASE WAS SET IN MOTION MANY MONTHS AGO.
BY OUR MUTUAL FRIEND.
DEV, YOU SON OF A BITCH.
AH-AH! DO NOT COME ANY CLOSER YOUNG MAN. HAVE NO WISHES TO KILL YOU.
YOUR WEAPONS, PLEASE.
NOW YOUR WALLETS AND SHOES. YOU MAY KEEP YOUR STOCKINGS.
I'LL KILL YOU, DEV. YOU HEAR ME? RUN WHEREVER YOU WANT.
DID ESTACADO NOT THREATEN ME TO JOIN HIS INSANE CRUSADE? WITH HIS LITTLE MONSTERS IN MY VERY HOME?
THE NEXT TIME I SEE YOU WILL BE THE LAST.
AH, THAT DAY HAS ALREADY COME, KIM. THIS PLANE WILL TAKE ME WHERE NO LIVING SOUL WILL FIND ME.
YEAH, WELL, LIVING SOULS AREN'T ALL YOU HAVE TO WORRY ABOUT.

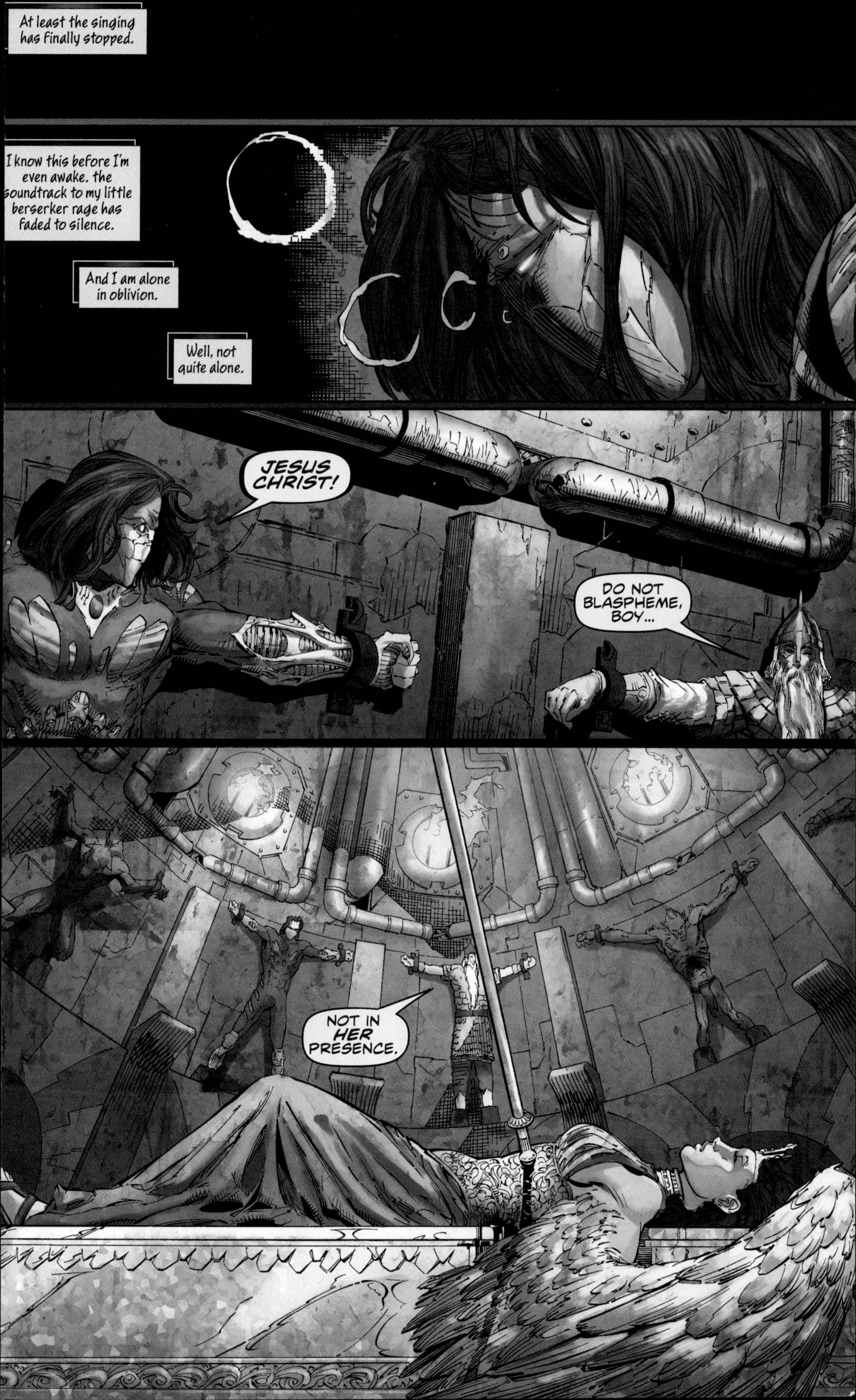
At least the singing has finally stopped.
I know this before I'm even awake. the soundtrack to my little berserker rage has faded to silence.
And I am alone in oblivion.
Well, not quite alone.
JESUS CHRIST!
DO NOT BLASPHEME, BOY...
NOT IN HER PRESENCE.

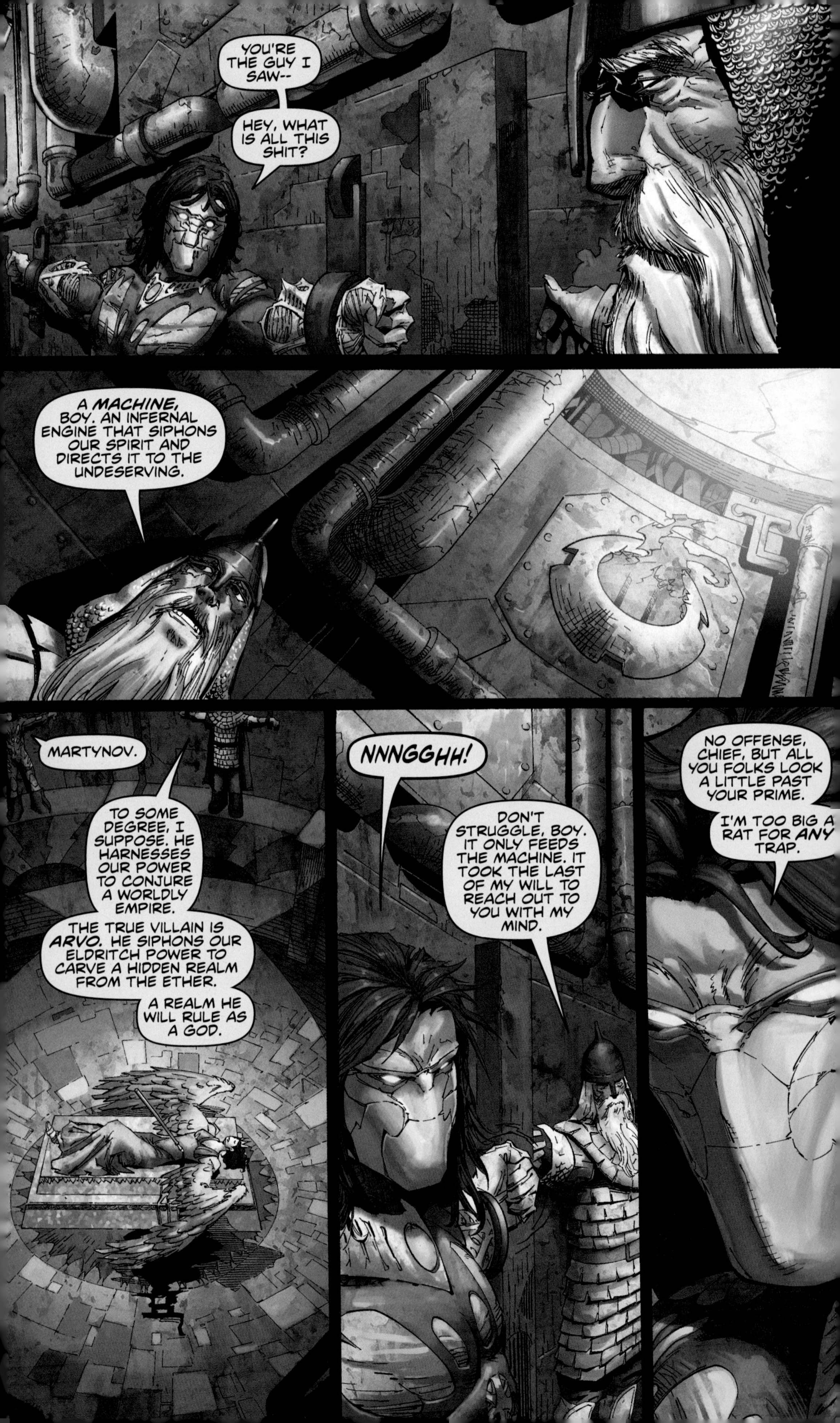

YOU'RE THE GUY I SAW--
HEY, WHAT IS ALL THIS SHIT?
A MACHINE, BOY. AN INFERNAL ENGINE THAT SIPHONS OUR SPIRIT AND DIRECTS IT TO THE UNDESERVING.
MARTYNOV.
TO SOME DEGREE, I SUPPOSE. HE HARNESSES OUR POWER TO CONJURE A WORLDLY EMPIRE.
THE TRUE VILLAIN IS ARVO. HE SIPHONS OUR ELDRITCH POWER TO CARVE A HIDDEN REALM FROM THE ETHER.
A REALM HE WILL RULE AS A GOD.
NNNGGHH!
DON'T STRUGGLE, BOY. IT ONLY FEEDS THE MACHINE. IT TOOK THE LAST OF MY WILL TO REACH OUT TO YOU WITH MY MIND.
NO OFFENSE, CHIEF, BUT ALL YOU FOLKS LOOK A LITTLE PAST YOUR PRIME.
I'M TOO BIG A RAT FOR ANY TRAP.

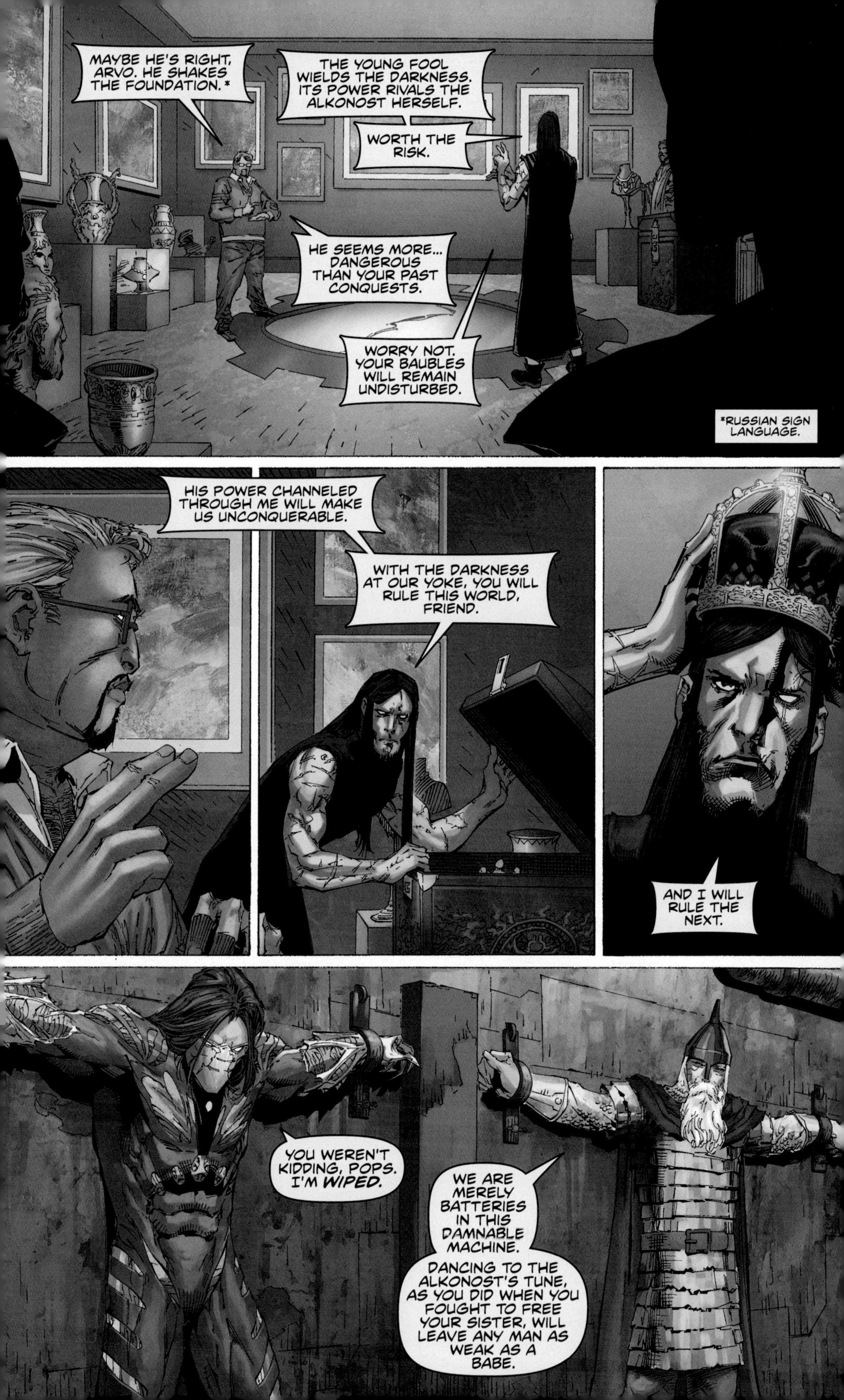
MAYBE HE'S RIGHT, ARVO. HE SHAKES THE FOUNDATION.*
THE YOUNG FOOL WIELDS THE DARKNESS. ITS POWER RIVALS THE ALKONOST HERSELF.
WORTH THE RISK.
HE SEEMS MORE... DANGEROUS THAN YOUR PAST CONQUESTS.
WORRY NOT. YOUR BAUBLES WILL REMAIN UNDISTURBED.
*RUSSIAN SIGN LANGUAGE.
HIS POWER CHANNELED THROUGH ME WILL MAKE US UNCONQUERABLE.
WITH THE DARKNESS AT OUR YOKE, YOU WILL RULE THIS WORLD, FRIEND.
AND I WILL RULE THE NEXT.
YOU WEREN'T KIDDING, POPS. I'M *WIPED*.
WE ARE MERELY BATTERIES IN THIS DAMNABLE MACHINE.
DANCING TO THE ALKONOST'S TUNE, AS YOU DID WHEN YOU FOUGHT TO FREE YOUR SISTER, WILL LEAVE ANY MAN AS WEAK AS A BABE.

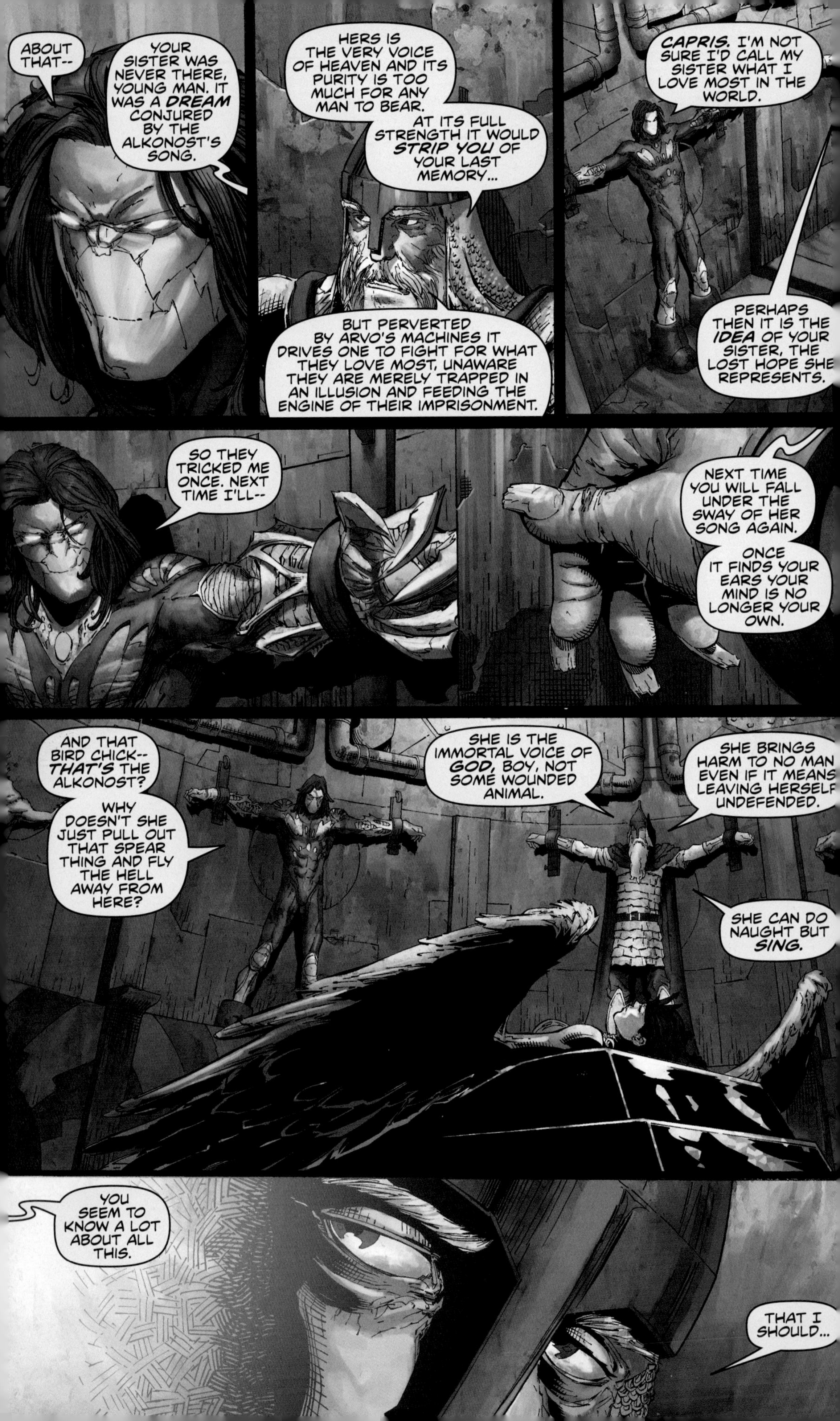
ABOUT THAT--
YOUR SISTER WAS NEVER THERE, YOUNG MAN. IT WAS A DREAM CONJURED BY THE ALKONOST'S SONG.
HERS IS THE VERY VOICE OF HEAVEN AND ITS PURITY IS TOO MUCH FOR ANY MAN TO BEAR.
AT ITS FULL STRENGTH IT WOULD STRIP YOU OF YOUR LAST MEMORY...
BUT PERVERTED BY ARVO'S MACHINES IT DRIVES ONE TO FIGHT FOR WHAT THEY LOVE MOST, UNAWARE THEY ARE MERELY TRAPPED IN AN ILLUSION AND FEEDING THE ENGINE OF THEIR IMPRISONMENT.
CAPRIS. I'M NOT SURE I'D CALL MY SISTER WHAT I LOVE MOST IN THE WORLD.
PERHAPS THEN IT IS THE IDEA OF YOUR SISTER, THE LOST HOPE SHE REPRESENTS.
SO THEY TRICKED ME ONCE. NEXT TIME I'LL--
NEXT TIME YOU WILL FALL UNDER THE SWAY OF HER SONG AGAIN.
ONCE IT FINDS YOUR EARS YOUR MIND IS NO LONGER YOUR OWN.
AND THAT BIRD CHICK-- THAT'S THE ALKONOST?
WHY DOESN'T SHE JUST PULL OUT THAT SPEAR THING AND FLY THE HELL AWAY FROM HERE?
SHE IS THE IMMORTAL VOICE OF GOD, BOY, NOT SOME WOUNDED ANIMAL.
SHE BRINGS HARM TO NO MAN EVEN IF IT MEANS LEAVING HERSELF UNDEFENDED.
SHE CAN DO NAUGHT BUT SING.
YOU SEEM TO KNOW A LOT ABOUT ALL THIS.
THAT I SHOULD...

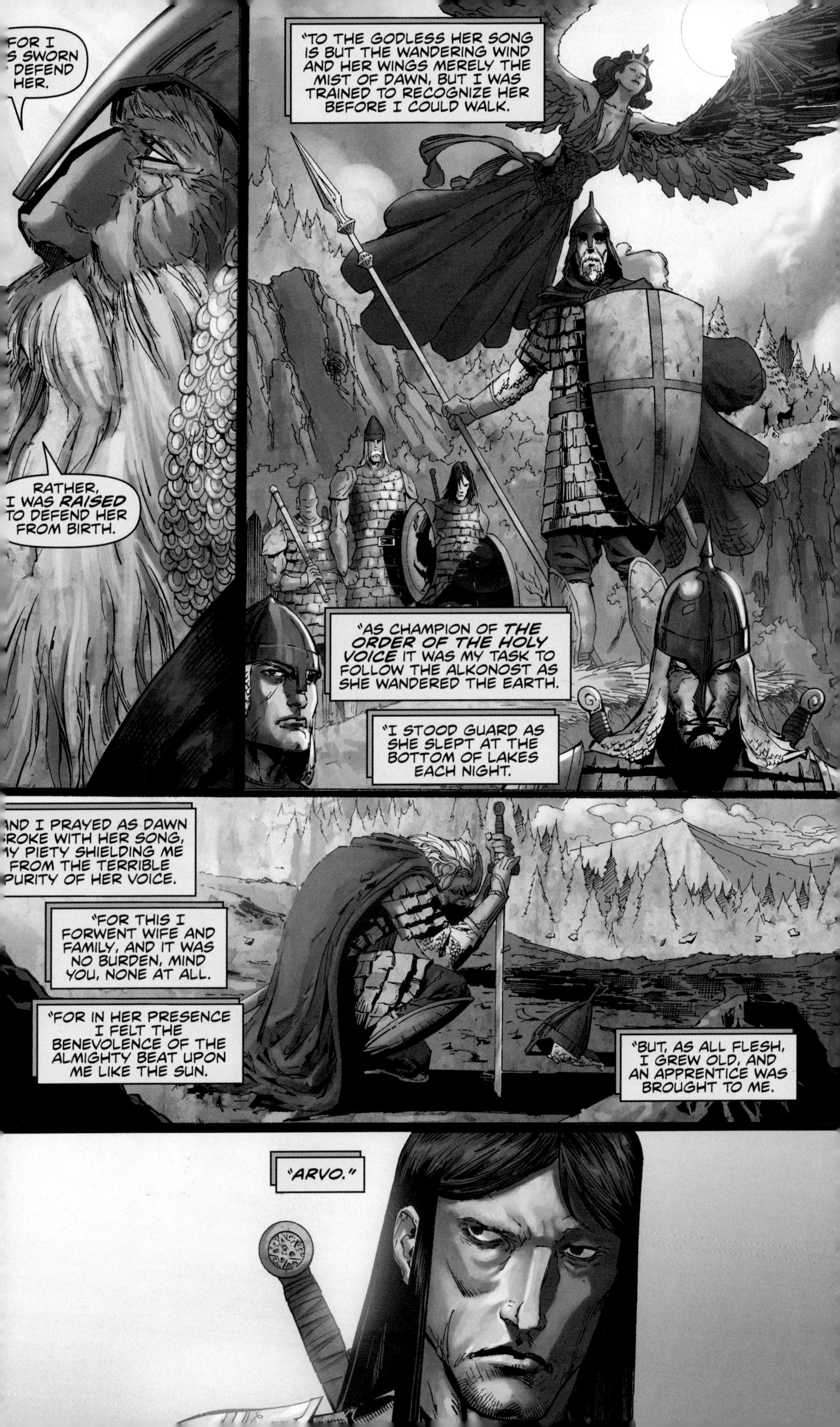
FOR I S SWORN DEFEND HER.
"TO THE GODLESS HER SONG IS BUT THE WANDERING WIND AND HER WINGS MERELY THE MIST OF DAWN, BUT I WAS TRAINED TO RECOGNIZE HER BEFORE I COULD WALK.
RATHER, I WAS ***RAISED*** TO DEFEND HER FROM BIRTH.
"AS CHAMPION OF ***THE ORDER OF THE HOLY VOICE*** IT WAS MY TASK TO FOLLOW THE ALKONOST AS SHE WANDERED THE EARTH.
"I STOOD GUARD AS SHE SLEPT AT THE BOTTOM OF LAKES EACH NIGHT.
ND I PRAYED AS DAWN ROKE WITH HER SONG, Y PIETY SHIELDING ME FROM THE TERRIBLE PURITY OF HER VOICE.
"FOR THIS I FORWENT WIFE AND FAMILY, AND IT WAS NO BURDEN, MIND YOU, NONE AT ALL.
"FOR IN HER PRESENCE I FELT THE BENEVOLENCE OF THE ALMIGHTY BEAT UPON ME LIKE THE SUN.
"BUT, AS ALL FLESH, I GREW OLD, AND AN APPRENTICE WAS BROUGHT TO ME.
"ARVO."

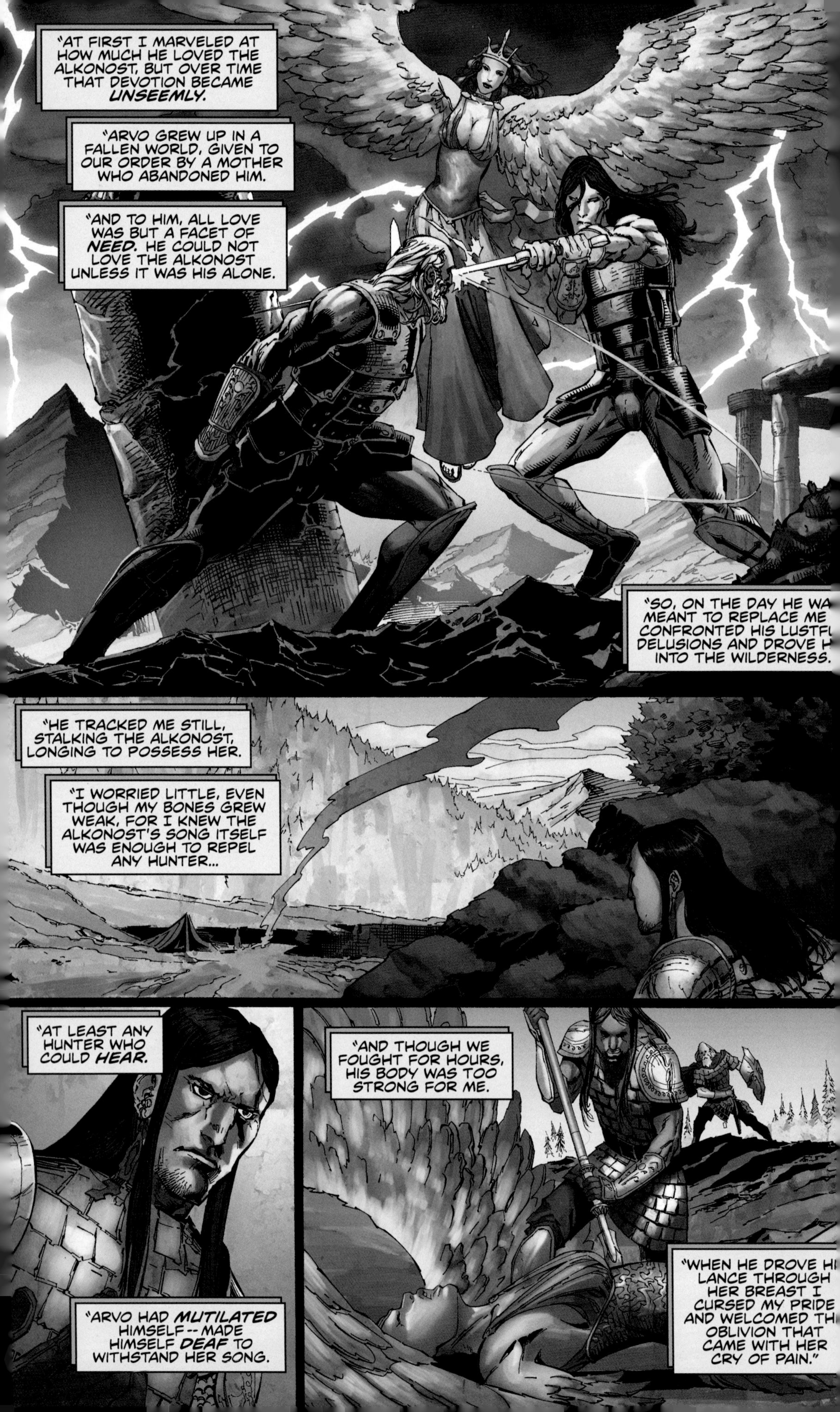
"AT FIRST I MARVELED AT HOW MUCH HE LOVED THE ALKONOST, BUT OVER TIME THAT DEVOTION BECAME UNSEEMLY.
"ARVO GREW UP IN A FALLEN WORLD, GIVEN TO OUR ORDER BY A MOTHER WHO ABANDONED HIM.
"AND TO HIM, ALL LOVE WAS BUT A FACET OF NEED. HE COULD NOT LOVE THE ALKONOST UNLESS IT WAS HIS ALONE.
"SO, ON THE DAY HE WA MEANT TO REPLACE ME CONFRONTED HIS LUSTF DELUSIONS AND DROVE H INTO THE WILDERNESS.
"HE TRACKED ME STILL, STALKING THE ALKONOST, LONGING TO POSSESS HER.
"I WORRIED LITTLE, EVEN THOUGH MY BONES GREW WEAK, FOR I KNEW THE ALKONOST'S SONG ITSELF WAS ENOUGH TO REPEL ANY HUNTER...
"AT LEAST ANY HUNTER WHO COULD HEAR.
"ARVO HAD MUTILATED HIMSELF--MADE HIMSELF DEAF TO WITHSTAND HER SONG.
"AND THOUGH WE FOUGHT FOR HOURS, HIS BODY WAS TOO STRONG FOR ME.
"WHEN HE DROVE HI LANCE THROUGH HER BREAST I CURSED MY PRIDE AND WELCOMED TH OBLIVION THAT CAME WITH HER CRY OF PAIN."

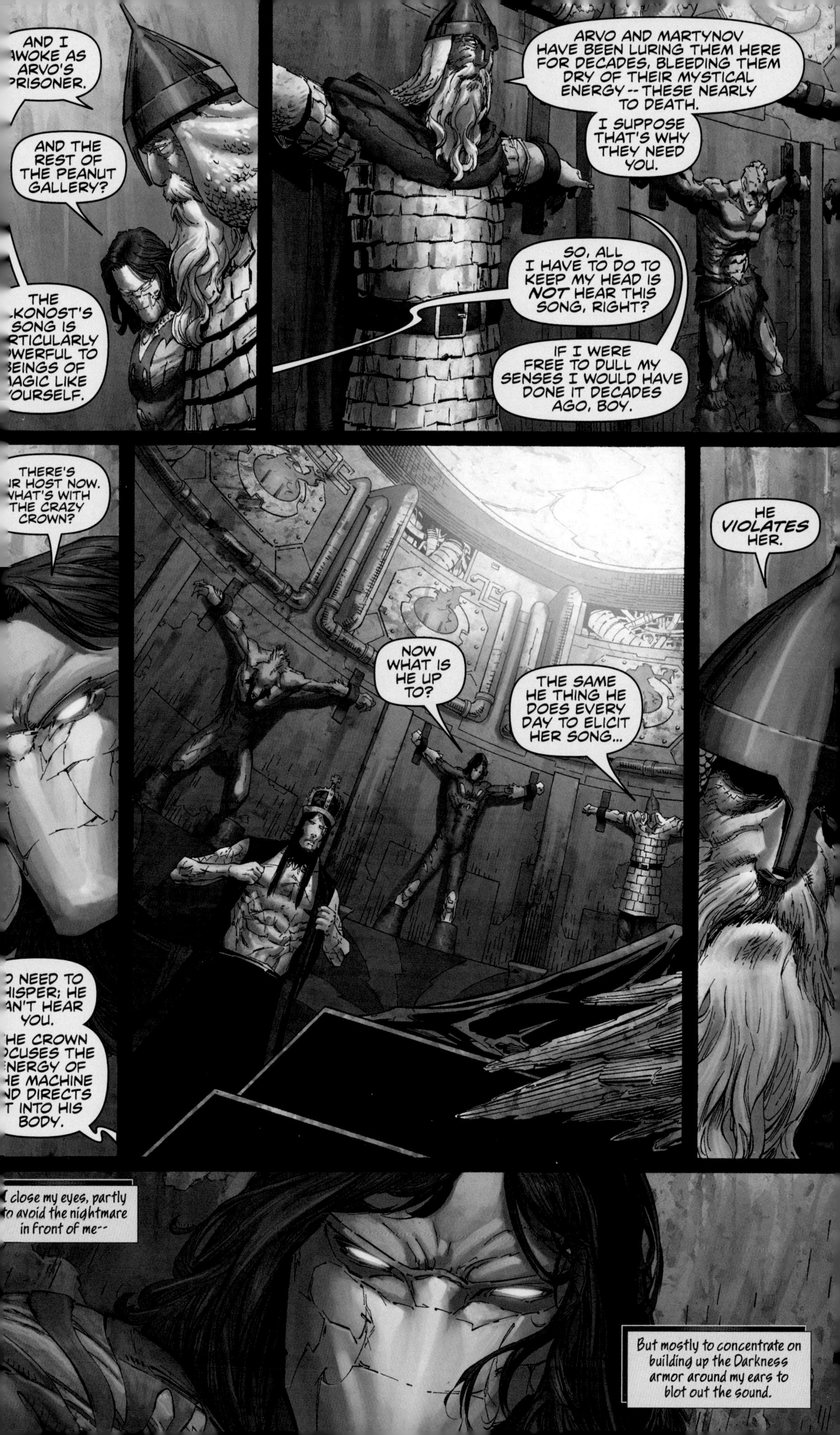
AND I AWOKE AS ARVO'S PRISONER.
AND THE REST OF THE PEANUT GALLERY?
THE ALKONOST'S SONG IS PARTICULARLY POWERFUL TO BEINGS OF MAGIC LIKE YOURSELF.
ARVO AND MARTYNOV HAVE BEEN LURING THEM HERE FOR DECADES, BLEEDING THEM DRY OF THEIR MYSTICAL ENERGY -- THESE NEARLY TO DEATH.
I SUPPOSE THAT'S WHY THEY NEED YOU.
SO, ALL I HAVE TO DO TO KEEP MY HEAD IS NOT HEAR THIS SONG, RIGHT?
IF I WERE FREE TO DULL MY SENSES I WOULD HAVE DONE IT DECADES AGO, BOY.
THERE'S OUR HOST NOW. WHAT'S WITH THE CRAZY CROWN?
NOW WHAT IS HE UP TO?
THE SAME HE THING HE DOES EVERY DAY TO ELICIT HER SONG...
HE VIOLATES HER.
NO NEED TO WHISPER; HE CAN'T HEAR YOU.
THE CROWN FOCUSES THE ENERGY OF THE MACHINE AND DIRECTS IT INTO HIS BODY.
I close my eyes, partly to avoid the nightmare in front of me--
But mostly to concentrate on building up the Darkness armor around my ears to blot out the sound.

I almost make it.

I can feel the Darkness matter filling my ear canal, stopping up all sound, but just before that last seal is closed--

A single note reaches my brain.

And I'm chasing Capris again. Fighting to save her, to save what she represents--

The family I never had.

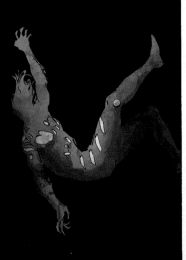

The family I keep trying to recreate, be it the Franchettis, Sierra Muñoz--

Or even the second rate A-Team I just put together.

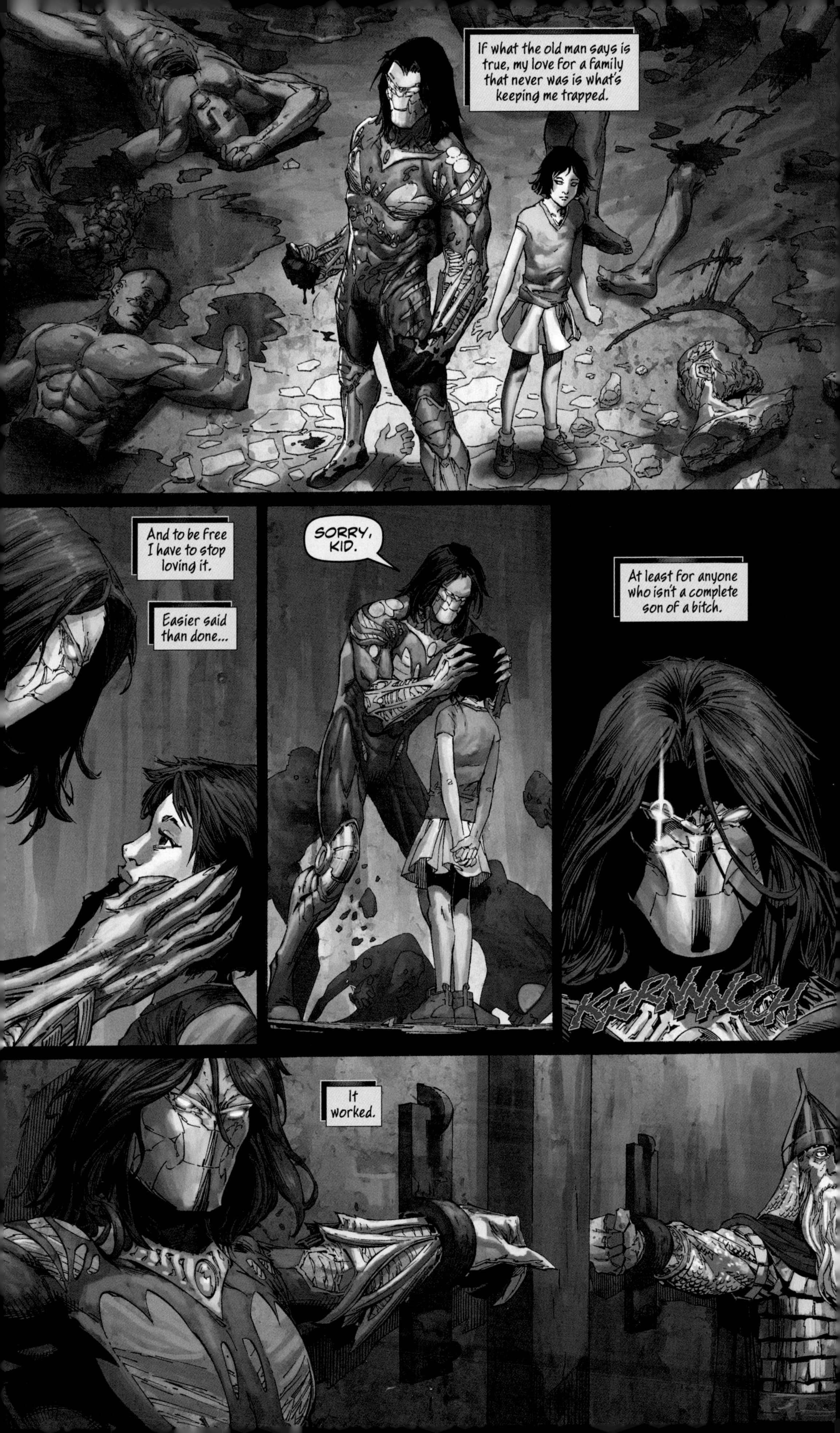
If what the old man says is true, my love for a family that never was is what's keeping me trapped.
And to be free I have to stop loving it.
Easier said than done...
SORRY, KID.
At least for anyone who isn't a complete son of a bitch.
KRRNNNCCH
It worked.

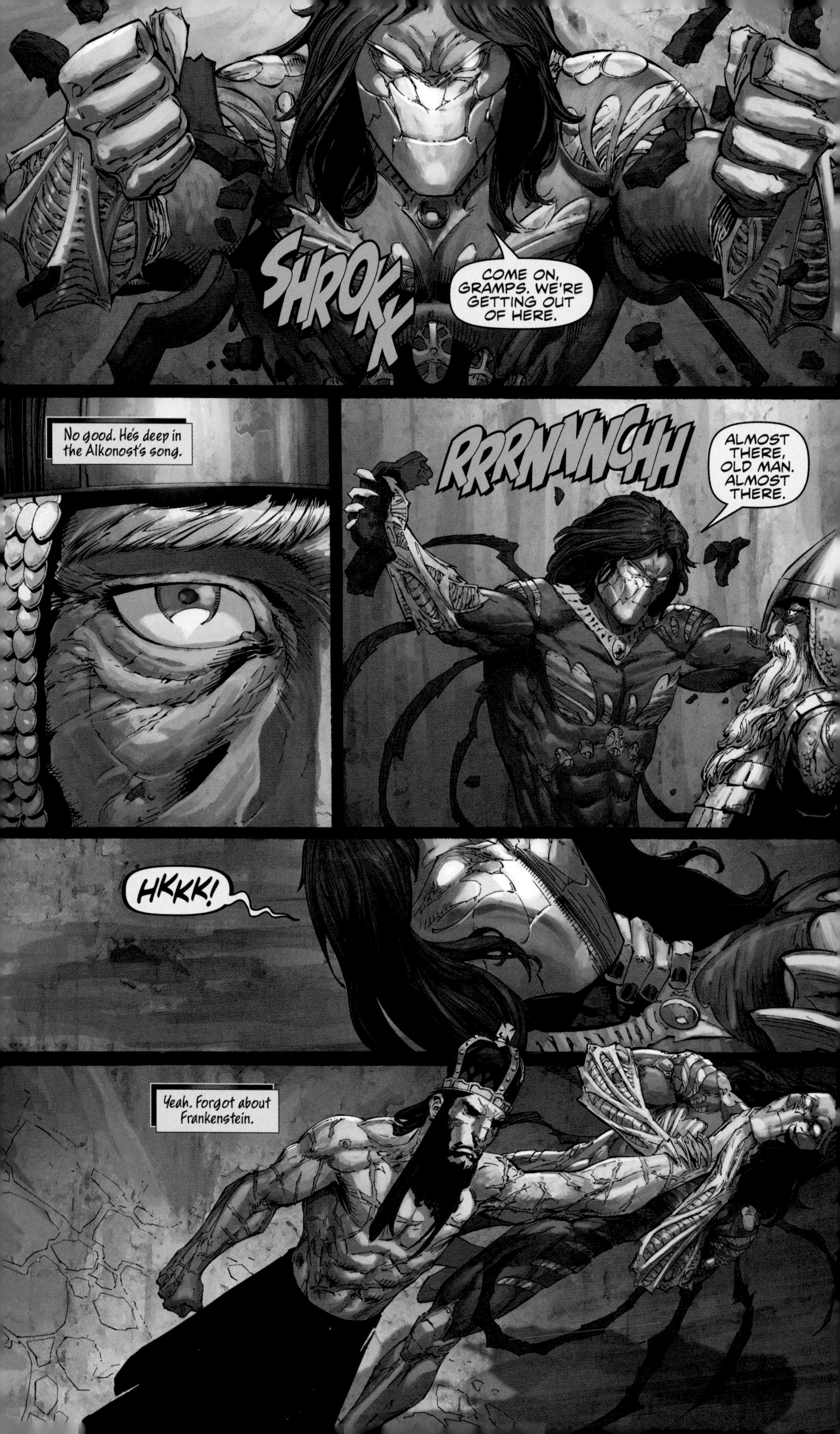
SHROKK
COME ON, GRAMPS. WE'RE GETTING OUT OF HERE.
No good. He's deep in the Alkonost's song.
RRRNNNCHH
ALMOST THERE, OLD MAN. ALMOST THERE.
HKKK!
Yeah. Forgot about Frankenstein.

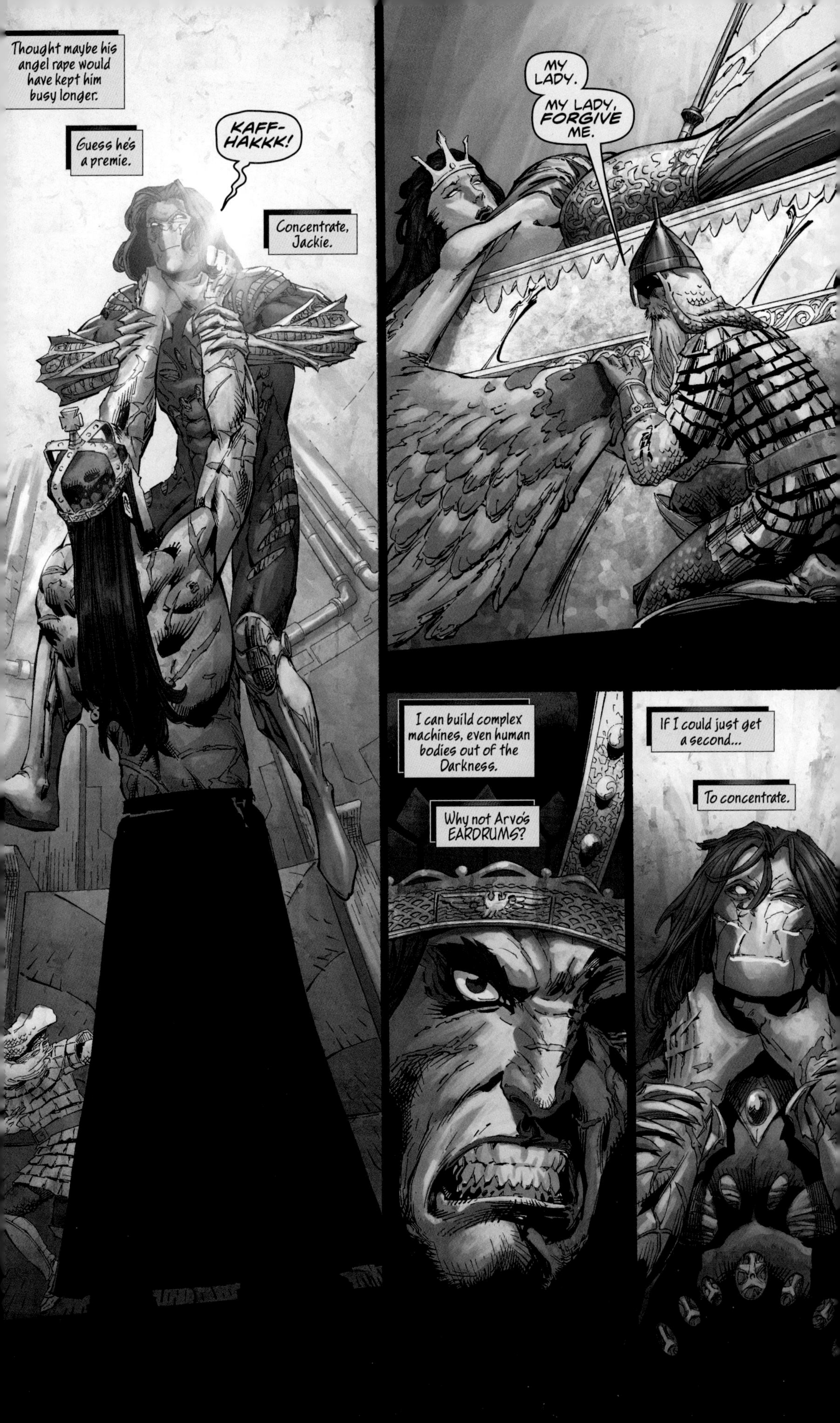
Thought maybe his angel rape would have kept him busy longer.
Guess he's a premie.
KAFF-HAKKK!
Concentrate, Jackie.
MY LADY.
MY LADY, FORGIVE ME.
I can build complex machines, even human bodies out of the Darkness.
Why not Arvo's EARDRUMS?
If I could just get a second...
To concentrate.

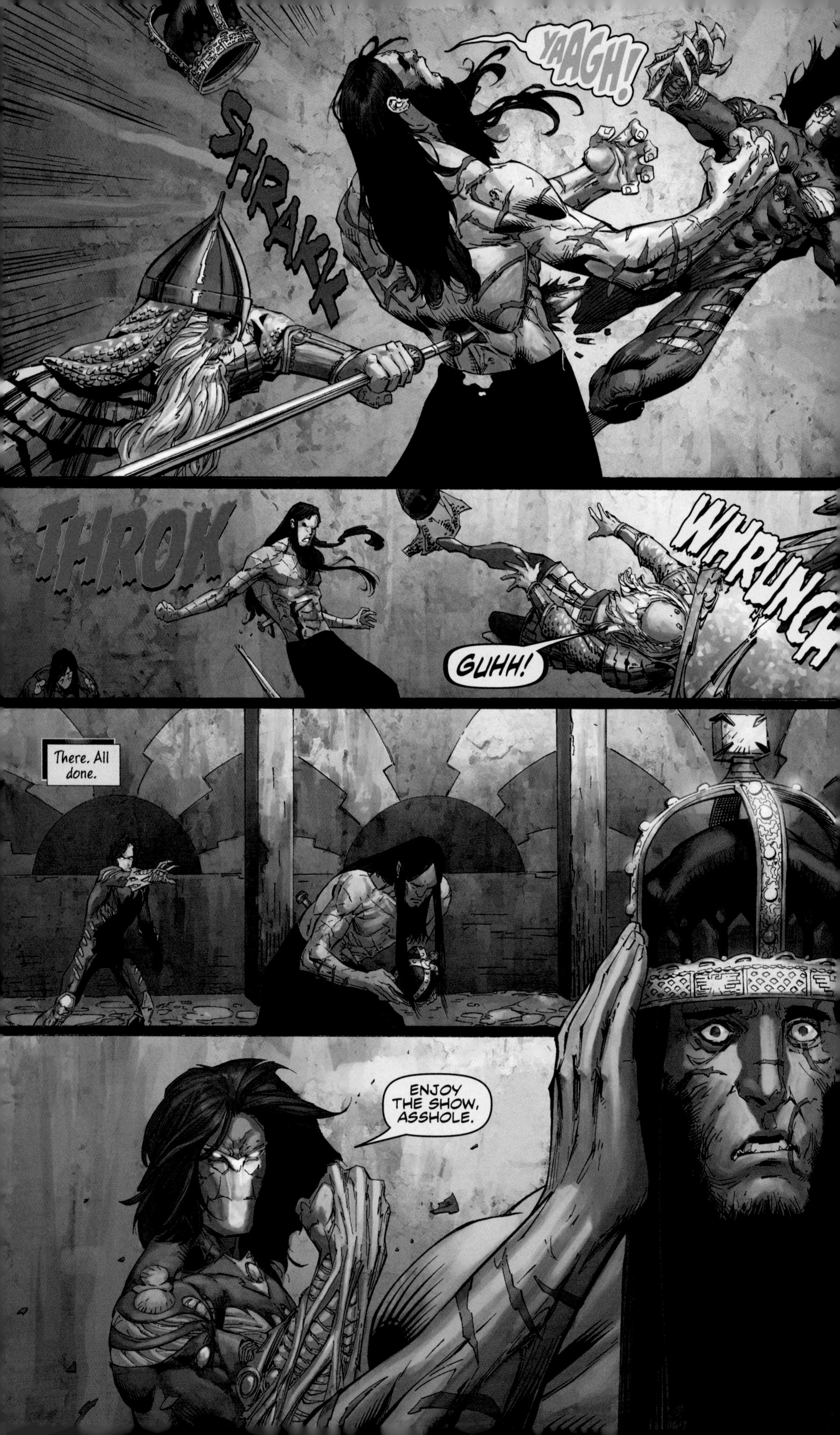
YAAGH!
SHRAKK
THROK
WHRUNCH
GUHH!
There. All done.
ENJOY THE SHOW, ASSHOLE.

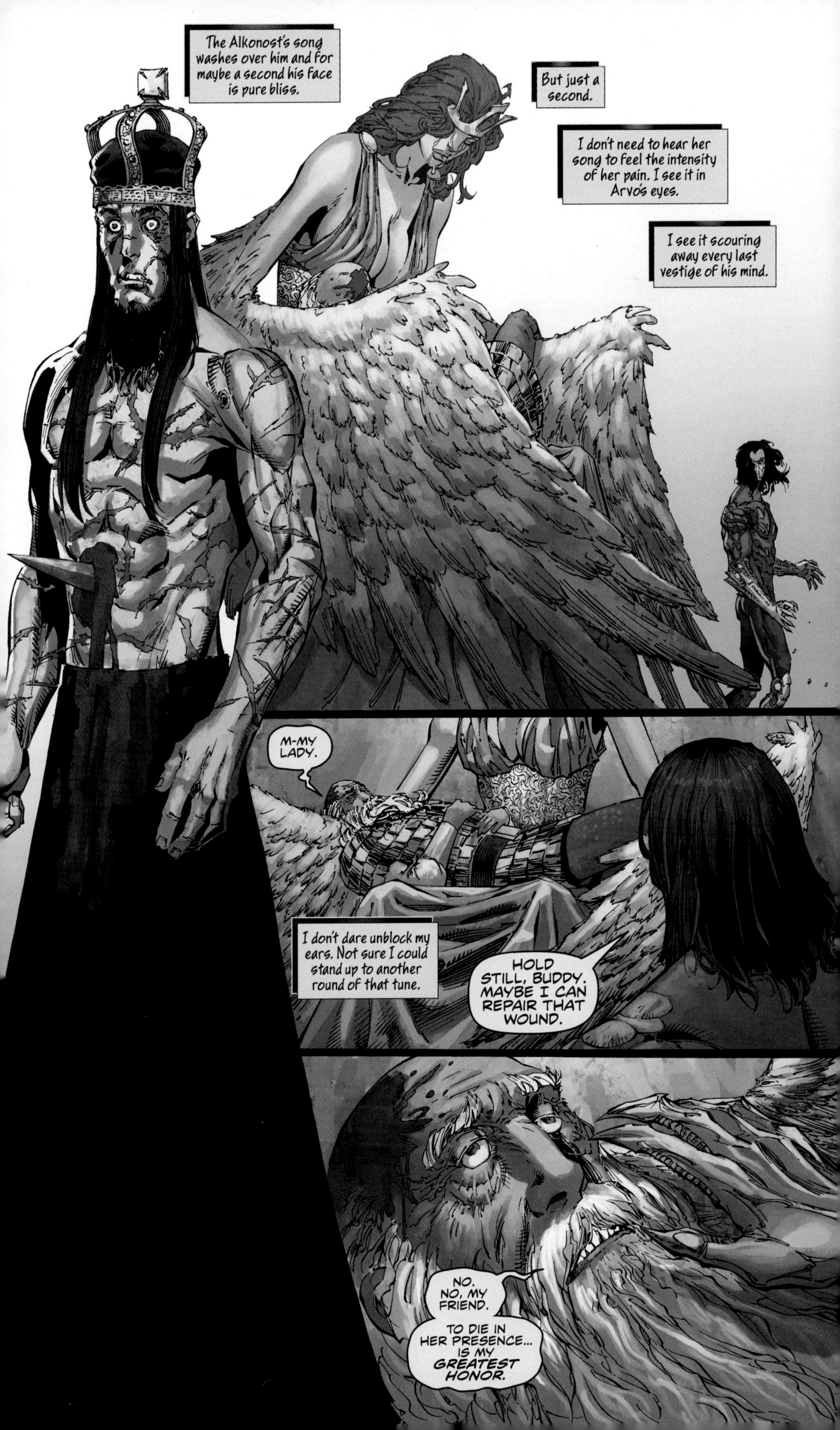

The Alkonost's song washes over him and for maybe a second his face is pure bliss.
But just a second.
I don't need to hear her song to feel the intensity of her pain. I see it in Arvo's eyes.
I see it scouring away every last vestige of his mind.
M-MY LADY.
I don't dare unblock my ears. Not sure I could stand up to another round of that tune.
HOLD STILL, BUDDY. MAYBE I CAN REPAIR THAT WOUND.
NO. NO, MY FRIEND.
TO DIE IN HER PRESENCE... IS MY GREATEST HONOR.

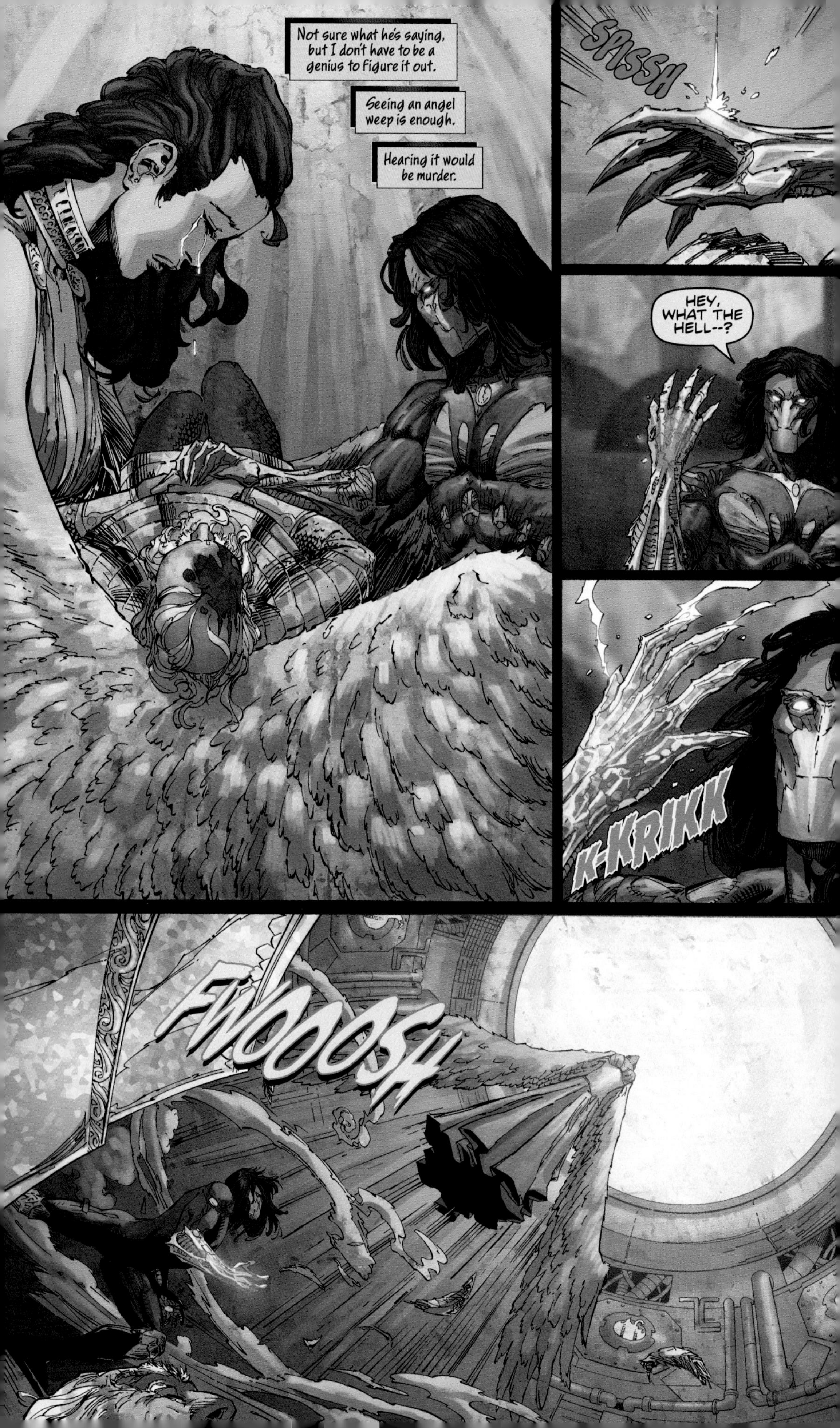
Not sure what he's saying, but I don't have to be a genius to figure it out.
Seeing an angel weep is enough.
Hearing it would be murder.
SPSSH
HEY, WHAT THE HELL--?
K-KRIKK
FWOOOSH

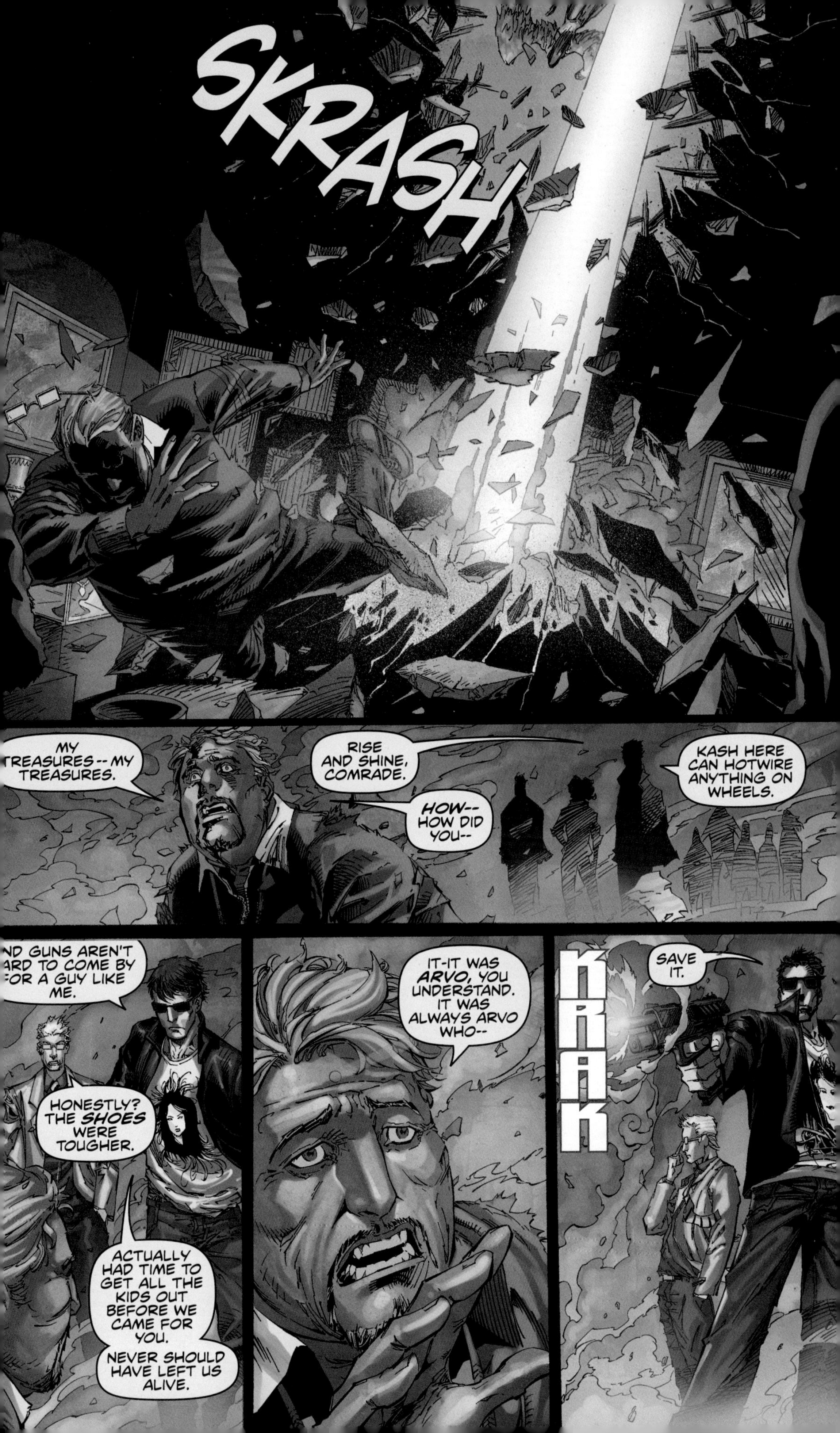
SKRASH
MY TREASURES--MY TREASURES.
RISE AND SHINE, COMRADE.
HOW--HOW DID YOU--
KASH HERE CAN HOTWIRE ANYTHING ON WHEELS.
ND GUNS AREN'T ARD TO COME BY FOR A GUY LIKE ME.
HONESTLY? THE SHOES WERE TOUGHER.
ACTUALLY HAD TIME TO GET ALL THE KIDS OUT BEFORE WE CAME FOR YOU.
NEVER SHOULD HAVE LEFT US ALIVE.
IT-IT WAS ARVO, YOU UNDERSTAND. IT WAS ALWAYS ARVO WHO--
KRAK
SAVE IT.

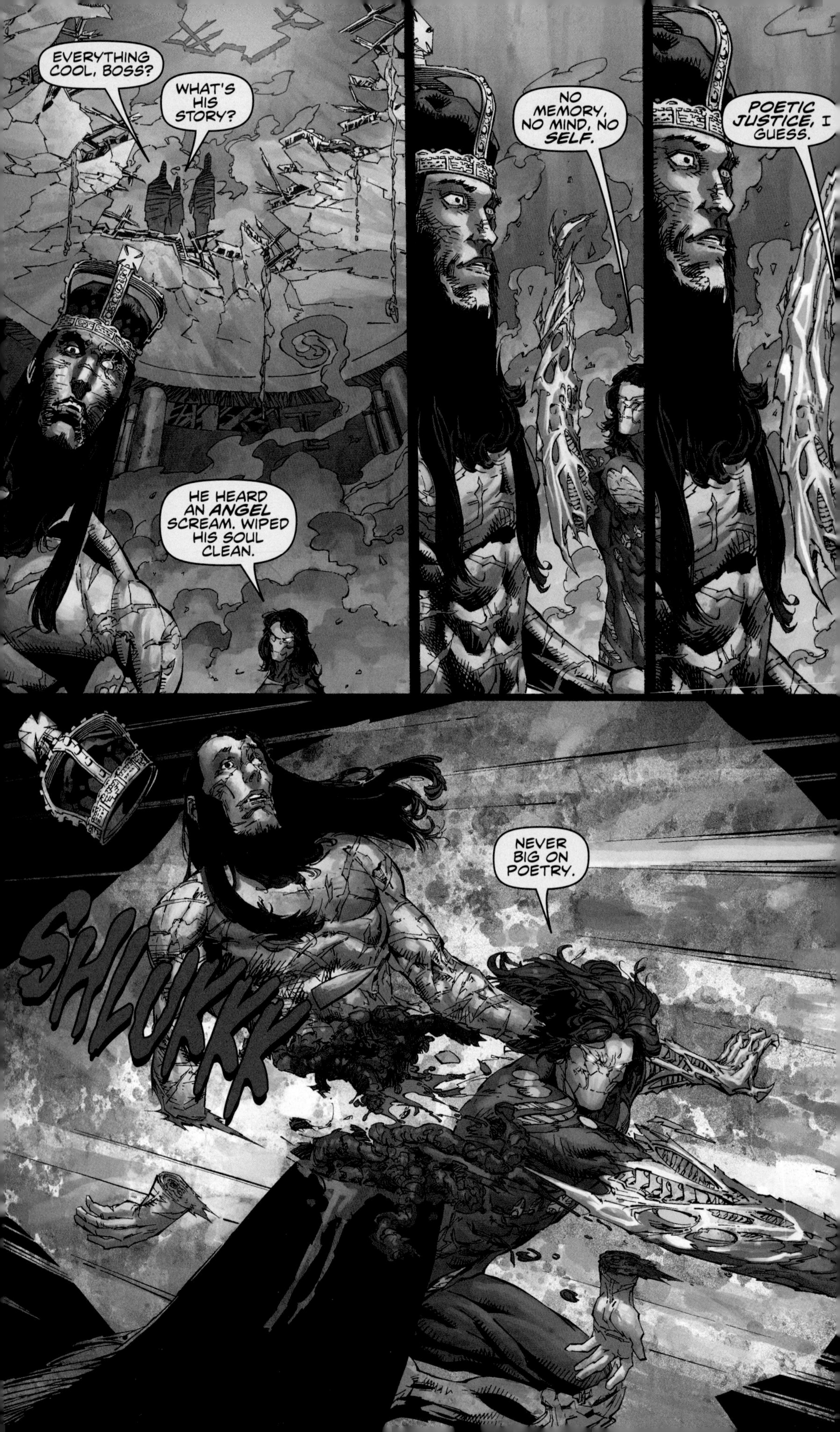
EVERYTHING COOL, BOSS?
WHAT'S HIS STORY?
HE HEARD AN ANGEL SCREAM. WIPED HIS SOUL CLEAN.
NO MEMORY, NO MIND, NO SELF.
POETIC JUSTICE, I GUESS.
NEVER BIG ON POETRY.
SHLUKK

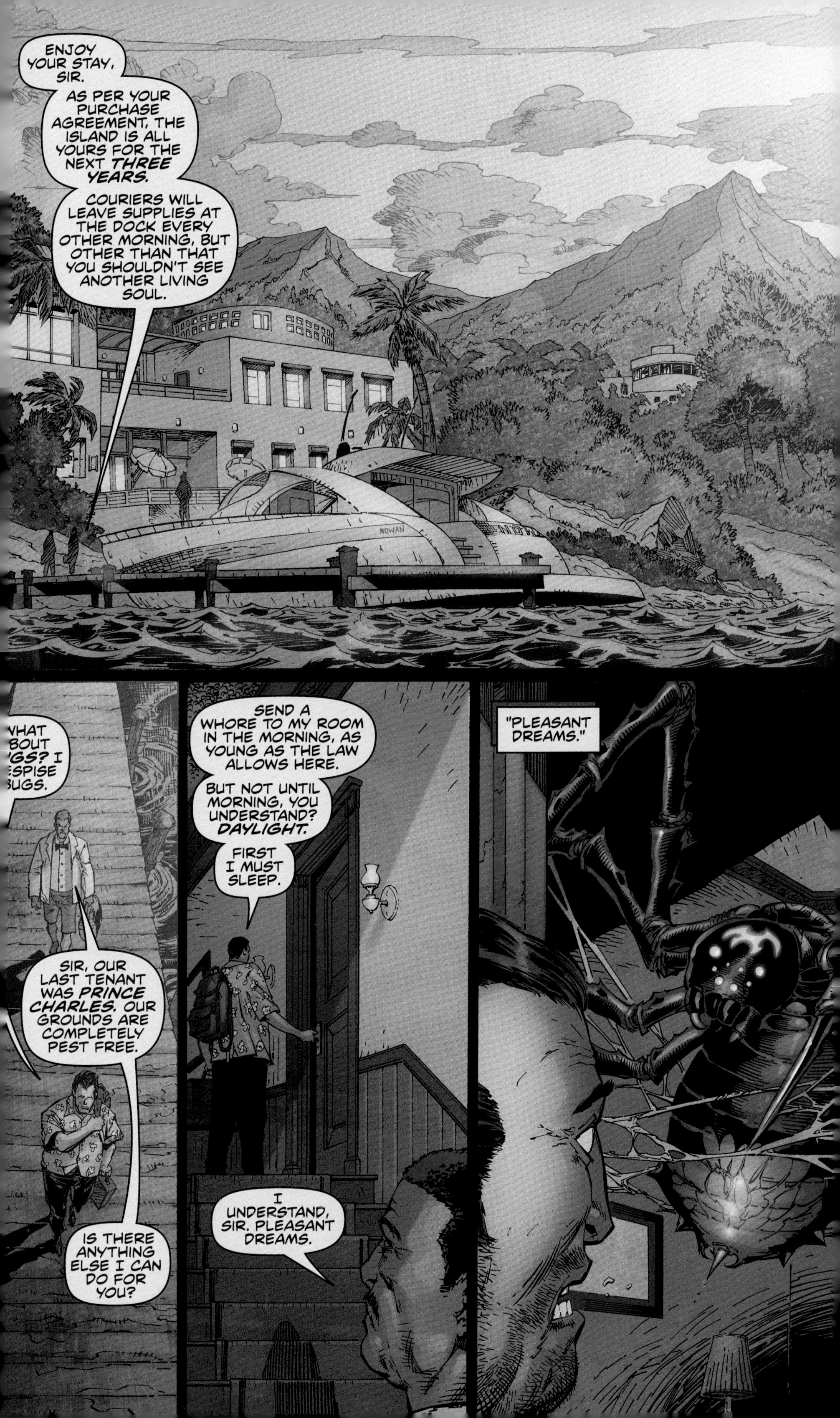
ENJOY YOUR STAY, SIR.
AS PER YOUR PURCHASE AGREEMENT, THE ISLAND IS ALL YOURS FOR THE NEXT ***THREE YEARS.***
COURIERS WILL LEAVE SUPPLIES AT THE DOCK EVERY OTHER MORNING, BUT OTHER THAN THAT YOU SHOULDN'T SEE ANOTHER LIVING SOUL.
NOWAN
WHAT BOUT GS? I ESPISE BUGS.
SIR, OUR LAST TENANT WAS ***PRINCE CHARLES.*** OUR GROUNDS ARE COMPLETELY PEST FREE.
IS THERE ANYTHING ELSE I CAN DO FOR YOU?
SEND A WHORE TO MY ROOM IN THE MORNING, AS YOUNG AS THE LAW ALLOWS HERE.
BUT NOT UNTIL MORNING, YOU UNDERSTAND? ***DAYLIGHT.***
FIRST I MUST SLEEP.
I UNDERSTAND, SIR. PLEASANT DREAMS.
"PLEASANT DREAMS."

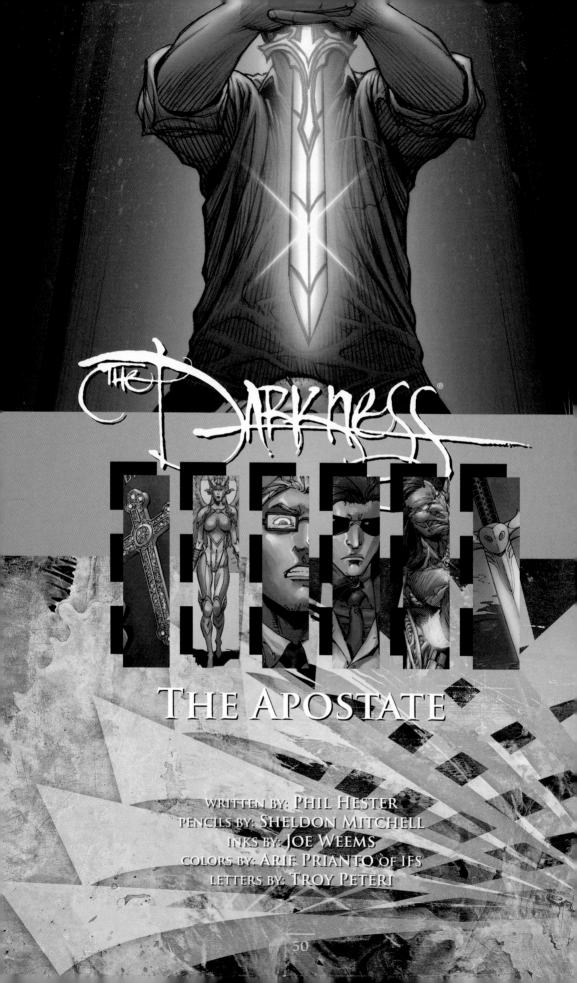

THE DARKNESS

THE APOSTATE

WRITTEN BY: PHIL HESTER
PENCILS BY: SHELDON MITCHELL
INKS BY: JOE WEEMS
COLORS BY: ARIF PRIANTO OF IFS
LETTERS BY: TROY PETERI

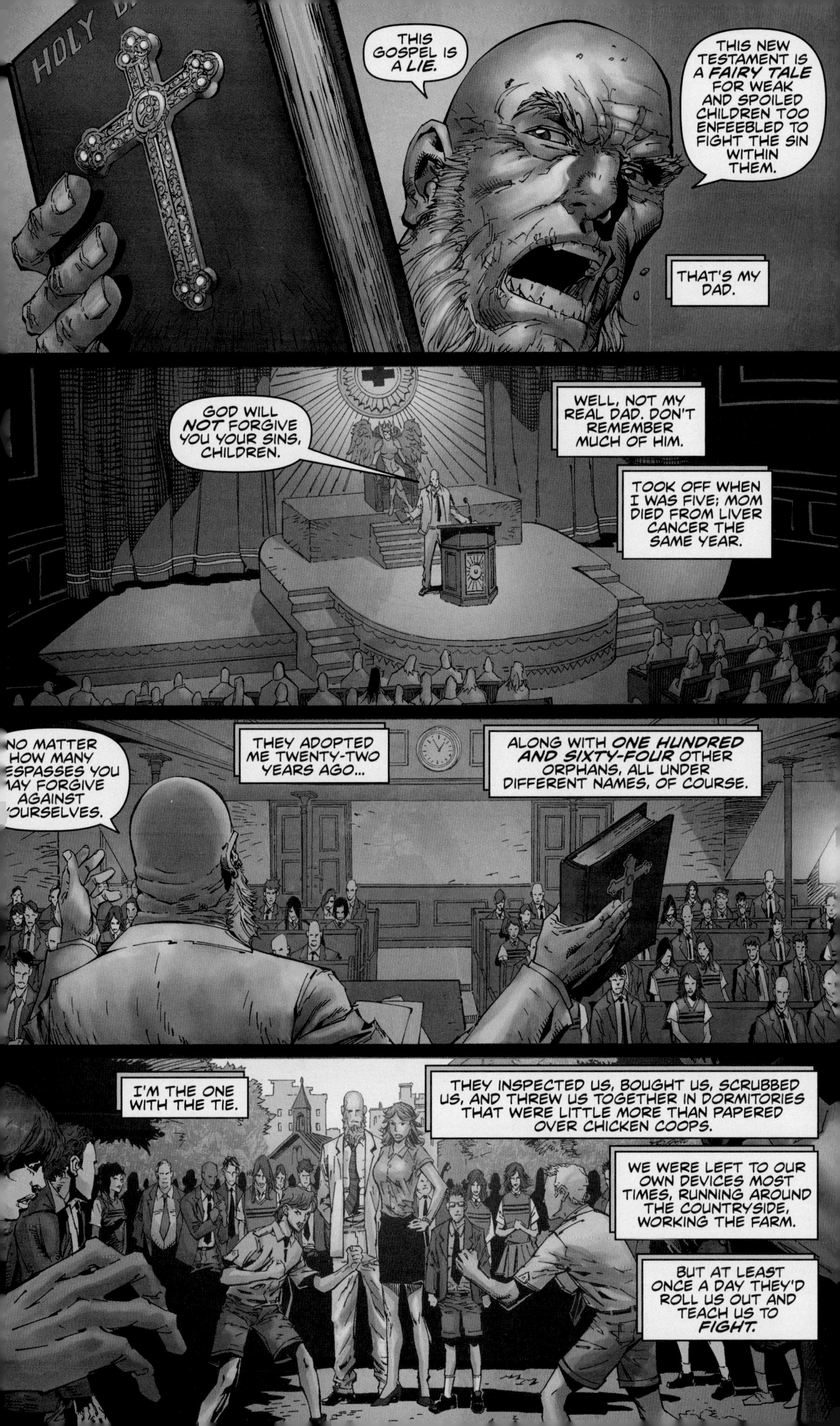
HOLY
THIS GOSPEL IS A LIE.
THIS NEW TESTAMENT IS A FAIRY TALE FOR WEAK AND SPOILED CHILDREN TOO ENFEEBLED TO FIGHT THE SIN WITHIN THEM.
THAT'S MY DAD.
GOD WILL NOT FORGIVE YOU YOUR SINS, CHILDREN.
WELL, NOT MY REAL DAD. DON'T REMEMBER MUCH OF HIM.
TOOK OFF WHEN I WAS FIVE; MOM DIED FROM LIVER CANCER THE SAME YEAR.
NO MATTER HOW MANY ESPASSES YOU AY FORGIVE AGAINST OURSELVES.
THEY ADOPTED ME TWENTY-TWO YEARS AGO...
ALONG WITH ONE HUNDRED AND SIXTY-FOUR OTHER ORPHANS, ALL UNDER DIFFERENT NAMES, OF COURSE.
I'M THE ONE WITH THE TIE.
THEY INSPECTED US, BOUGHT US, SCRUBBED US, AND THREW US TOGETHER IN DORMITORIES THAT WERE LITTLE MORE THAN PAPERED OVER CHICKEN COOPS.
WE WERE LEFT TO OUR OWN DEVICES MOST TIMES, RUNNING AROUND THE COUNTRYSIDE, WORKING THE FARM.
BUT AT LEAST ONCE A DAY THEY'D ROLL US OUT AND TEACH US TO FIGHT.

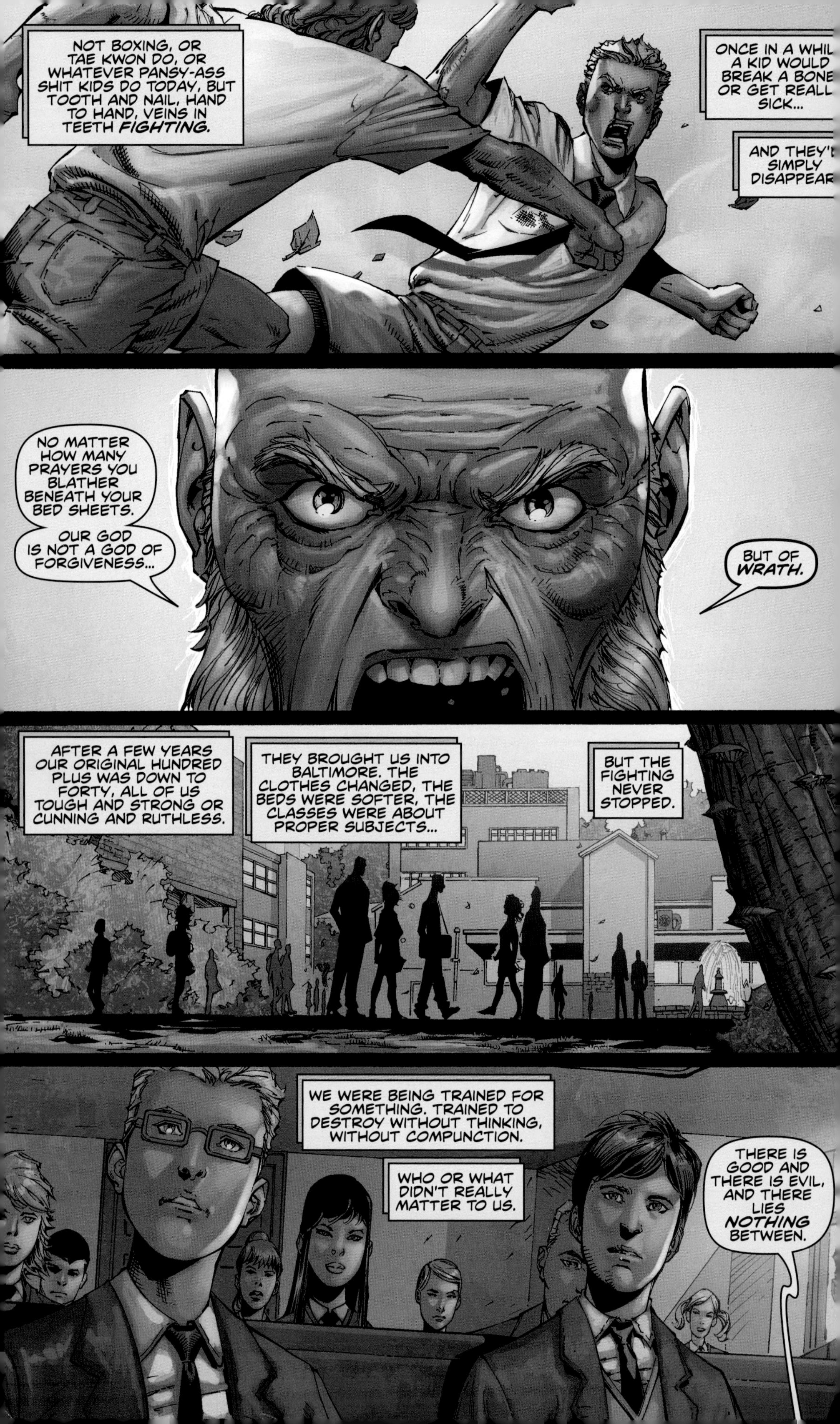
NOT BOXING, OR TAE KWON DO, OR WHATEVER PANSY-ASS SHIT KIDS DO TODAY, BUT TOOTH AND NAIL, HAND TO HAND, VEINS IN TEETH FIGHTING.
ONCE IN A WHIL A KID WOULD BREAK A BONE OR GET REALL SICK...
AND THEY'I SIMPLY DISAPPEAR
NO MATTER HOW MANY PRAYERS YOU BLATHER BENEATH YOUR BED SHEETS.
OUR GOD IS NOT A GOD OF FORGIVENESS...
BUT OF WRATH.
AFTER A FEW YEARS OUR ORIGINAL HUNDRED PLUS WAS DOWN TO FORTY, ALL OF US TOUGH AND STRONG OR CUNNING AND RUTHLESS.
THEY BROUGHT US INTO BALTIMORE. THE CLOTHES CHANGED, THE BEDS WERE SOFTER, THE CLASSES WERE ABOUT PROPER SUBJECTS...
BUT THE FIGHTING NEVER STOPPED.
WE WERE BEING TRAINED FOR SOMETHING. TRAINED TO DESTROY WITHOUT THINKING, WITHOUT COMPUNCTION.
WHO OR WHAT DIDN'T REALLY MATTER TO US.
THERE IS GOOD AND THERE IS EVIL, AND THERE LIES NOTHING BETWEEN.

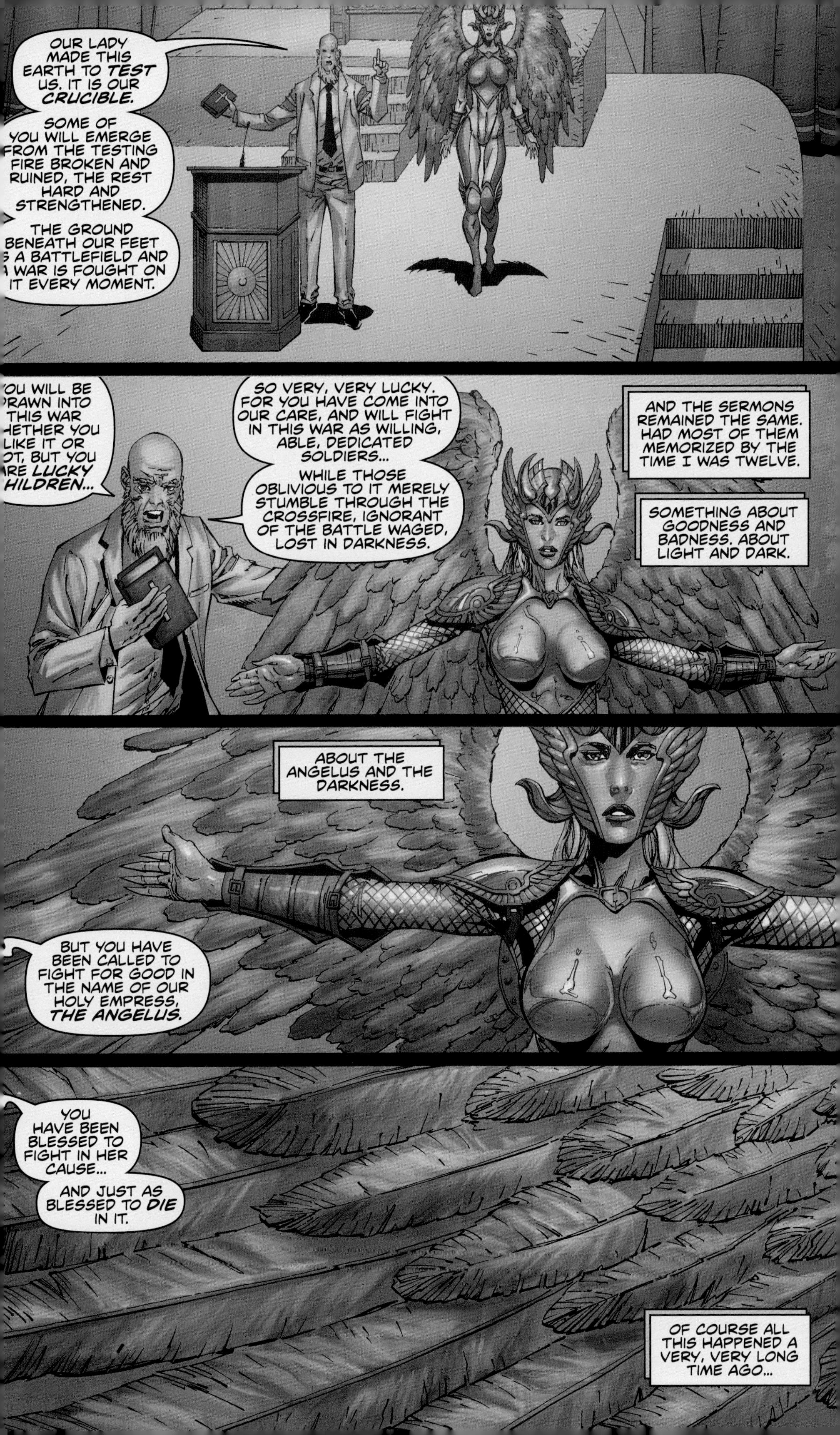

OUR LADY MADE THIS EARTH TO TEST US. IT IS OUR CRUCIBLE.
SOME OF YOU WILL EMERGE FROM THE TESTING FIRE BROKEN AND RUINED, THE REST HARD AND STRENGTHENED.
THE GROUND BENEATH OUR FEET IS A BATTLEFIELD AND A WAR IS FOUGHT ON IT EVERY MOMENT.
YOU WILL BE DRAWN INTO THIS WAR WHETHER YOU LIKE IT OR NOT, BUT YOU ARE LUCKY CHILDREN...
SO VERY, VERY LUCKY. FOR YOU HAVE COME INTO OUR CARE, AND WILL FIGHT IN THIS WAR AS WILLING, ABLE, DEDICATED SOLDIERS...
WHILE THOSE OBLIVIOUS TO IT MERELY STUMBLE THROUGH THE CROSSFIRE, IGNORANT OF THE BATTLE WAGED, LOST IN DARKNESS.
AND THE SERMONS REMAINED THE SAME. HAD MOST OF THEM MEMORIZED BY THE TIME I WAS TWELVE.
SOMETHING ABOUT GOODNESS AND BADNESS. ABOUT LIGHT AND DARK.
ABOUT THE ANGELUS AND THE DARKNESS.
BUT YOU HAVE BEEN CALLED TO FIGHT FOR GOOD IN THE NAME OF OUR HOLY EMPRESS, THE ANGELUS.
YOU HAVE BEEN BLESSED TO FIGHT IN HER CAUSE...
AND JUST AS BLESSED TO DIE IN IT.
OF COURSE ALL THIS HAPPENED A VERY, VERY LONG TIME AGO...

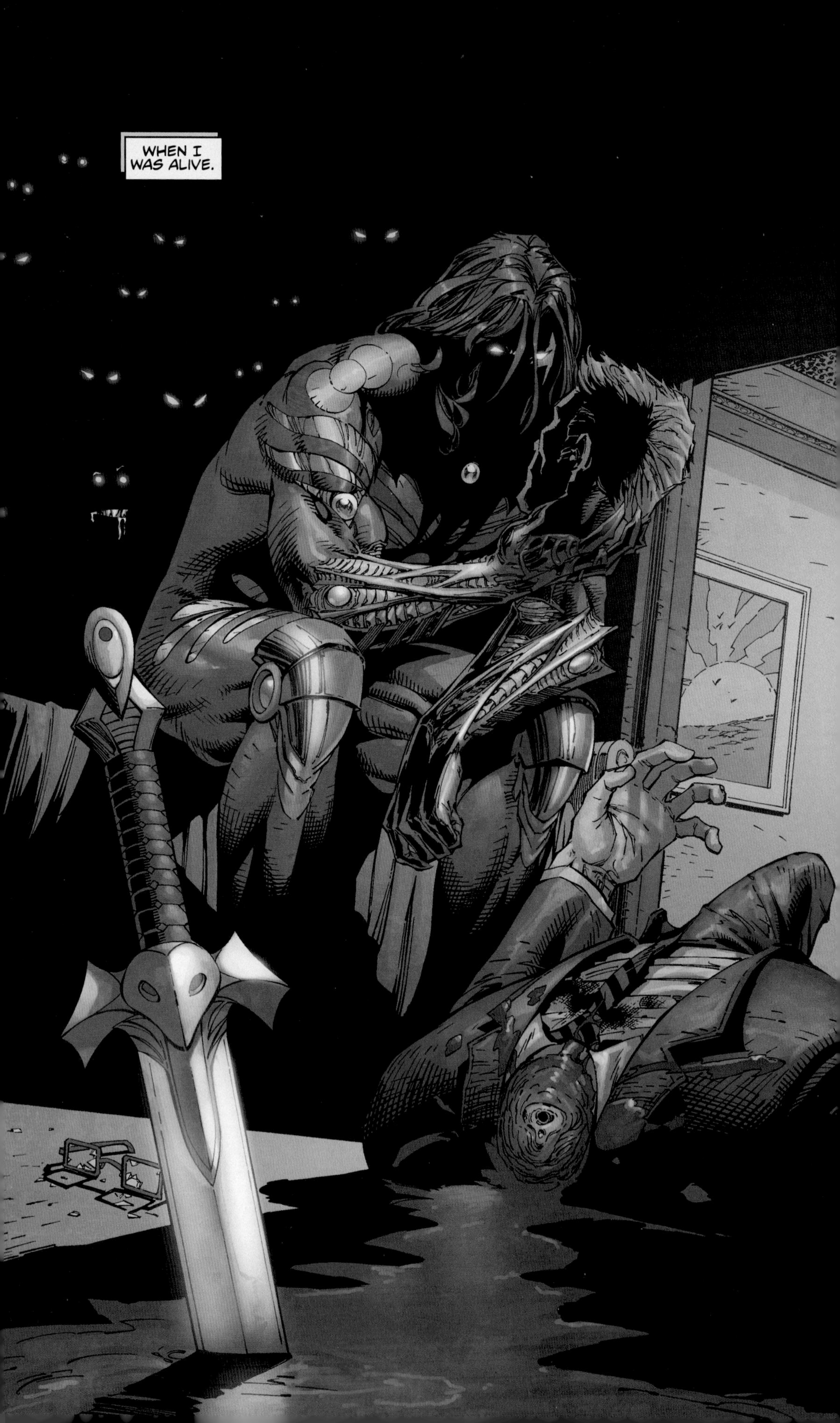
WHEN I WAS ALIVE.

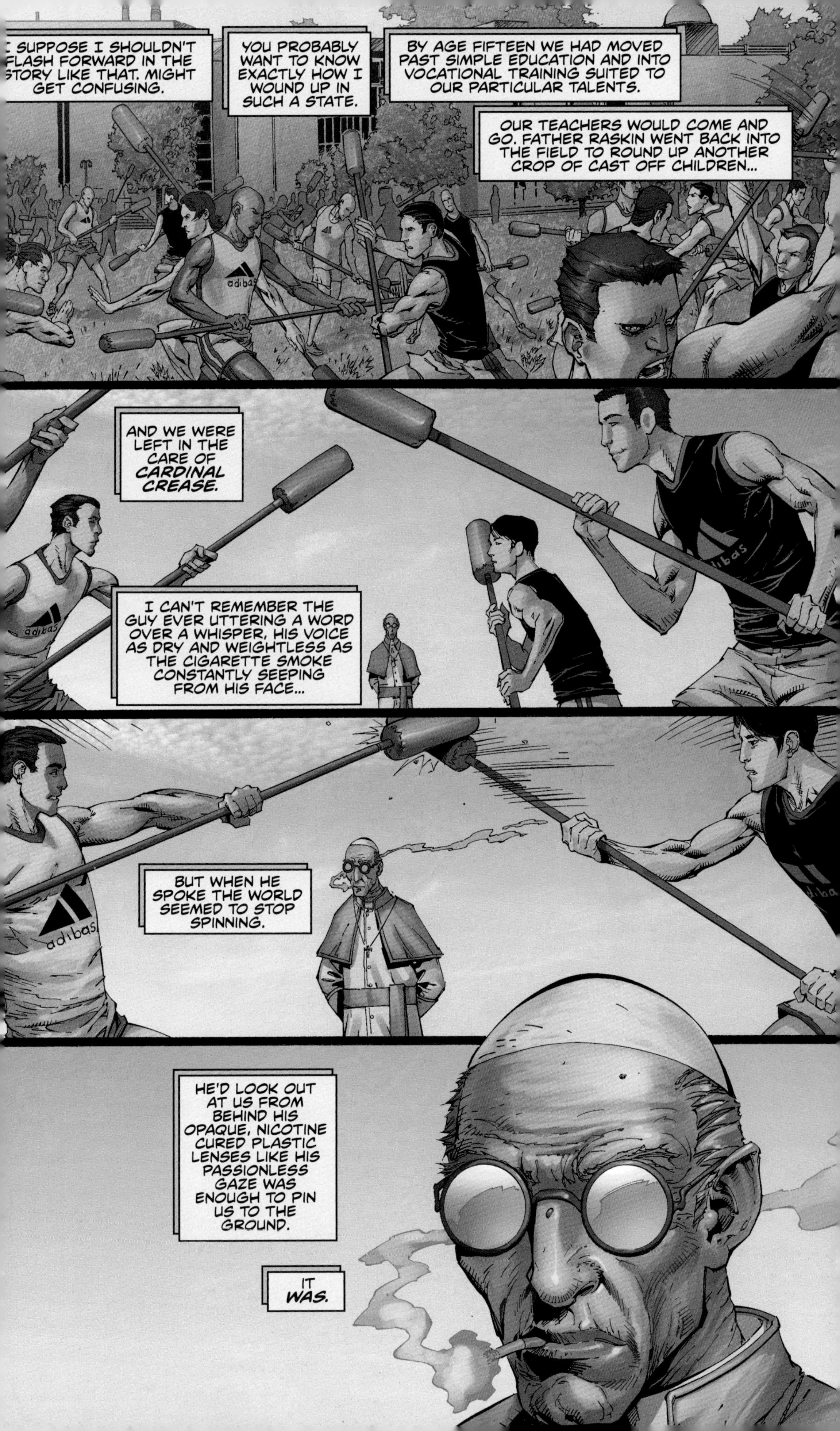
I SUPPOSE I SHOULDN'T FLASH FORWARD IN THE STORY LIKE THAT. MIGHT GET CONFUSING.
YOU PROBABLY WANT TO KNOW EXACTLY HOW I WOUND UP IN SUCH A STATE.
BY AGE FIFTEEN WE HAD MOVED PAST SIMPLE EDUCATION AND INTO VOCATIONAL TRAINING SUITED TO OUR PARTICULAR TALENTS.
OUR TEACHERS WOULD COME AND GO. FATHER RASKIN WENT BACK INTO THE FIELD TO ROUND UP ANOTHER CROP OF CAST OFF CHILDREN...
AND WE WERE LEFT IN THE CARE OF *CARDINAL CREASE.*
I CAN'T REMEMBER THE GUY EVER UTTERING A WORD OVER A WHISPER, HIS VOICE AS DRY AND WEIGHTLESS AS THE CIGARETTE SMOKE CONSTANTLY SEEPING FROM HIS FACE...
BUT WHEN HE SPOKE THE WORLD SEEMED TO STOP SPINNING.
HE'D LOOK OUT AT US FROM BEHIND HIS OPAQUE, NICOTINE CURED PLASTIC LENSES LIKE HIS PASSIONLESS GAZE WAS ENOUGH TO PIN US TO THE GROUND.
IT *WAS.*

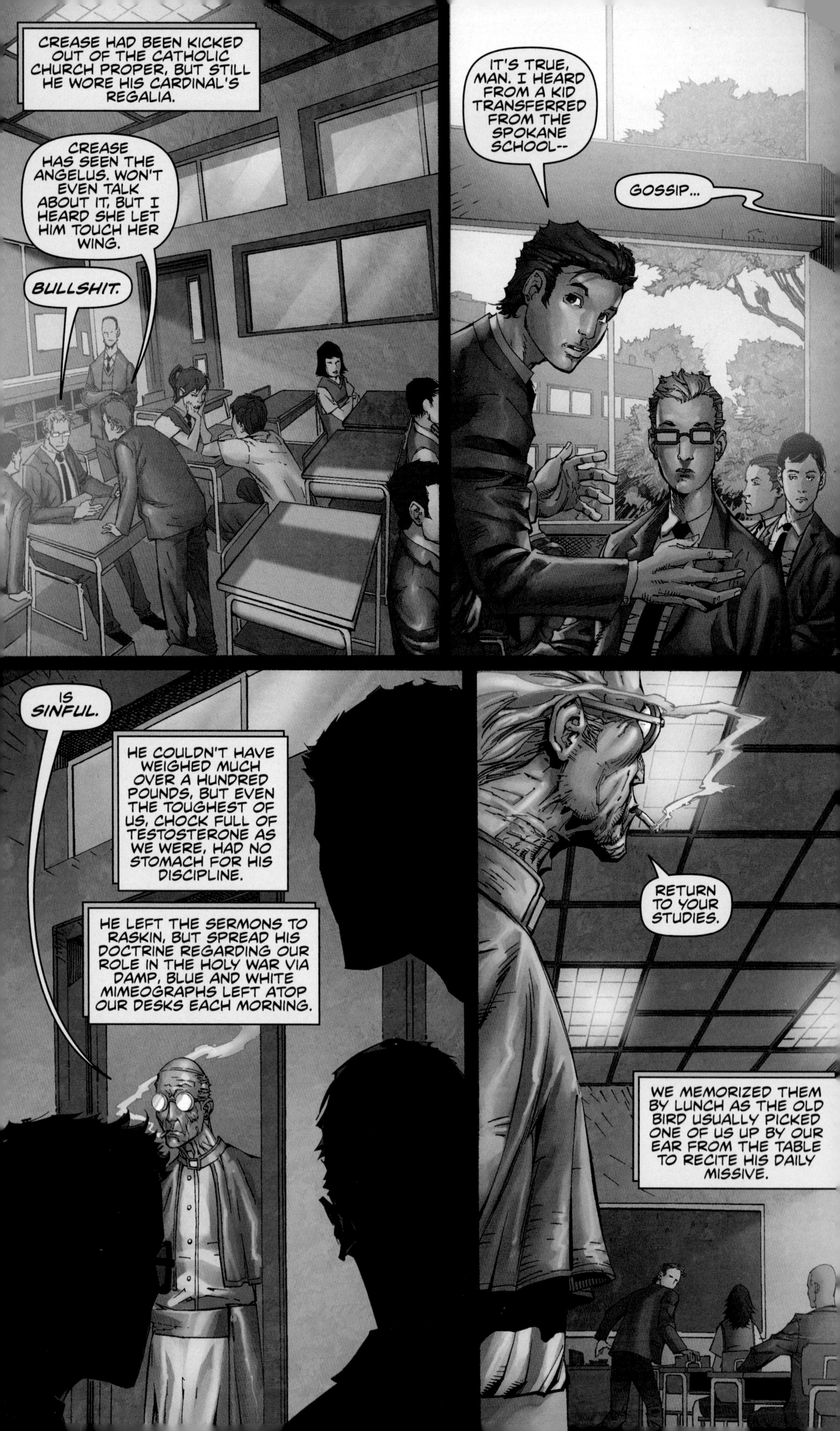
CREASE HAD BEEN KICKED OUT OF THE CATHOLIC CHURCH PROPER, BUT STILL HE WORE HIS CARDINAL'S REGALIA.
CREASE HAS SEEN THE ANGELUS. WON'T EVEN TALK ABOUT IT, BUT I HEARD SHE LET HIM TOUCH HER WING.
BULLSHIT.
IT'S TRUE, MAN. I HEARD FROM A KID TRANSFERRED FROM THE SPOKANE SCHOOL--
GOSSIP...
IS SINFUL.
HE COULDN'T HAVE WEIGHED MUCH OVER A HUNDRED POUNDS, BUT EVEN THE TOUGHEST OF US, CHOCK FULL OF TESTOSTERONE AS WE WERE, HAD NO STOMACH FOR HIS DISCIPLINE.
HE LEFT THE SERMONS TO RASKIN, BUT SPREAD HIS DOCTRINE REGARDING OUR ROLE IN THE HOLY WAR VIA DAMP, BLUE AND WHITE MIMEOGRAPHS LEFT ATOP OUR DESKS EACH MORNING.
RETURN TO YOUR STUDIES.
WE MEMORIZED THEM BY LUNCH AS THE OLD BIRD USUALLY PICKED ONE OF US UP BY OUR EAR FROM THE TABLE TO RECITE HIS DAILY MISSIVE.

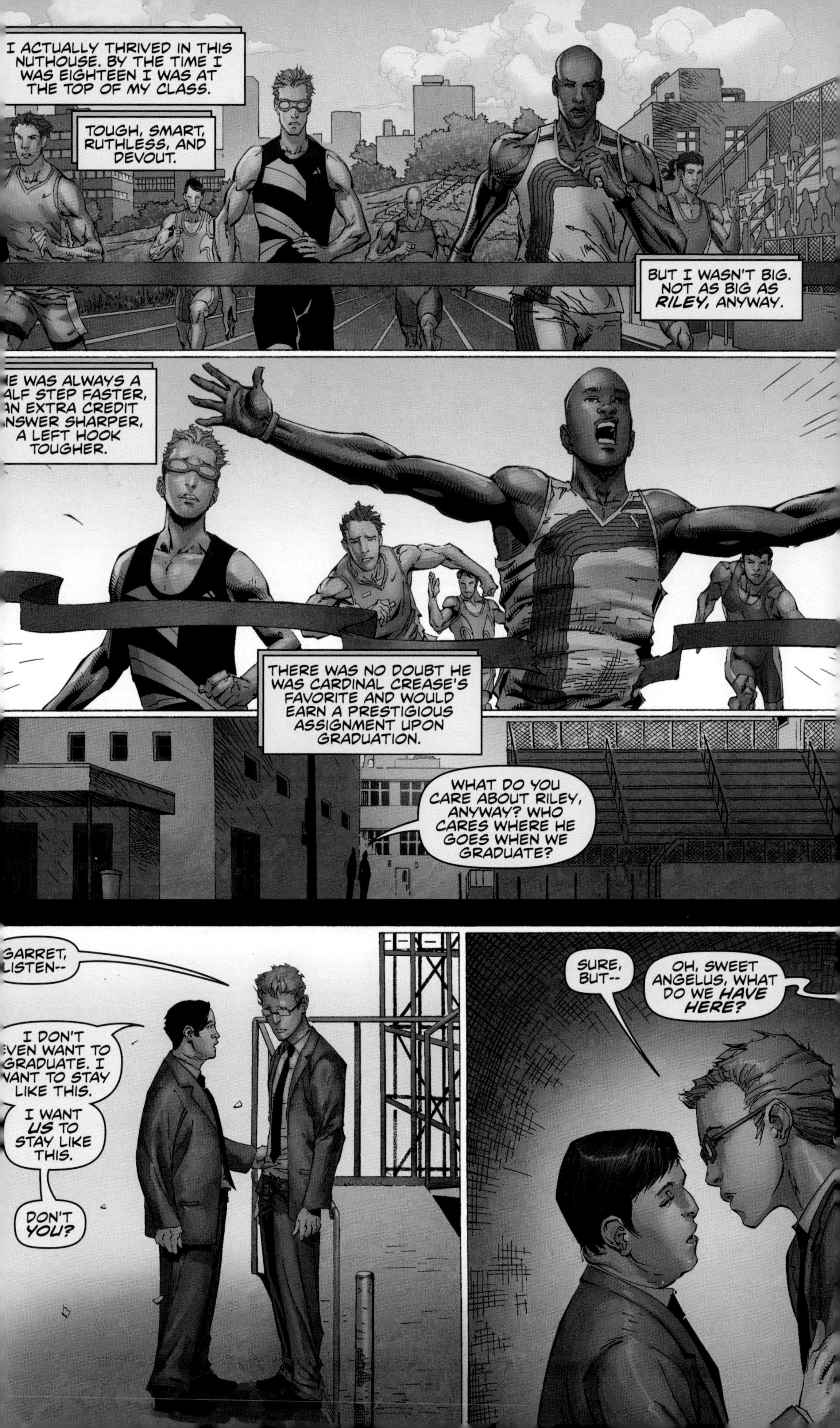
I ACTUALLY THRIVED IN THIS NUTHOUSE. BY THE TIME I WAS EIGHTEEN I WAS AT THE TOP OF MY CLASS.
TOUGH, SMART, RUTHLESS, AND DEVOUT.
BUT I WASN'T BIG. NOT AS BIG AS RILEY, ANYWAY.
HE WAS ALWAYS A HALF STEP FASTER, AN EXTRA CREDIT ANSWER SHARPER, A LEFT HOOK TOUGHER.
THERE WAS NO DOUBT HE WAS CARDINAL CREASE'S FAVORITE AND WOULD EARN A PRESTIGIOUS ASSIGNMENT UPON GRADUATION.
WHAT DO YOU CARE ABOUT RILEY, ANYWAY? WHO CARES WHERE HE GOES WHEN WE GRADUATE?
GARRET, LISTEN--
I DON'T EVEN WANT TO GRADUATE. I WANT TO STAY LIKE THIS.
I WANT US TO STAY LIKE THIS.
DON'T YOU?
SURE, BUT--
OH, SWEET ANGELUS, WHAT DO WE HAVE HERE?

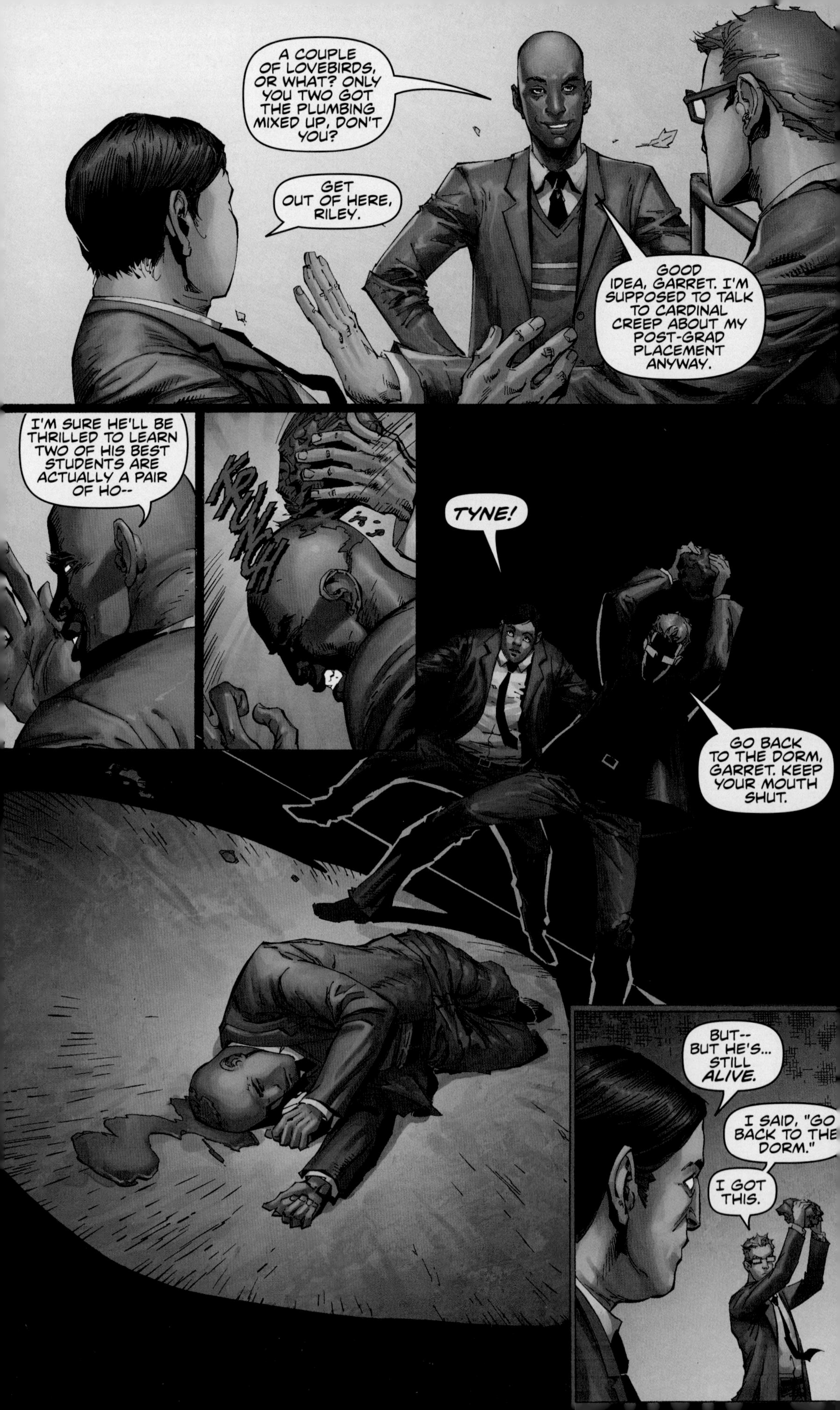
A COUPLE OF LOVEBIRDS, OR WHAT? ONLY YOU TWO GOT THE PLUMBING MIXED UP, DON'T YOU?
GET OUT OF HERE, RILEY.
GOOD IDEA, GARRET. I'M SUPPOSED TO TALK TO CARDINAL CREEP ABOUT MY POST-GRAD PLACEMENT ANYWAY.
I'M SURE HE'LL BE THRILLED TO LEARN TWO OF HIS BEST STUDENTS ARE ACTUALLY A PAIR OF HO--
KRUNCH
TYNE!
GO BACK TO THE DORM, GARRET. KEEP YOUR MOUTH SHUT.
BUT-- BUT HE'S... STILL ALIVE.
I SAID, "GO BACK TO THE DORM."
I GOT THIS.

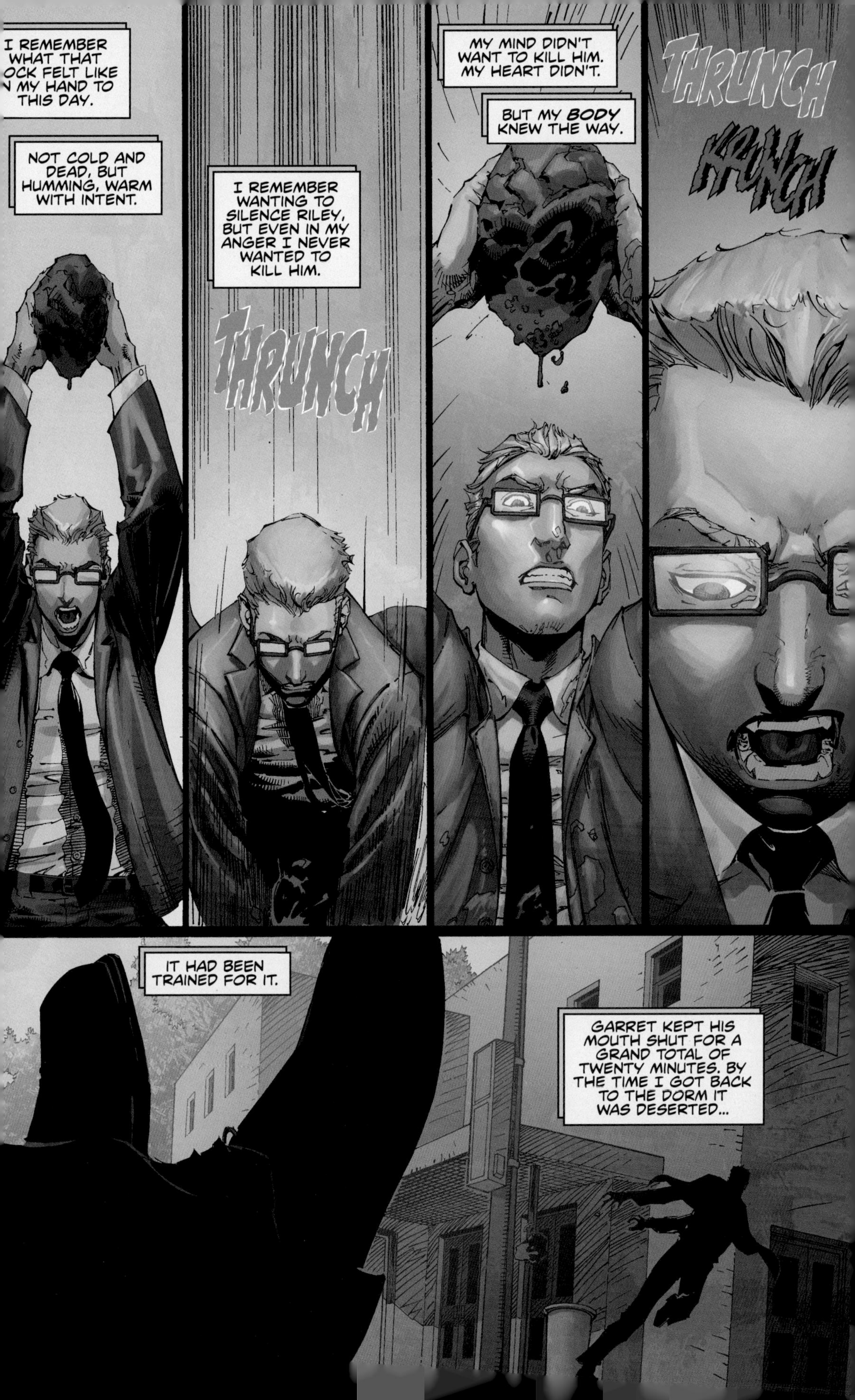
I REMEMBER WHAT THAT OCK FELT LIKE N MY HAND TO THIS DAY.
NOT COLD AND DEAD, BUT HUMMING, WARM WITH INTENT.
I REMEMBER WANTING TO SILENCE RILEY, BUT EVEN IN MY ANGER I NEVER WANTED TO KILL HIM.
THRUNCH
MY MIND DIDN'T WANT TO KILL HIM. MY HEART DIDN'T.
BUT MY BODY KNEW THE WAY.
THRUNCH
KRUNCH
IT HAD BEEN TRAINED FOR IT.
GARRET KEPT HIS MOUTH SHUT FOR A GRAND TOTAL OF TWENTY MINUTES. BY THE TIME I GOT BACK TO THE DORM IT WAS DESERTED...

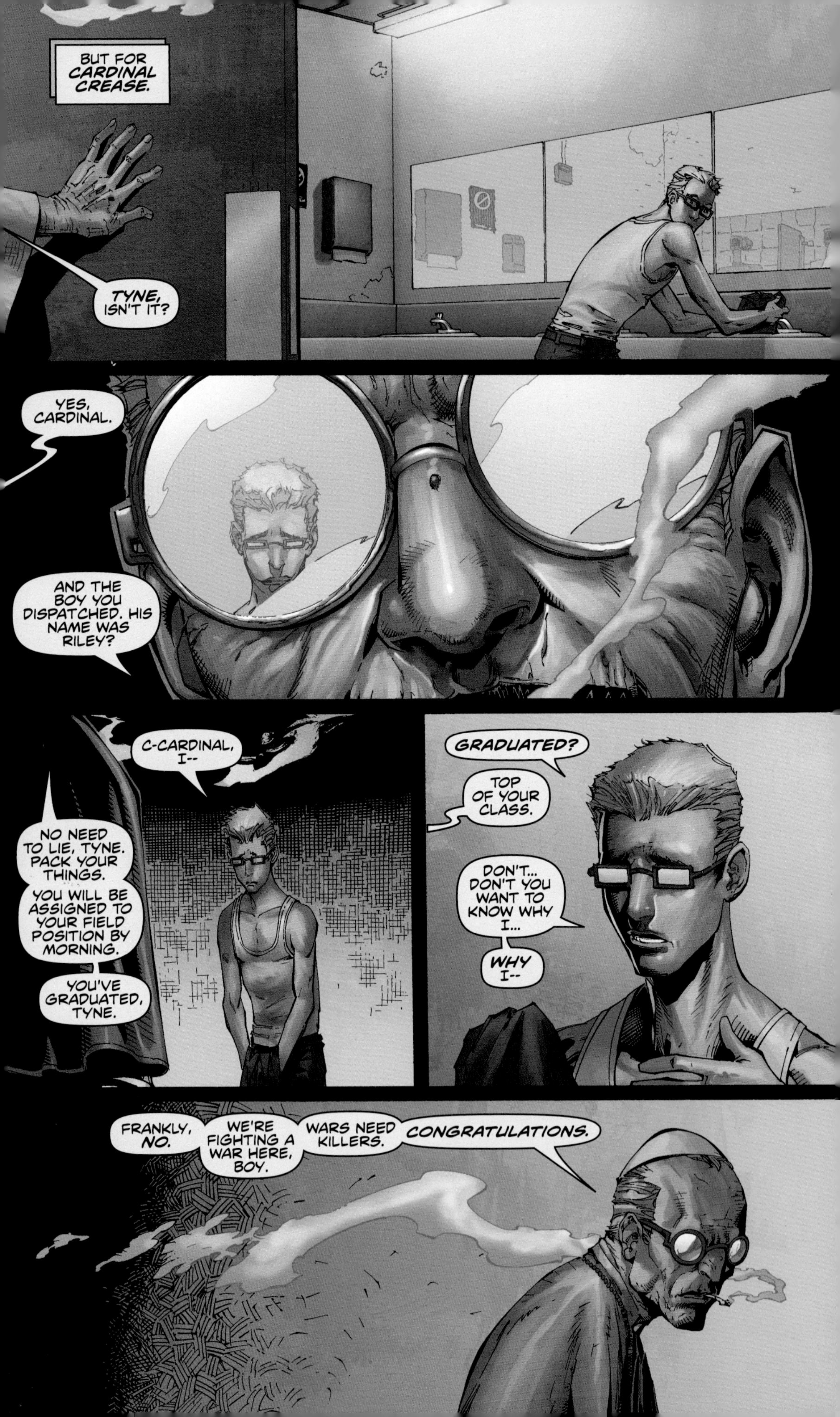
BUT FOR CARDINAL CREASE.
TYNE, ISN'T IT?
YES, CARDINAL.
AND THE BOY YOU DISPATCHED. HIS NAME WAS RILEY?
C-CARDINAL, I--
NO NEED TO LIE, TYNE. PACK YOUR THINGS.
YOU WILL BE ASSIGNED TO YOUR FIELD POSITION BY MORNING.
YOU'VE GRADUATED, TYNE.
GRADUATED?
TOP OF YOUR CLASS.
DON'T... DON'T YOU WANT TO KNOW WHY I...
WHY I--
FRANKLY, NO.
WE'RE FIGHTING A WAR HERE, BOY.
WARS NEED KILLERS.
CONGRATULATIONS.

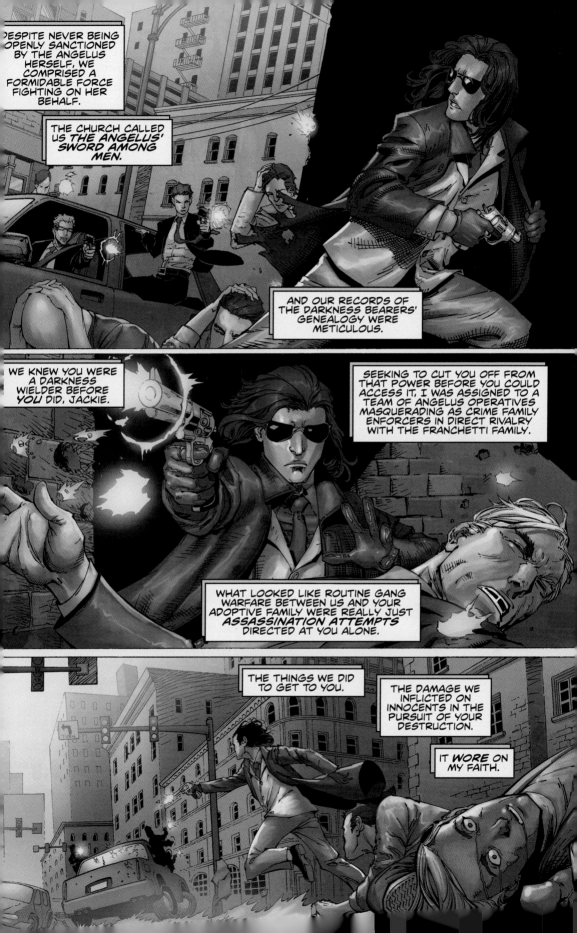

DESPITE NEVER BEING OPENLY SANCTIONED BY THE ANGELUS HERSELF, WE COMPRISED A FORMIDABLE FORCE FIGHTING ON HER BEHALF.

THE CHURCH CALLED US *THE ANGELUS' SWORD AMONG MEN.*

AND OUR RECORDS OF THE DARKNESS BEARERS' GENEALOGY WERE METICULOUS.

WE KNEW YOU WERE A DARKNESS WIELDER BEFORE *YOU* DID, JACKIE.

SEEKING TO CUT YOU OFF FROM THAT POWER BEFORE YOU COULD ACCESS IT, I WAS ASSIGNED TO A TEAM OF ANGELUS OPERATIVES MASQUERADING AS CRIME FAMILY ENFORCERS IN DIRECT RIVALRY WITH THE FRANCHETTI FAMILY.

WHAT LOOKED LIKE ROUTINE GANG WARFARE BETWEEN US AND YOUR ADOPTIVE FAMILY WERE REALLY JUST *ASSASSINATION ATTEMPTS* DIRECTED AT YOU ALONE.

THE THINGS WE DID TO GET TO YOU.

THE DAMAGE WE INFLICTED ON INNOCENTS IN THE PURSUIT OF YOUR DESTRUCTION.

IT *WORE* ON MY FAITH.

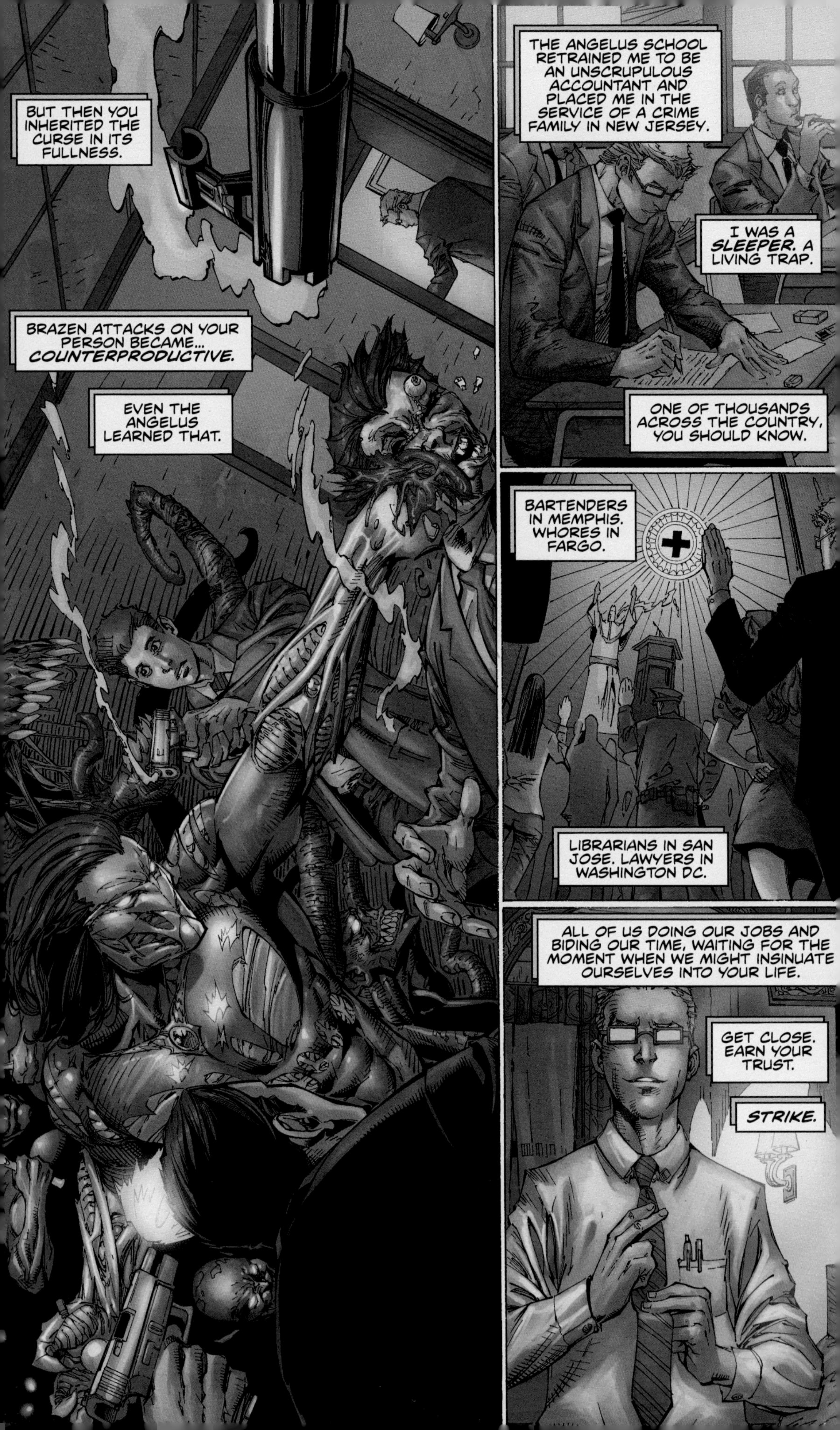
BUT THEN YOU INHERITED THE CURSE IN ITS FULLNESS.
BRAZEN ATTACKS ON YOUR PERSON BECAME... *COUNTERPRODUCTIVE.*
EVEN THE ANGELUS LEARNED THAT.
THE ANGELUS SCHOOL RETRAINED ME TO BE AN UNSCRUPULOUS ACCOUNTANT AND PLACED ME IN THE SERVICE OF A CRIME FAMILY IN NEW JERSEY.
I WAS A *SLEEPER.* A LIVING TRAP.
ONE OF THOUSANDS ACROSS THE COUNTRY, YOU SHOULD KNOW.
BARTENDERS IN MEMPHIS. WHORES IN FARGO.
LIBRARIANS IN SAN JOSE. LAWYERS IN WASHINGTON DC.
ALL OF US DOING OUR JOBS AND BIDING OUR TIME, WAITING FOR THE MOMENT WHEN WE MIGHT INSINUATE OURSELVES INTO YOUR LIFE.
GET CLOSE. EARN YOUR TRUST.
STRIKE.

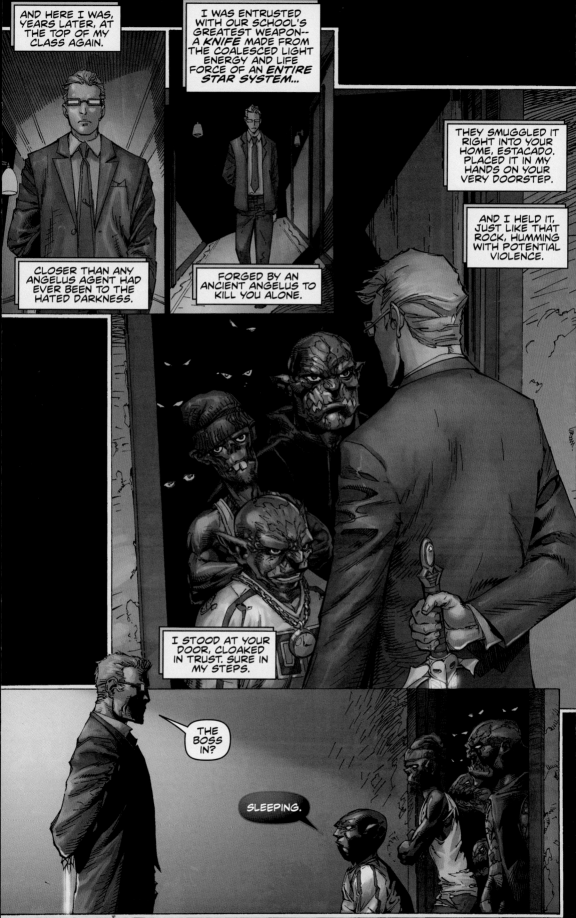

AND HERE I WAS, YEARS LATER, AT THE TOP OF MY CLASS AGAIN.

I WAS ENTRUSTED WITH OUR SCHOOL'S GREATEST WEAPON-- A *KNIFE* MADE FROM THE COALESCED LIGHT ENERGY AND LIFE FORCE OF AN *ENTIRE STAR SYSTEM...*

THEY SMUGGLED IT RIGHT INTO YOUR HOME, ESTACADO. PLACED IT IN MY HANDS ON YOUR VERY DOORSTEP.

AND I HELD IT, JUST LIKE THAT ROCK, HUMMING WITH POTENTIAL VIOLENCE.

CLOSER THAN ANY ANGELUS AGENT HAD EVER BEEN TO THE HATED DARKNESS.

FORGED BY AN ANCIENT ANGELUS TO KILL YOU ALONE.

I STOOD AT YOUR DOOR, CLOAKED IN TRUST. SURE IN MY STEPS.

THE BOSS IN?

SLEEPING.

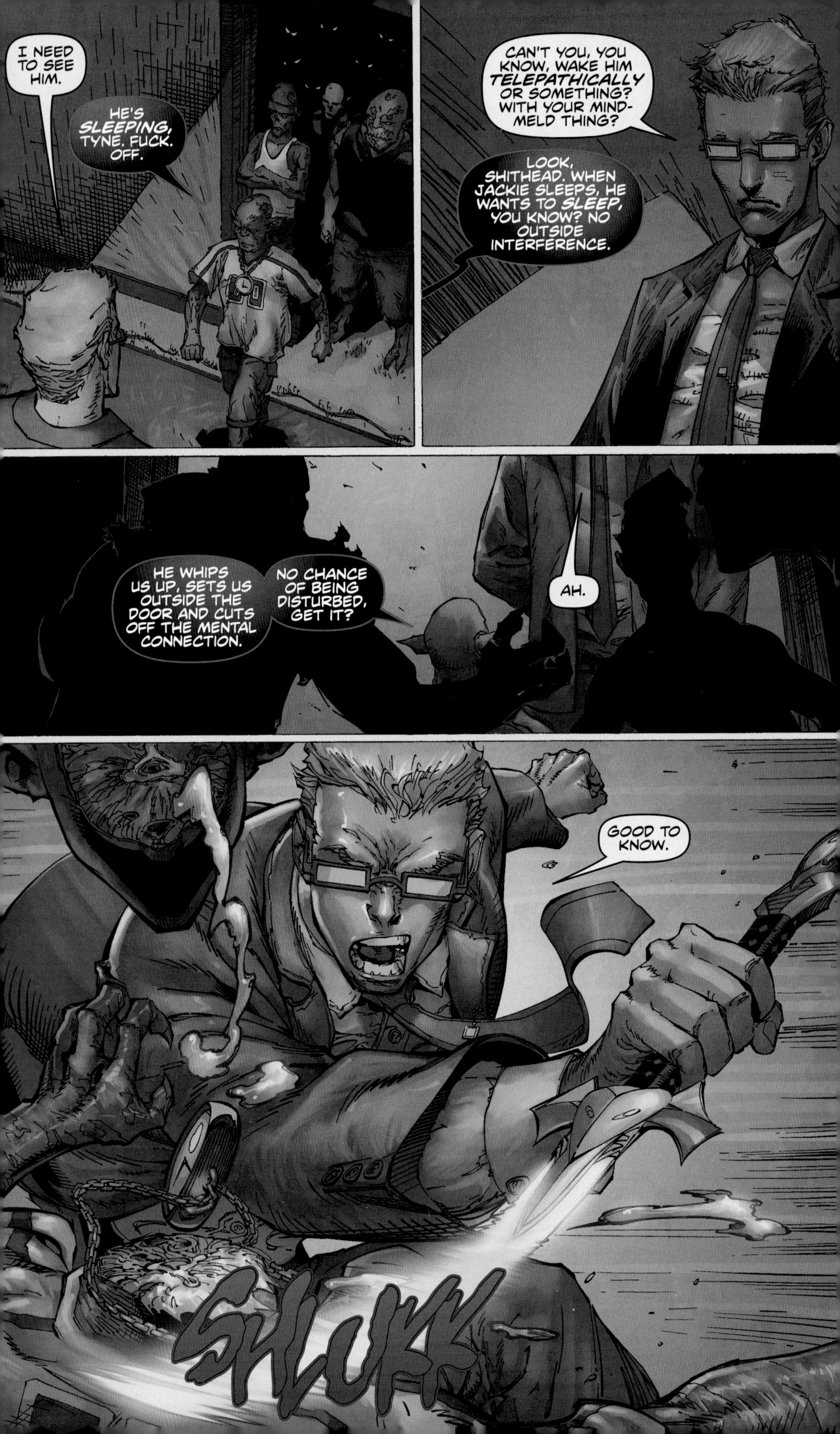
I NEED TO SEE HIM.
HE'S SLEEPING, TYNE. FUCK. OFF.
CAN'T YOU, YOU KNOW, WAKE HIM TELEPATHICALLY OR SOMETHING? WITH YOUR MIND-MELD THING?
LOOK, SHITHEAD. WHEN JACKIE SLEEPS, HE WANTS TO SLEEP, YOU KNOW? NO OUTSIDE INTERFERENCE.
HE WHIPS US UP, SETS US OUTSIDE THE DOOR AND CUTS OFF THE MENTAL CONNECTION.
NO CHANCE OF BEING DISTURBED, GET IT?
AH.
GOOD TO KNOW.
SHLUKK

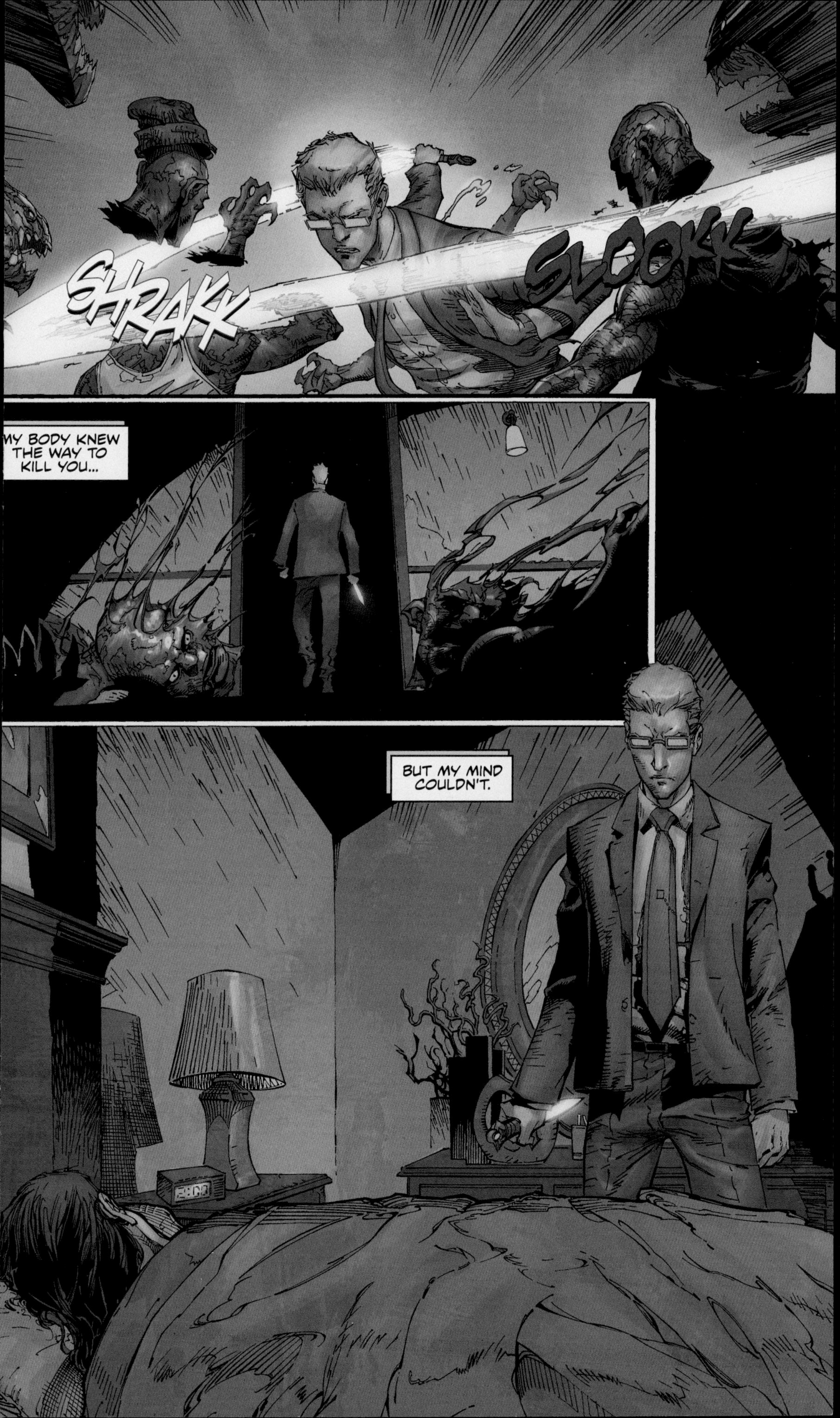
SHRAKK
SLOOKK
MY BODY KNEW THE WAY TO KILL YOU...
BUT MY MIND COULDN'T.

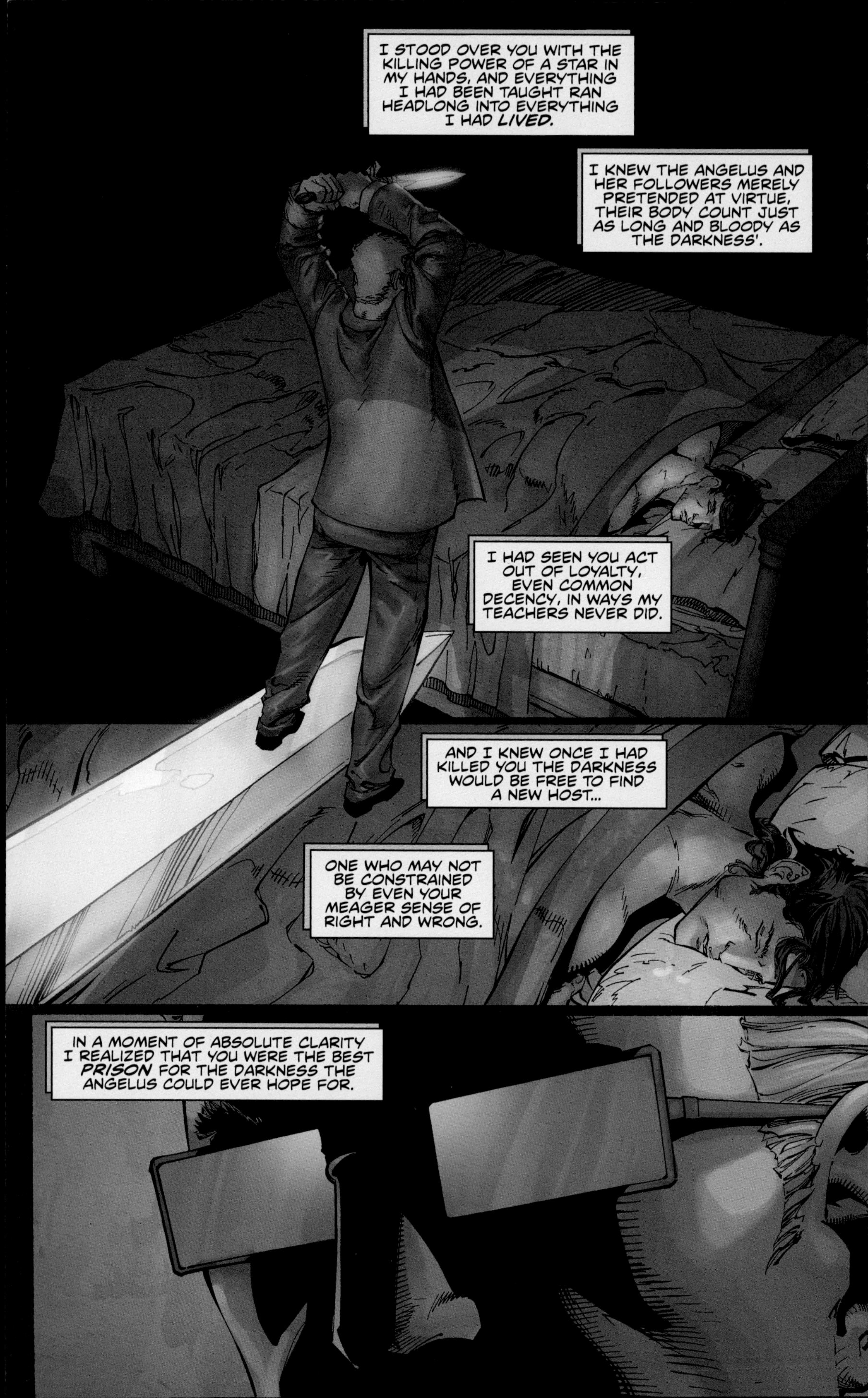
I STOOD OVER YOU WITH THE KILLING POWER OF A STAR IN MY HANDS, AND EVERYTHING I HAD BEEN TAUGHT RAN HEADLONG INTO EVERYTHING I HAD *LIVED.*
I KNEW THE ANGELUS AND HER FOLLOWERS MERELY PRETENDED AT VIRTUE, THEIR BODY COUNT JUST AS LONG AND BLOODY AS THE DARKNESS'.
I HAD SEEN YOU ACT OUT OF LOYALTY, EVEN COMMON DECENCY, IN WAYS MY TEACHERS NEVER DID.
AND I KNEW ONCE I HAD KILLED YOU THE DARKNESS WOULD BE FREE TO FIND A NEW HOST...
ONE WHO MAY NOT BE CONSTRAINED BY EVEN YOUR MEAGER SENSE OF RIGHT AND WRONG.
IN A MOMENT OF ABSOLUTE CLARITY I REALIZED THAT YOU WERE THE BEST *PRISON* FOR THE DARKNESS THE ANGELUS COULD EVER HOPE FOR.

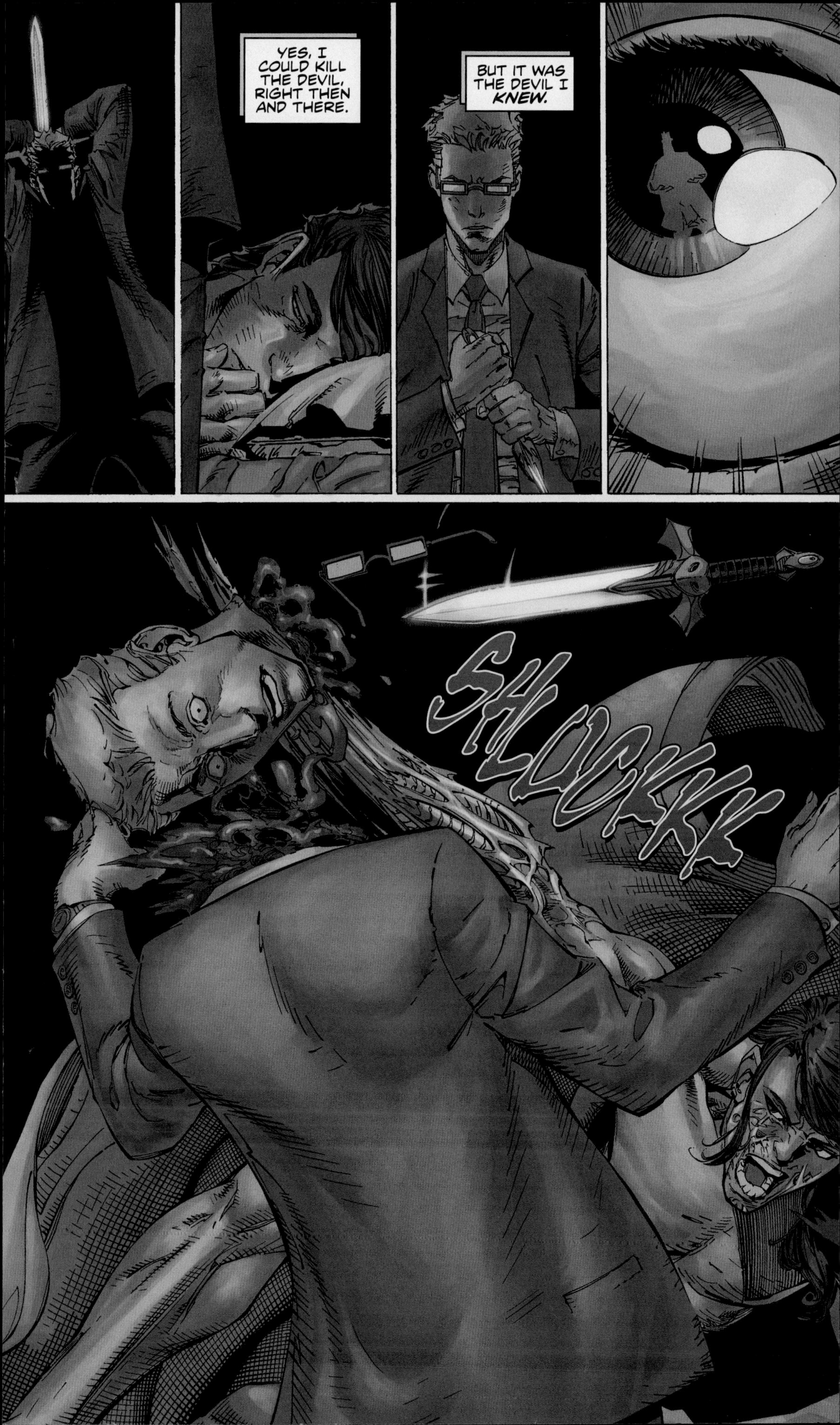
YES, I COULD KILL THE DEVIL, RIGHT THEN AND THERE.
BUT IT WAS THE DEVIL I *KNEW.*
SHLOCKKK

THUMP

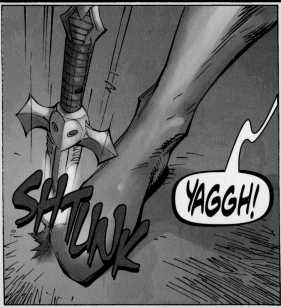

SHTUNK

YAGGH!

GOD DAMN IT, TYNE. WHAT WERE YOU TRYING TO DO?

BUT I COULDN'T ANSWER YOU.

NOT IN THAT STATE.

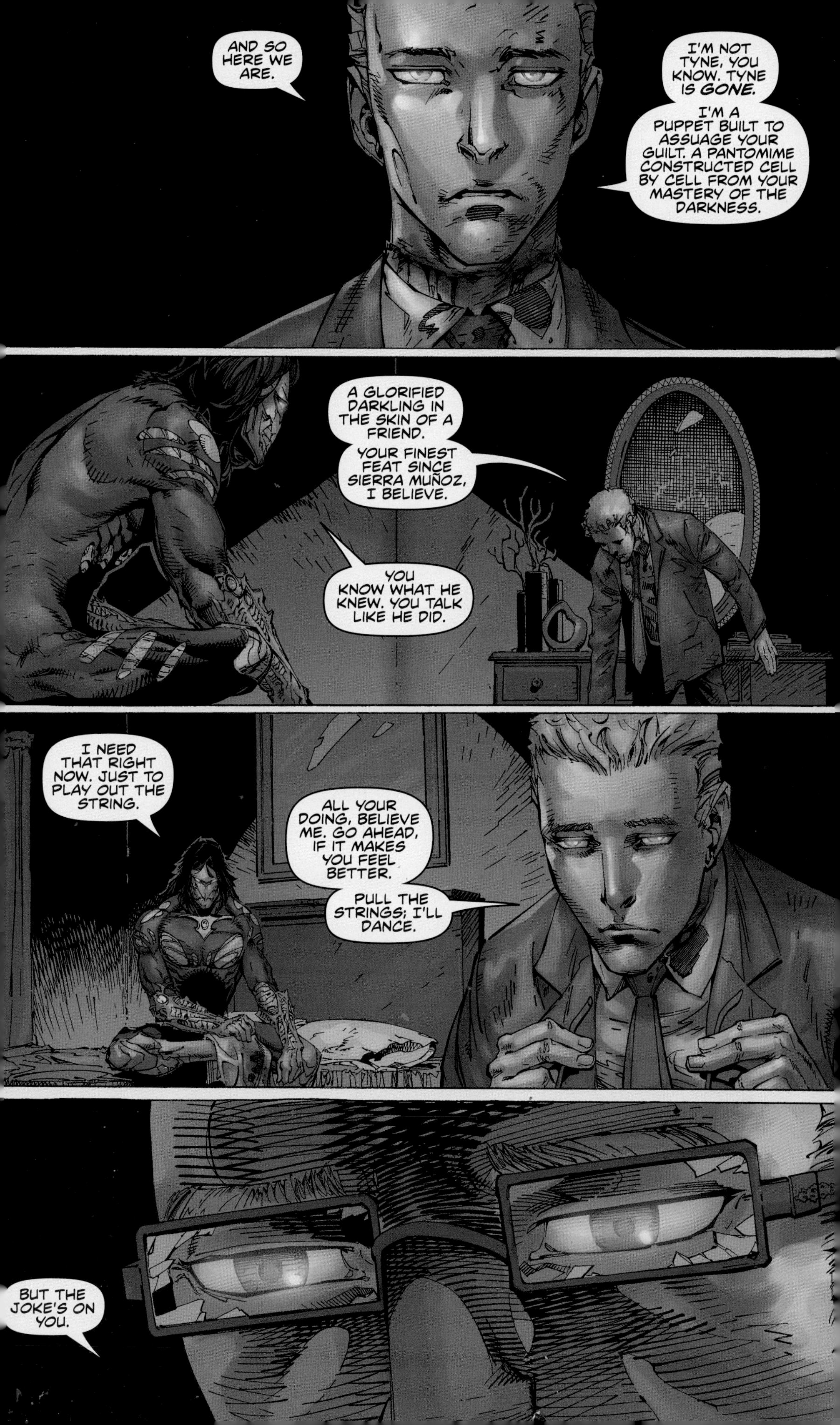
AND SO HERE WE ARE.
I'M NOT TYNE, YOU KNOW. TYNE IS GONE.
I'M A PUPPET BUILT TO ASSUAGE YOUR GUILT. A PANTOMIME CONSTRUCTED CELL BY CELL FROM YOUR MASTERY OF THE DARKNESS.
A GLORIFIED DARKLING IN THE SKIN OF A FRIEND.
YOUR FINEST FEAT SINCE SIERRA MUÑOZ, I BELIEVE.
YOU KNOW WHAT HE KNEW. YOU TALK LIKE HE DID.
I NEED THAT RIGHT NOW. JUST TO PLAY OUT THE STRING.
ALL YOUR DOING, BELIEVE ME. GO AHEAD, IF IT MAKES YOU FEEL BETTER.
PULL THE STRINGS; I'LL DANCE.
BUT THE JOKE'S ON YOU.

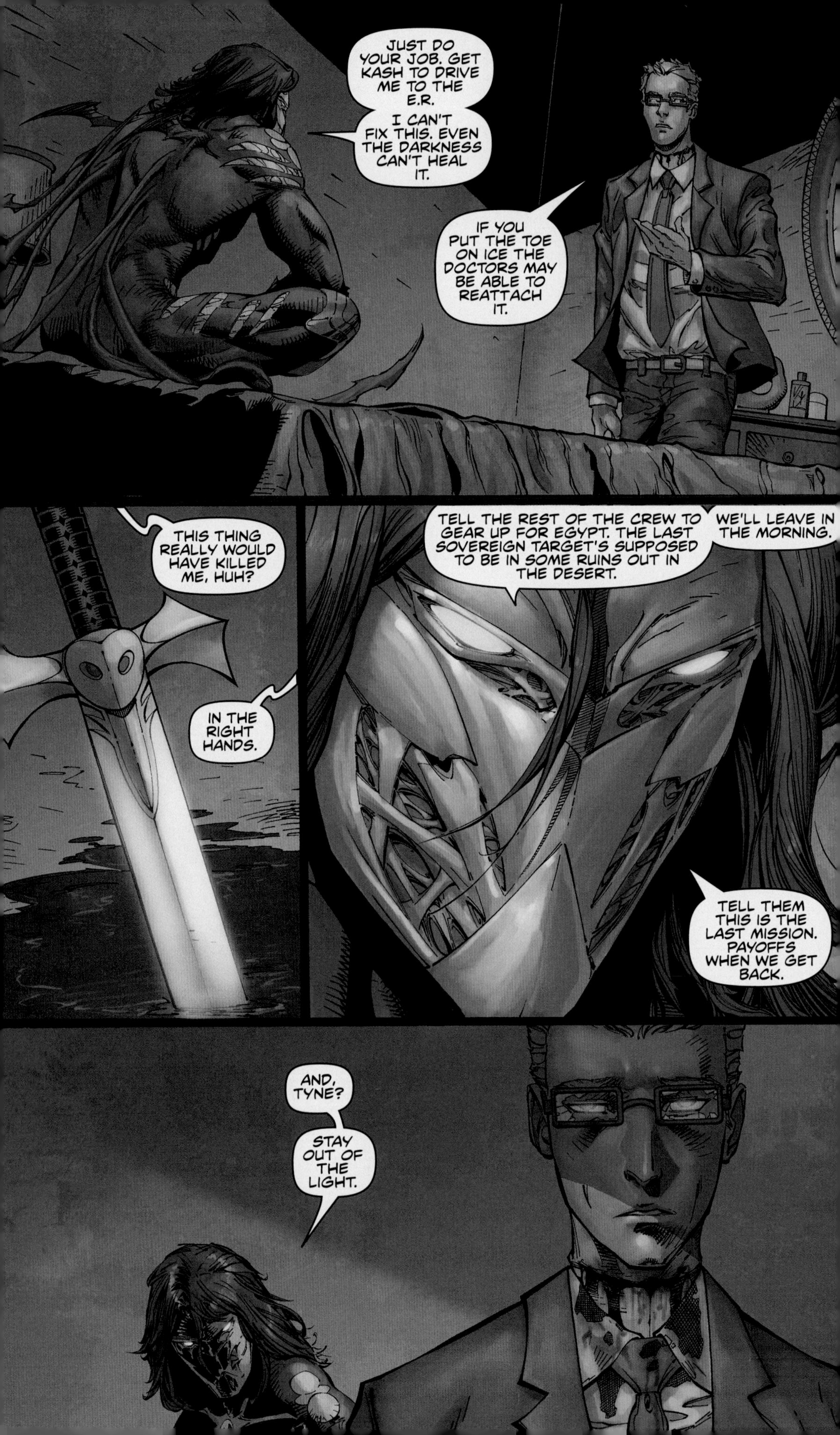
JUST DO YOUR JOB. GET KASH TO DRIVE ME TO THE E.R.
I CAN'T FIX THIS. EVEN THE DARKNESS CAN'T HEAL IT.
IF YOU PUT THE TOE ON ICE THE DOCTORS MAY BE ABLE TO REATTACH IT.
THIS THING REALLY WOULD HAVE KILLED ME, HUH?
IN THE RIGHT HANDS.
TELL THE REST OF THE CREW TO GEAR UP FOR EGYPT. THE LAST SOVEREIGN TARGET'S SUPPOSED TO BE IN SOME RUINS OUT IN THE DESERT.
WE'LL LEAVE IN THE MORNING.
TELL THEM THIS IS THE LAST MISSION. PAYOFFS WHEN WE GET BACK.
AND, TYNE?
STAY OUT OF THE LIGHT.

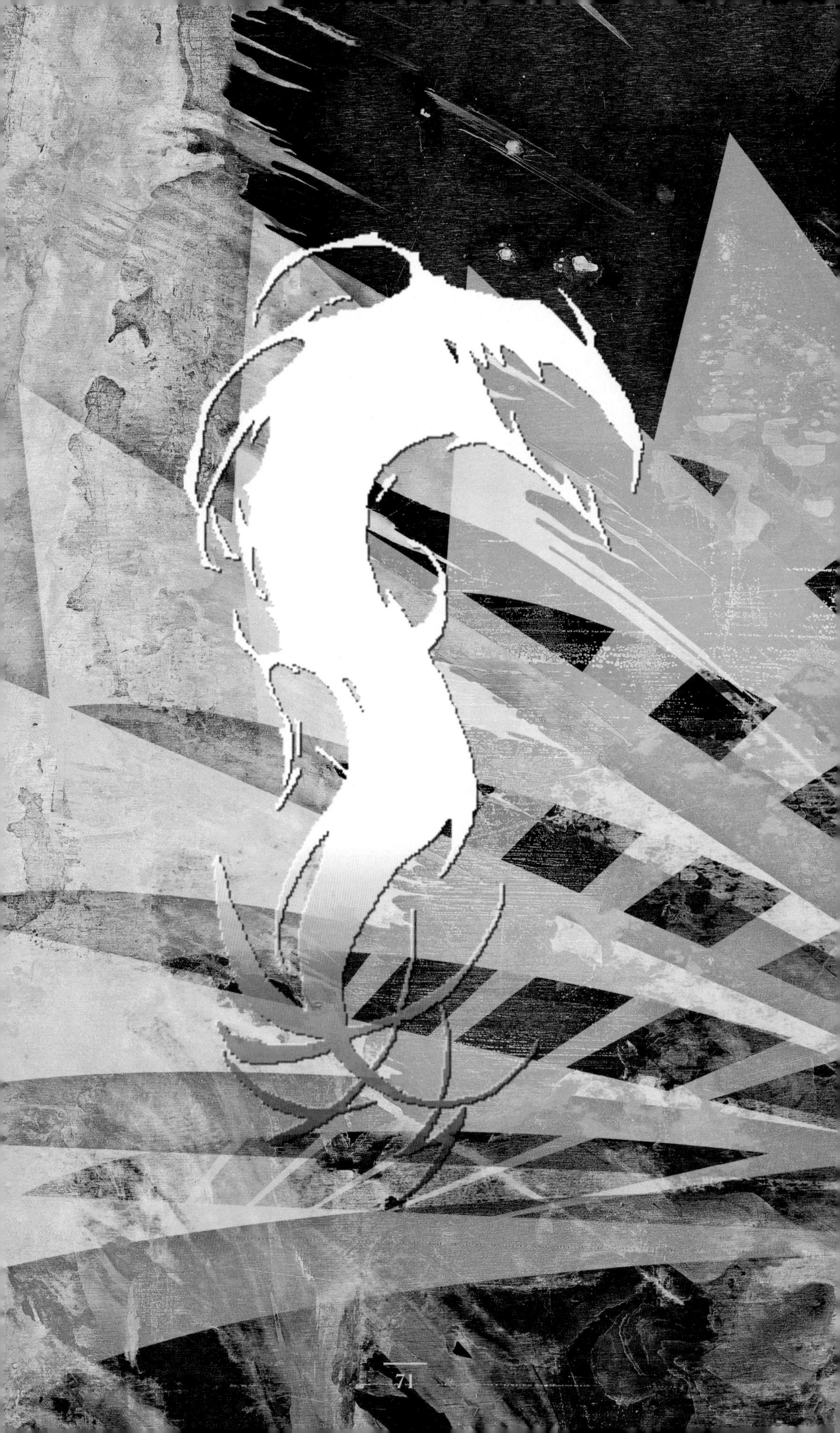

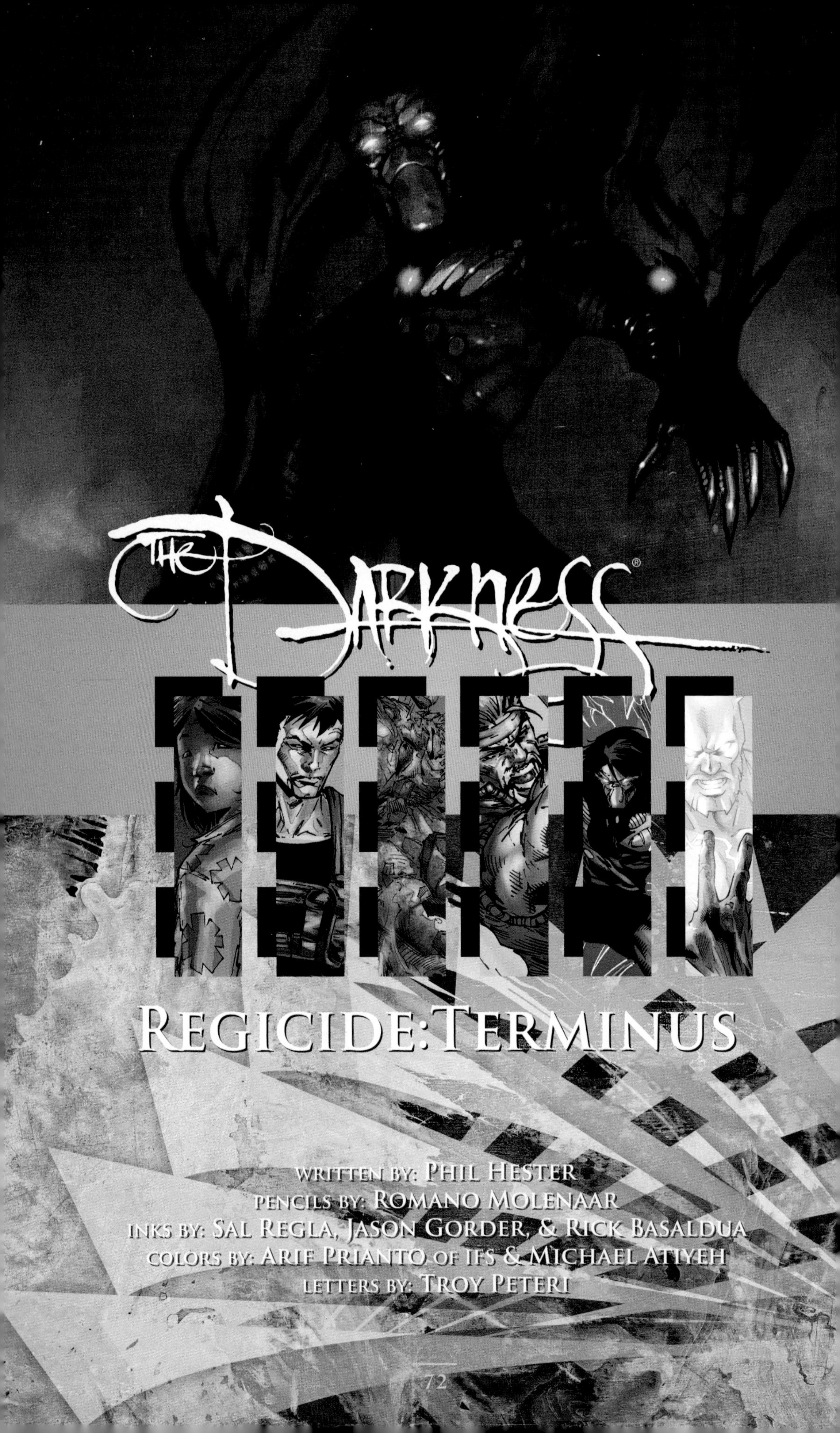
THE DARKNESS®
REGICIDE:TERMINUS
WRITTEN BY: PHIL HESTER
PENCILS BY: ROMANO MOLENAAR
INKS BY: SAL REGLA, JASON GORDER, & RICK BASALDUA
COLORS BY: ARIF PRIANTO OF IFS & MICHAEL ATIYEH
LETTERS BY: TROY PETERI

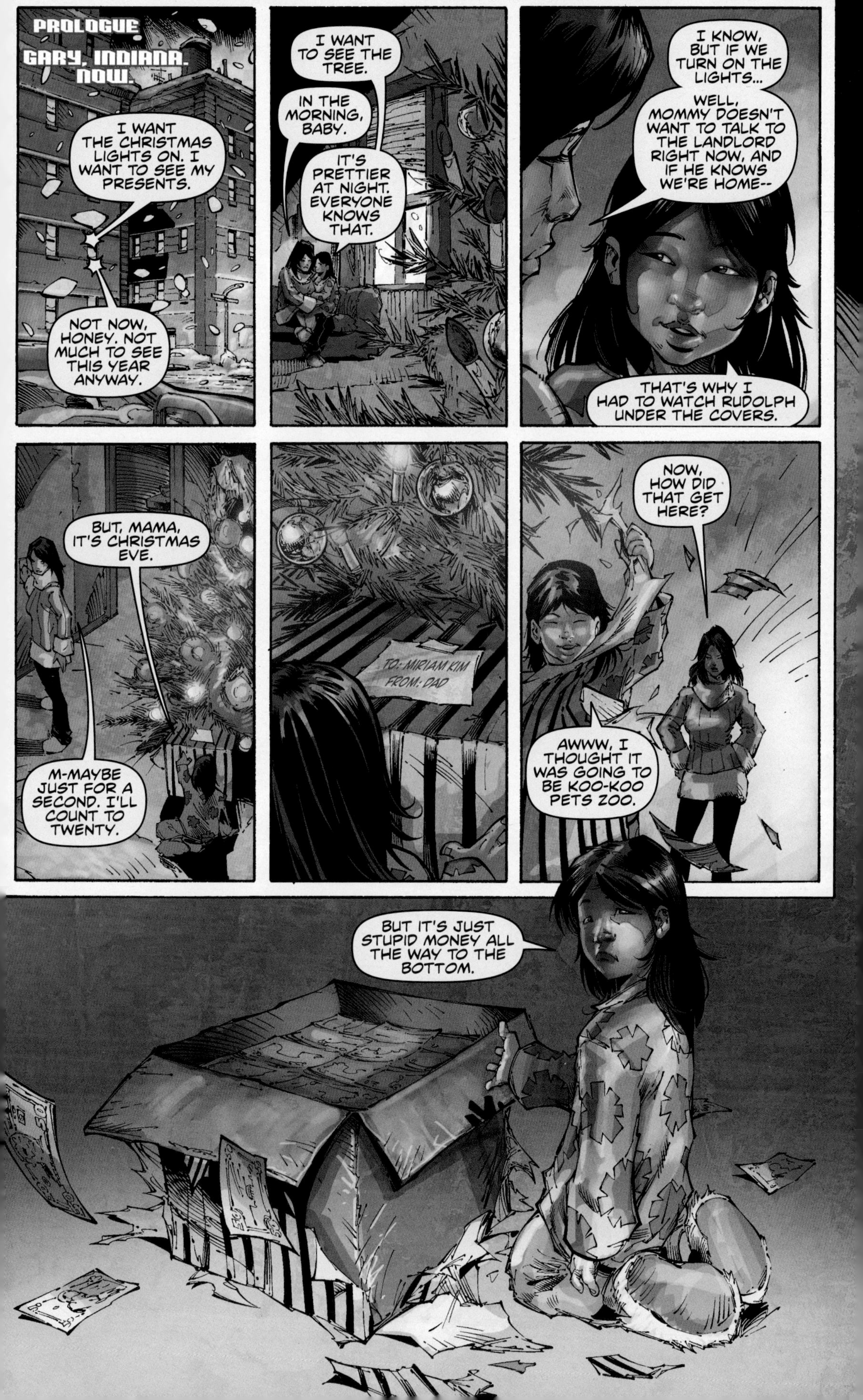
PROLOGUE
GARY, INDIANA. NOW.
I WANT THE CHRISTMAS LIGHTS ON. I WANT TO SEE MY PRESENTS.
NOT NOW, HONEY. NOT MUCH TO SEE THIS YEAR ANYWAY.
I WANT TO SEE THE TREE.
IN THE MORNING, BABY.
IT'S PRETTIER AT NIGHT. EVERYONE KNOWS THAT.
I KNOW, BUT IF WE TURN ON THE LIGHTS...
WELL, MOMMY DOESN'T WANT TO TALK TO THE LANDLORD RIGHT NOW, AND IF HE KNOWS WE'RE HOME--
THAT'S WHY I HAD TO WATCH RUDOLPH UNDER THE COVERS.
BUT, MAMA, IT'S CHRISTMAS EVE.
M-MAYBE JUST FOR A SECOND. I'LL COUNT TO TWENTY.
TO: MIRIAM KIM
FROM: DAD
NOW, HOW DID THAT GET HERE?
AWWW, I THOUGHT IT WAS GOING TO BE KOO-KOO PETS ZOO.
BUT IT'S JUST STUPID MONEY ALL THE WAY TO THE BOTTOM.

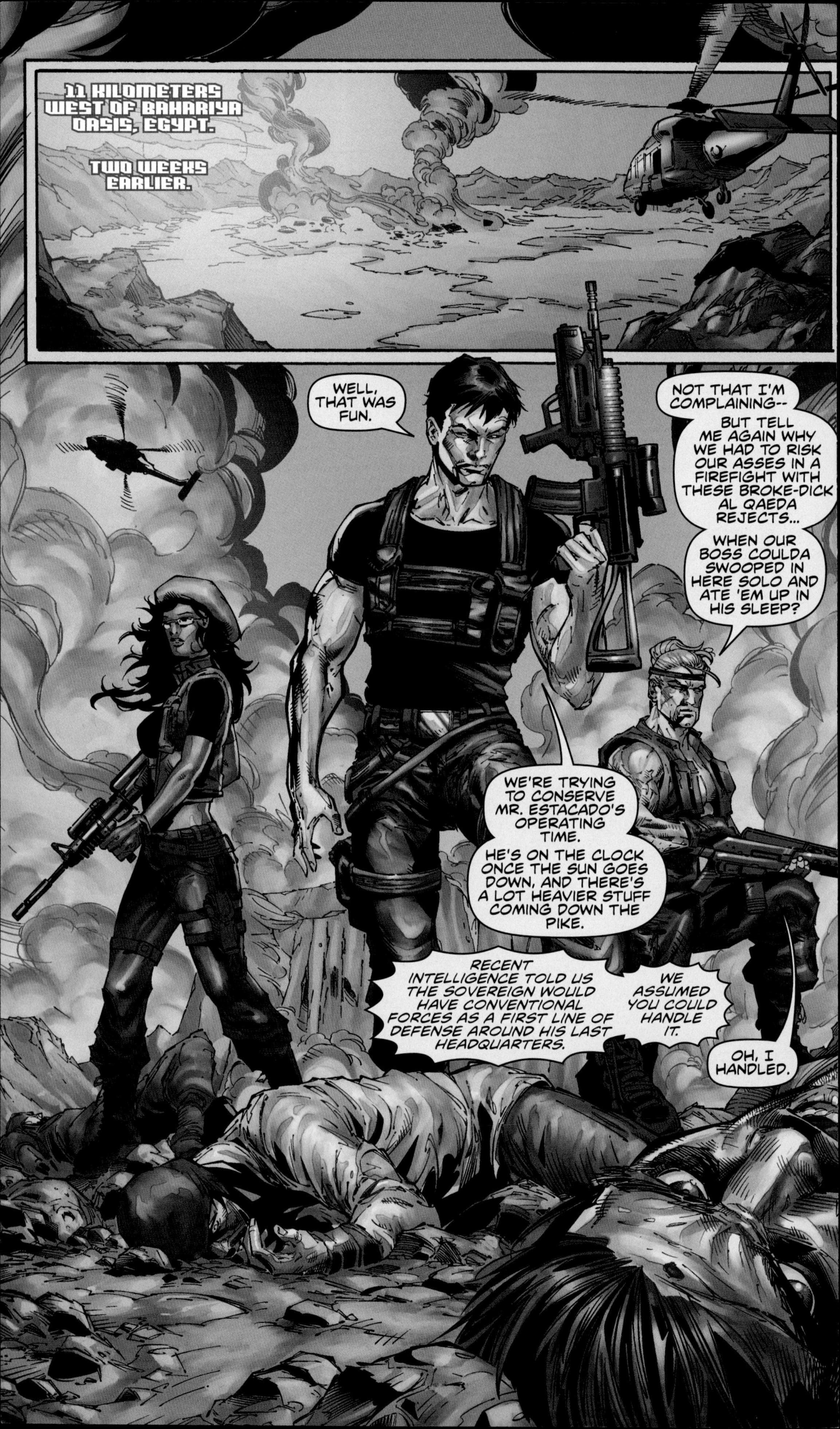
11 KILOMETERS WEST OF BAHARIYA OASIS, EGYPT.
TWO WEEKS EARLIER.
WELL, THAT WAS FUN.
NOT THAT I'M COMPLAINING--
BUT TELL ME AGAIN WHY WE HAD TO RISK OUR ASSES IN A FIREFIGHT WITH THESE BROKE-DICK AL QAEDA REJECTS...
WHEN OUR BOSS COULDA SWOOPED IN HERE SOLO AND ATE 'EM UP IN HIS SLEEP?
WE'RE TRYING TO CONSERVE MR. ESTACADO'S OPERATING TIME.
HE'S ON THE CLOCK ONCE THE SUN GOES DOWN, AND THERE'S A LOT HEAVIER STUFF COMING DOWN THE PIKE.
RECENT INTELLIGENCE TOLD US THE SOVEREIGN WOULD HAVE CONVENTIONAL FORCES AS A FIRST LINE OF DEFENSE AROUND HIS LAST HEADQUARTERS.
WE ASSUMED YOU COULD HANDLE IT.
OH, I HANDLED.

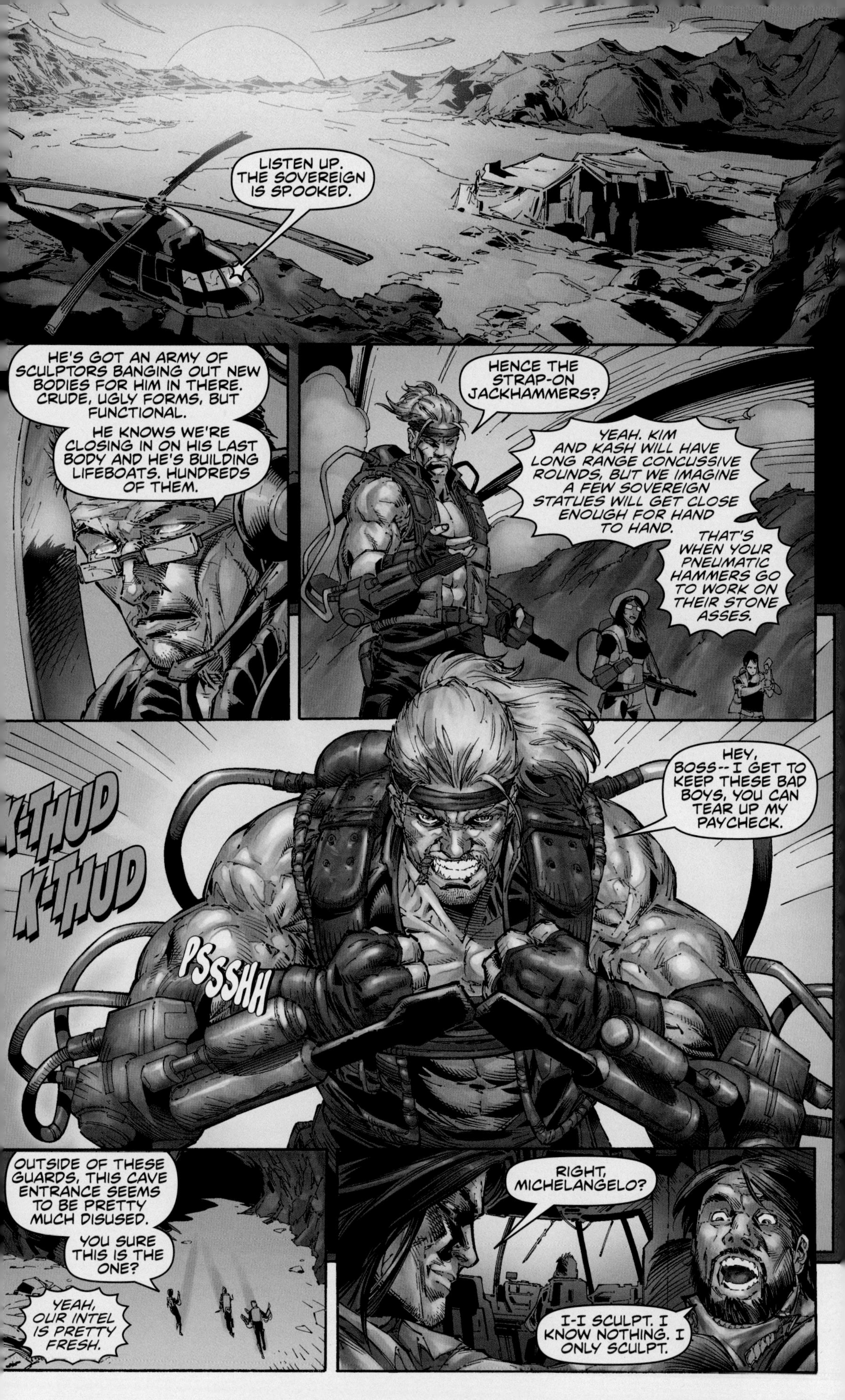
LISTEN UP. THE SOVEREIGN IS SPOOKED.
HE'S GOT AN ARMY OF SCULPTORS BANGING OUT NEW BODIES FOR HIM IN THERE. CRUDE, UGLY FORMS, BUT FUNCTIONAL.
HE KNOWS WE'RE CLOSING IN ON HIS LAST BODY AND HE'S BUILDING LIFEBOATS. HUNDREDS OF THEM.
HENCE THE STRAP-ON JACKHAMMERS?
YEAH. KIM AND KASH WILL HAVE LONG RANGE CONCUSSIVE ROUNDS, BUT WE IMAGINE A FEW SOVEREIGN STATUES WILL GET CLOSE ENOUGH FOR HAND TO HAND.
THAT'S WHEN YOUR PNEUMATIC HAMMERS GO TO WORK ON THEIR STONE ASSES.
K-THUD
K-THUD
PSSSHH
HEY, BOSS-- I GET TO KEEP THESE BAD BOYS, YOU CAN TEAR UP MY PAYCHECK.
OUTSIDE OF THESE GUARDS, THIS CAVE ENTRANCE SEEMS TO BE PRETTY MUCH DISUSED.
YOU SURE THIS IS THE ONE?
YEAH, OUR INTEL IS PRETTY FRESH.
RIGHT, MICHELANGELO?
I-I SCULPT. I KNOW NOTHING. I ONLY SCULPT.

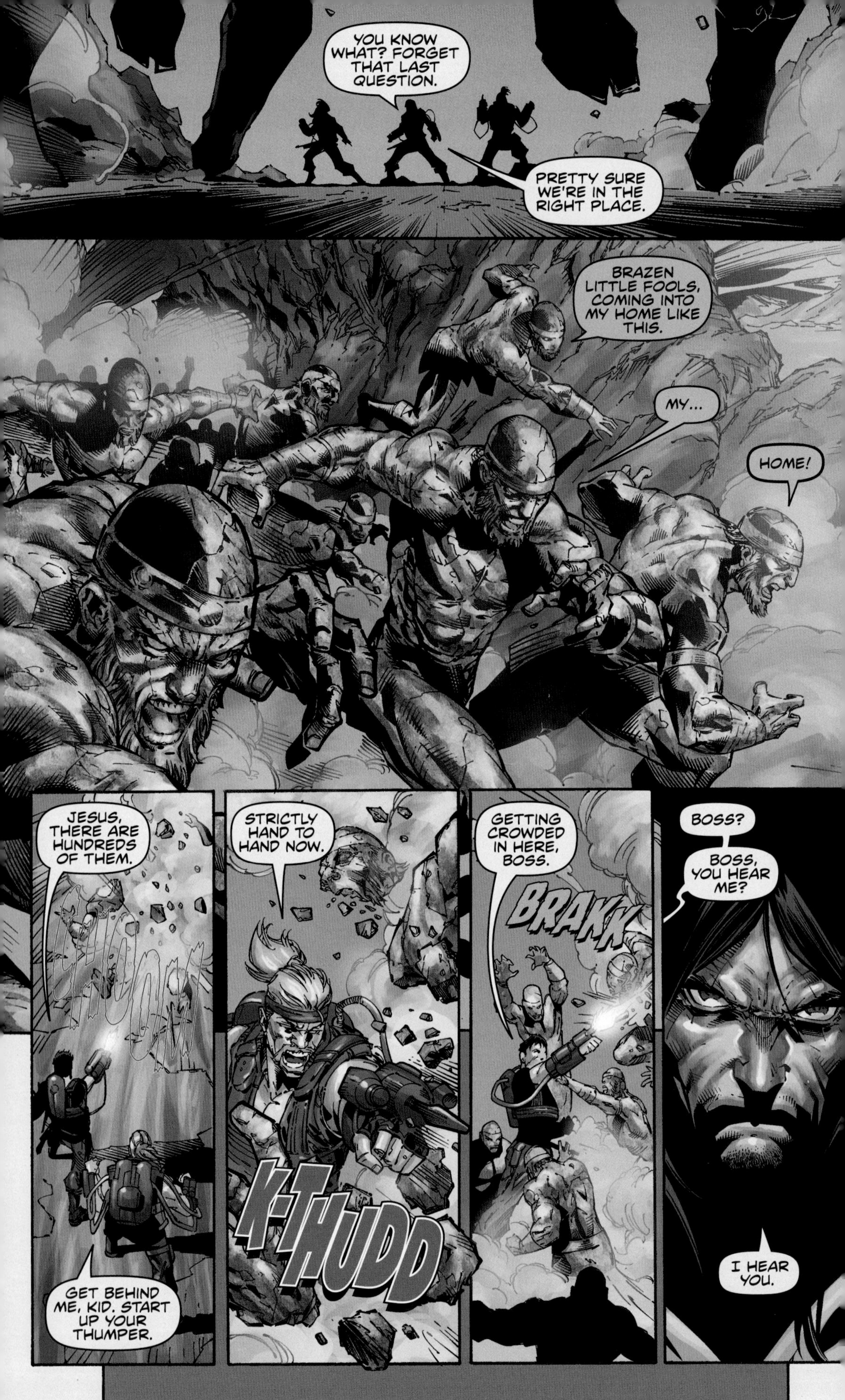
YOU KNOW WHAT? FORGET THAT LAST QUESTION.
PRETTY SURE WE'RE IN THE RIGHT PLACE.
BRAZEN LITTLE FOOLS, COMING INTO MY HOME LIKE THIS.
MY...
HOME!
JESUS, THERE ARE HUNDREDS OF THEM.
GET BEHIND ME, KID. START UP YOUR THUMPER.
STRICTLY HAND TO HAND NOW.
K-THUDD
GETTING CROWDED IN HERE, BOSS.
BRAKK
BOSS?
BOSS, YOU HEAR ME?
I HEAR YOU.

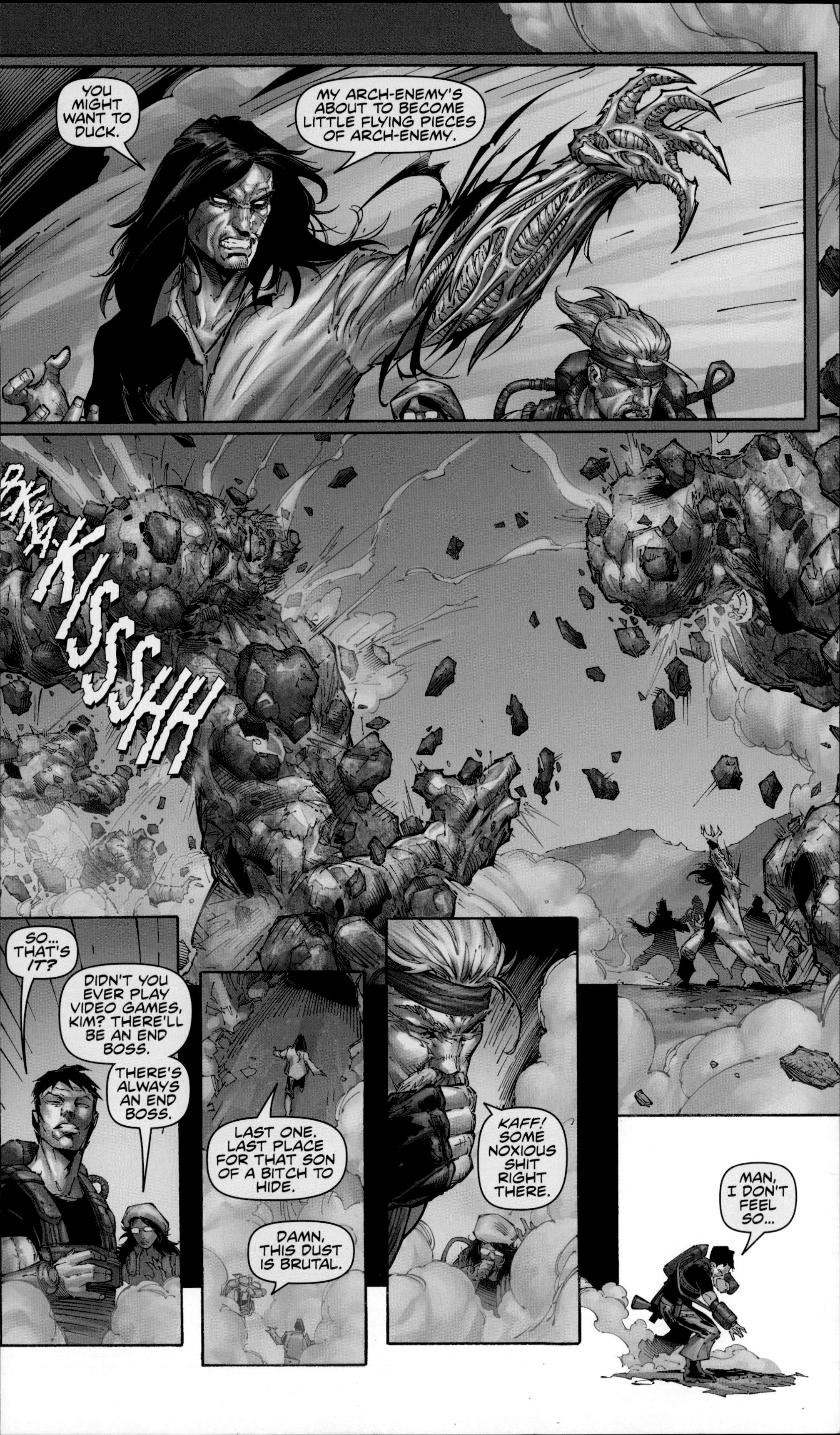
YOU MIGHT WANT TO DUCK.
MY ARCH-ENEMY'S ABOUT TO BECOME LITTLE FLYING PIECES OF ARCH-ENEMY.
BKA-KISSHH
SO... THAT'S IT?
DIDN'T YOU EVER PLAY VIDEO GAMES, KIM? THERE'LL BE AN END BOSS.
THERE'S ALWAYS AN END BOSS.
LAST ONE. LAST PLACE FOR THAT SON OF A BITCH TO HIDE.
DAMN, THIS DUST IS BRUTAL.
KAFF! SOME NOXIOUS SHIT RIGHT THERE.
MAN, I DON'T FEEL SO...

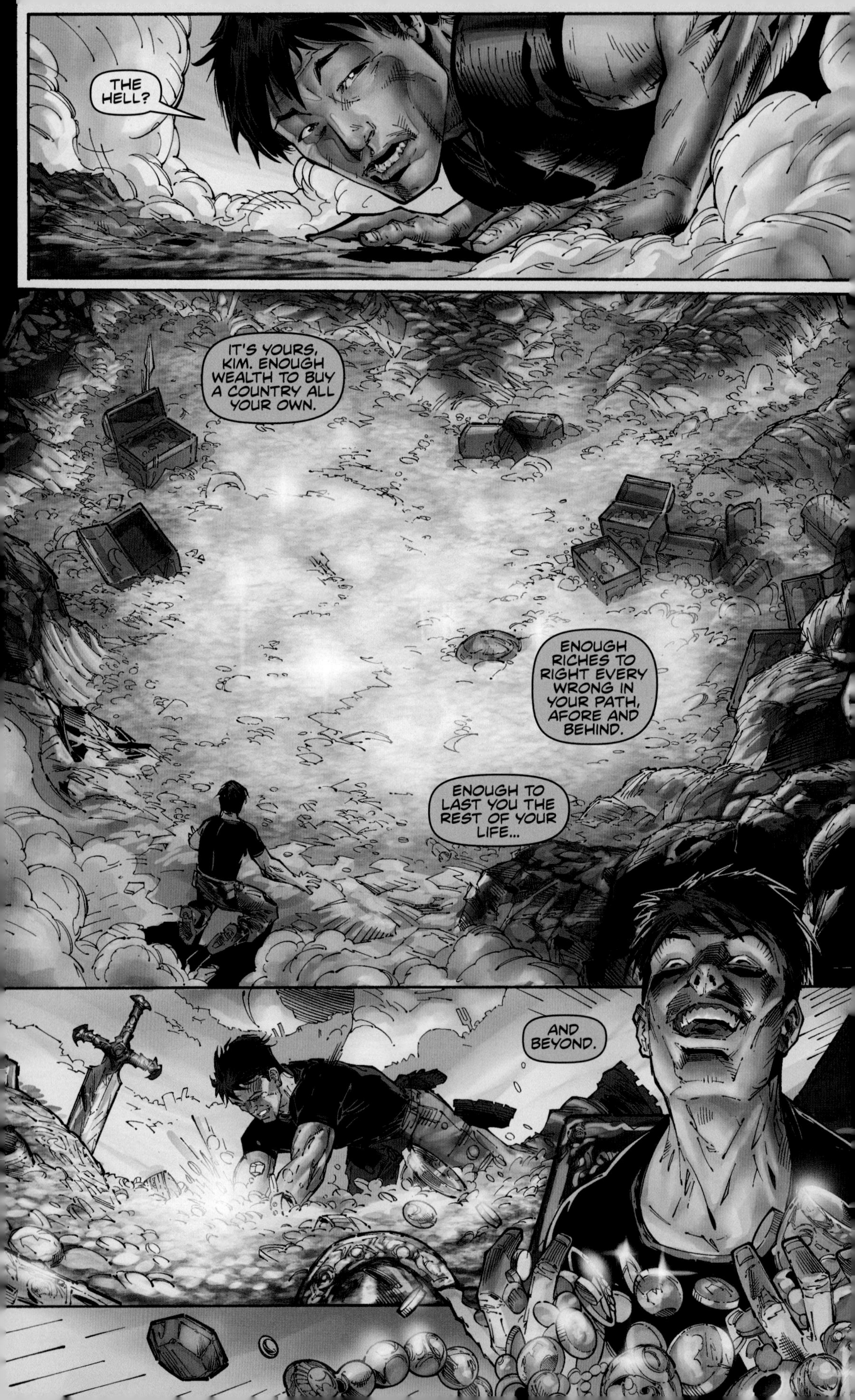
THE HELL?
IT'S YOURS, KIM. ENOUGH WEALTH TO BUY A COUNTRY ALL YOUR OWN.
ENOUGH RICHES TO RIGHT EVERY WRONG IN YOUR PATH, AFORE AND BEHIND.
ENOUGH TO LAST YOU THE REST OF YOUR LIFE...
AND BEYOND.

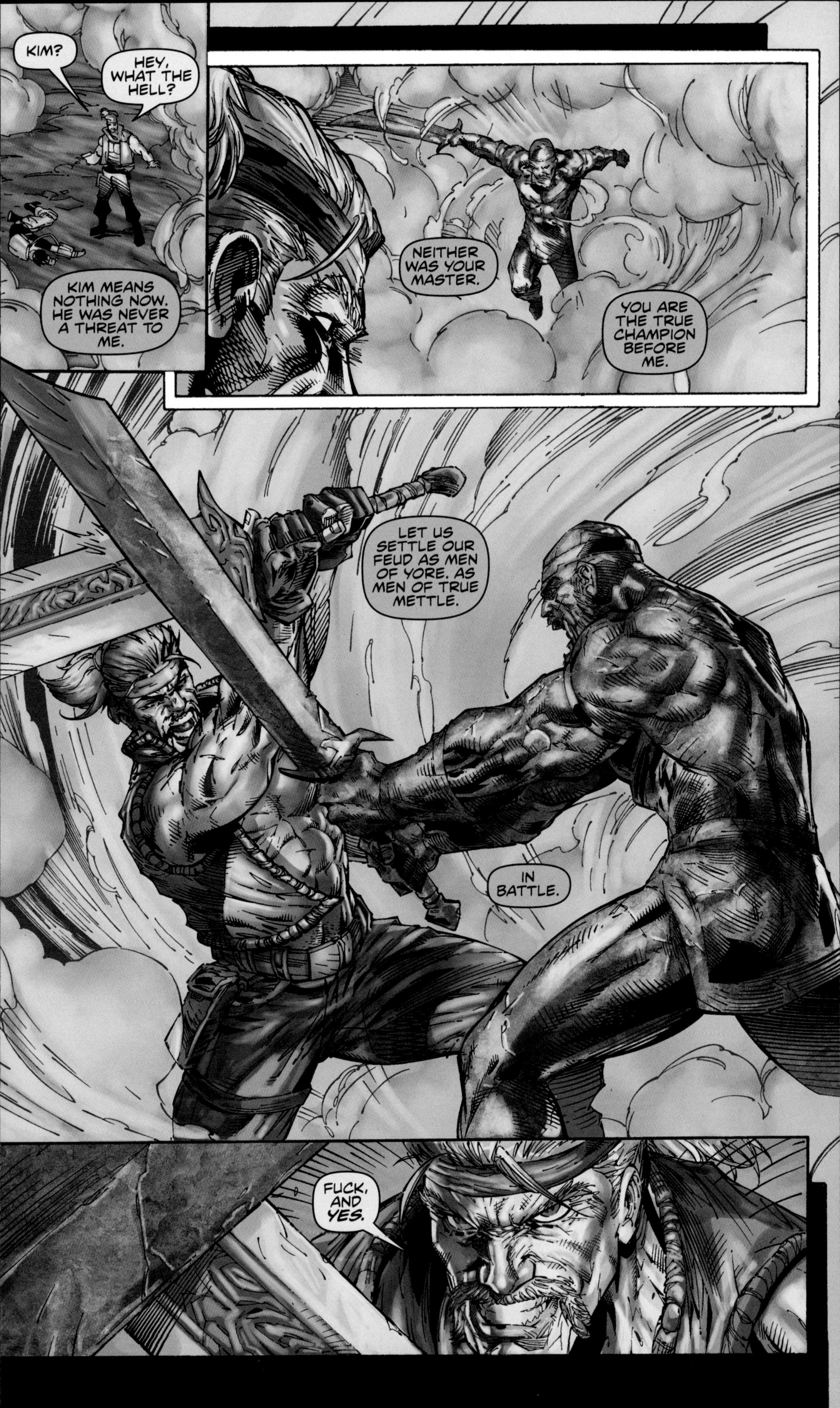
KIM?
HEY, WHAT THE HELL?
KIM MEANS NOTHING NOW. HE WAS NEVER A THREAT TO ME.
NEITHER WAS YOUR MASTER.
YOU ARE THE TRUE CHAMPION BEFORE ME.
LET US SETTLE OUR FEUD AS MEN OF YORE. AS MEN OF TRUE METTLE.
IN BATTLE.
FUCK, AND YES.

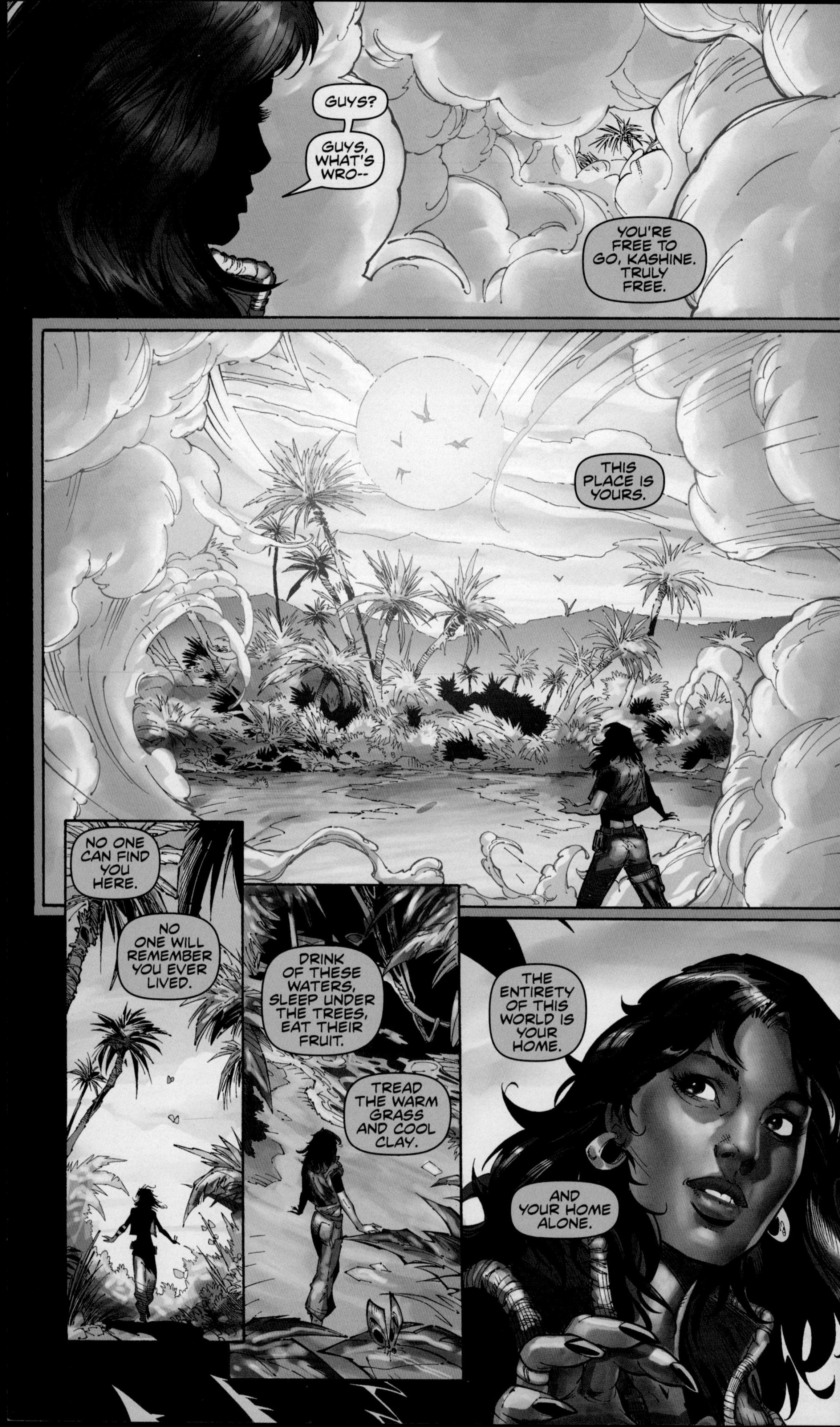
GUYS?
GUYS, WHAT'S WRO--
YOU'RE FREE TO GO, KASHINE. TRULY FREE.
THIS PLACE IS YOURS.
NO ONE CAN FIND YOU HERE.
NO ONE WILL REMEMBER YOU EVER LIVED.
DRINK OF THESE WATERS, SLEEP UNDER THE TREES, EAT THEIR FRUIT.
TREAD THE WARM GRASS AND COOL CLAY.
THE ENTIRETY OF THIS WORLD IS YOUR HOME.
AND YOUR HOME ALONE.

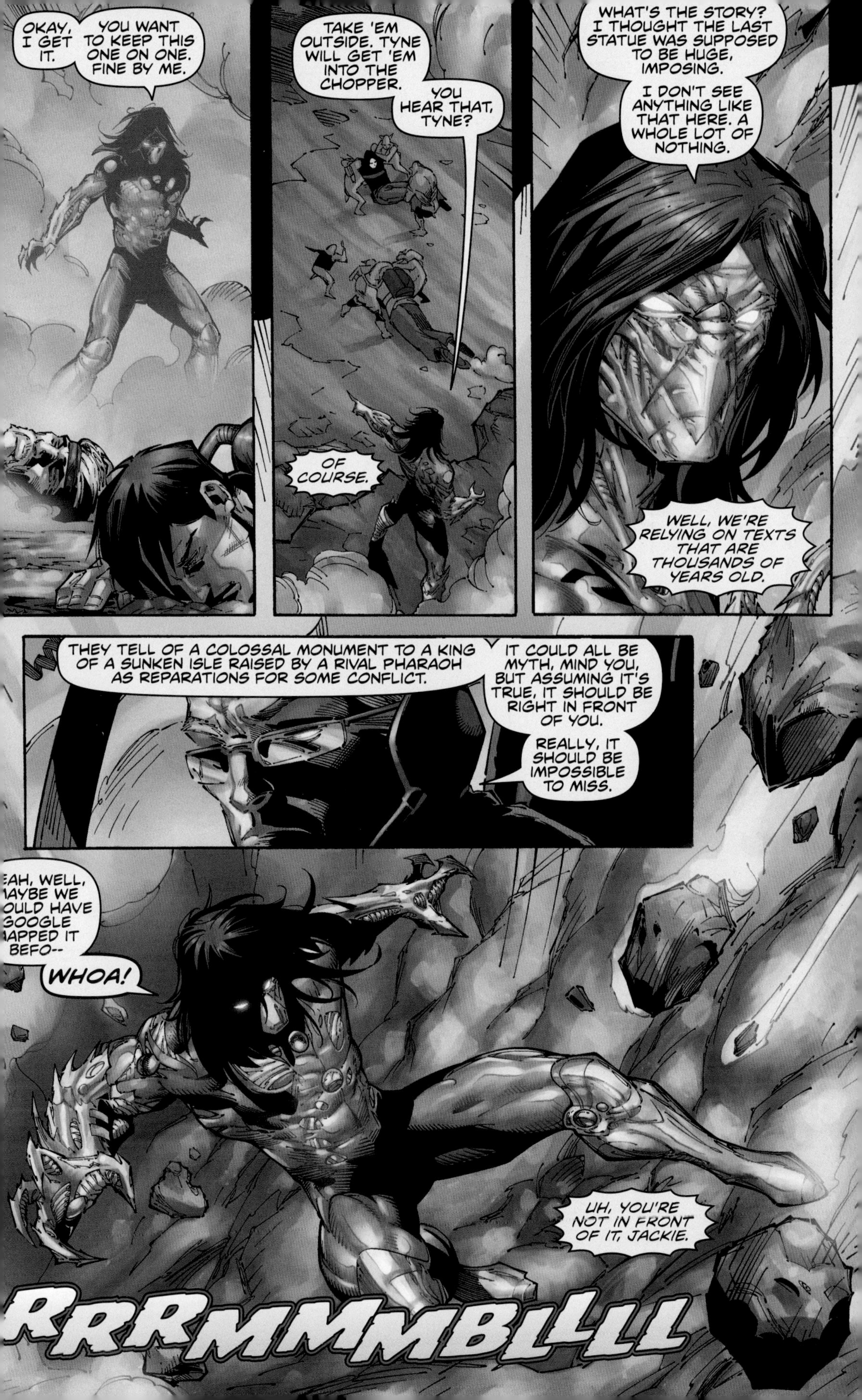
OKAY, I GET IT.
YOU WANT TO KEEP THIS ONE ON ONE. FINE BY ME.
TAKE 'EM OUTSIDE. TYNE WILL GET 'EM INTO THE CHOPPER.
YOU HEAR THAT, TYNE?
OF COURSE.
WHAT'S THE STORY? I THOUGHT THE LAST STATUE WAS SUPPOSED TO BE HUGE, IMPOSING.
I DON'T SEE ANYTHING LIKE THAT HERE. A WHOLE LOT OF NOTHING.
WELL, WE'RE RELYING ON TEXTS THAT ARE THOUSANDS OF YEARS OLD.
THEY TELL OF A COLOSSAL MONUMENT TO A KING OF A SUNKEN ISLE RAISED BY A RIVAL PHARAOH AS REPARATIONS FOR SOME CONFLICT.
IT COULD ALL BE MYTH, MIND YOU, BUT ASSUMING IT'S TRUE, IT SHOULD BE RIGHT IN FRONT OF YOU.
REALLY, IT SHOULD BE IMPOSSIBLE TO MISS.
EAH, WELL, MAYBE WE OULD HAVE GOOGLE MAPPED IT BEFO--
WHOA!
UH, YOU'RE NOT IN FRONT OF IT, JACKIE.
RRRMMMBLLLL

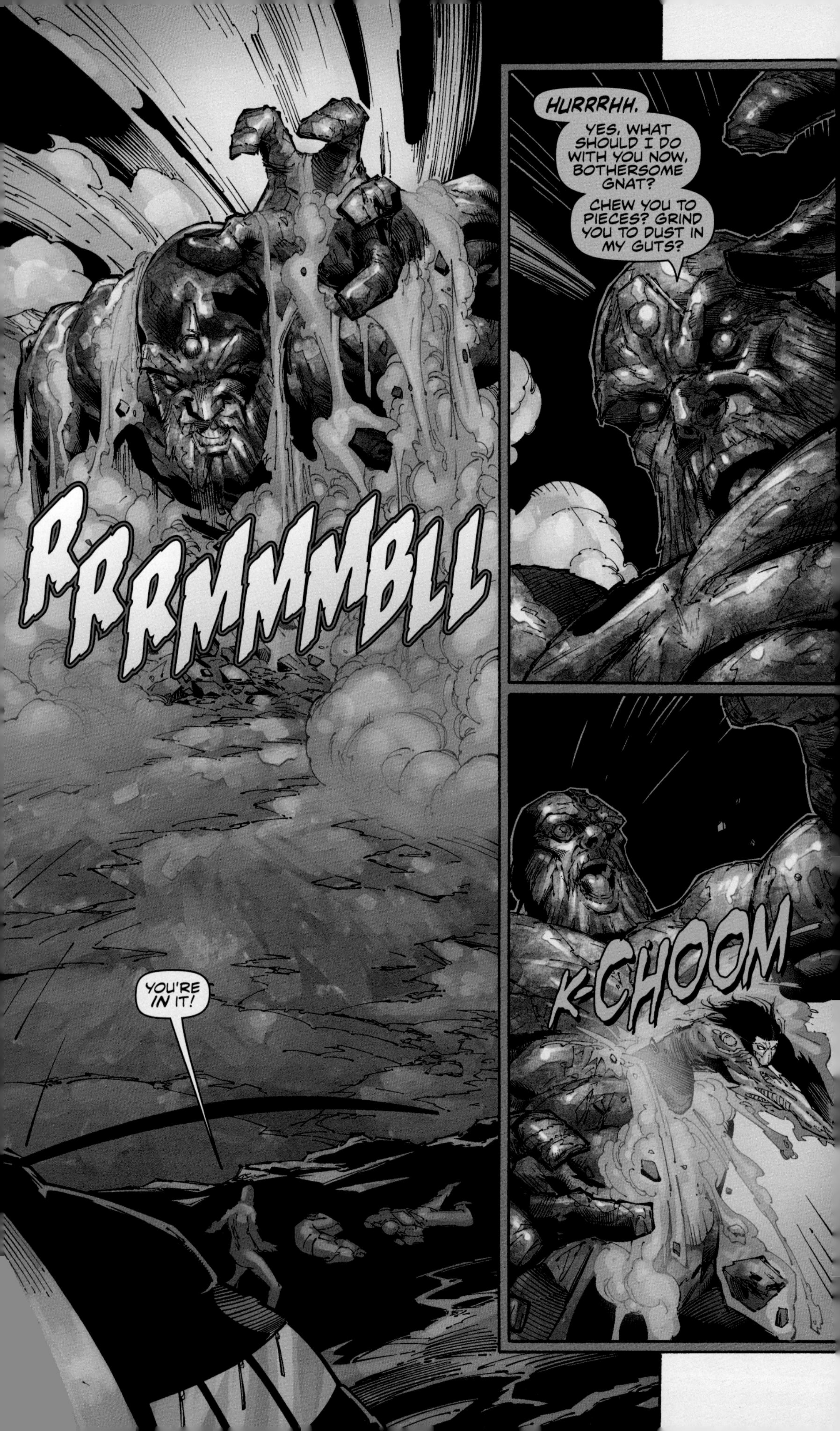
RRRMMMBLL
YOU'RE IN IT!
HURRRHH.
YES, WHAT SHOULD I DO WITH YOU NOW, BOTHERSOME GNAT?
CHEW YOU TO PIECES? GRIND YOU TO DUST IN MY GUTS?
K-CHOOM

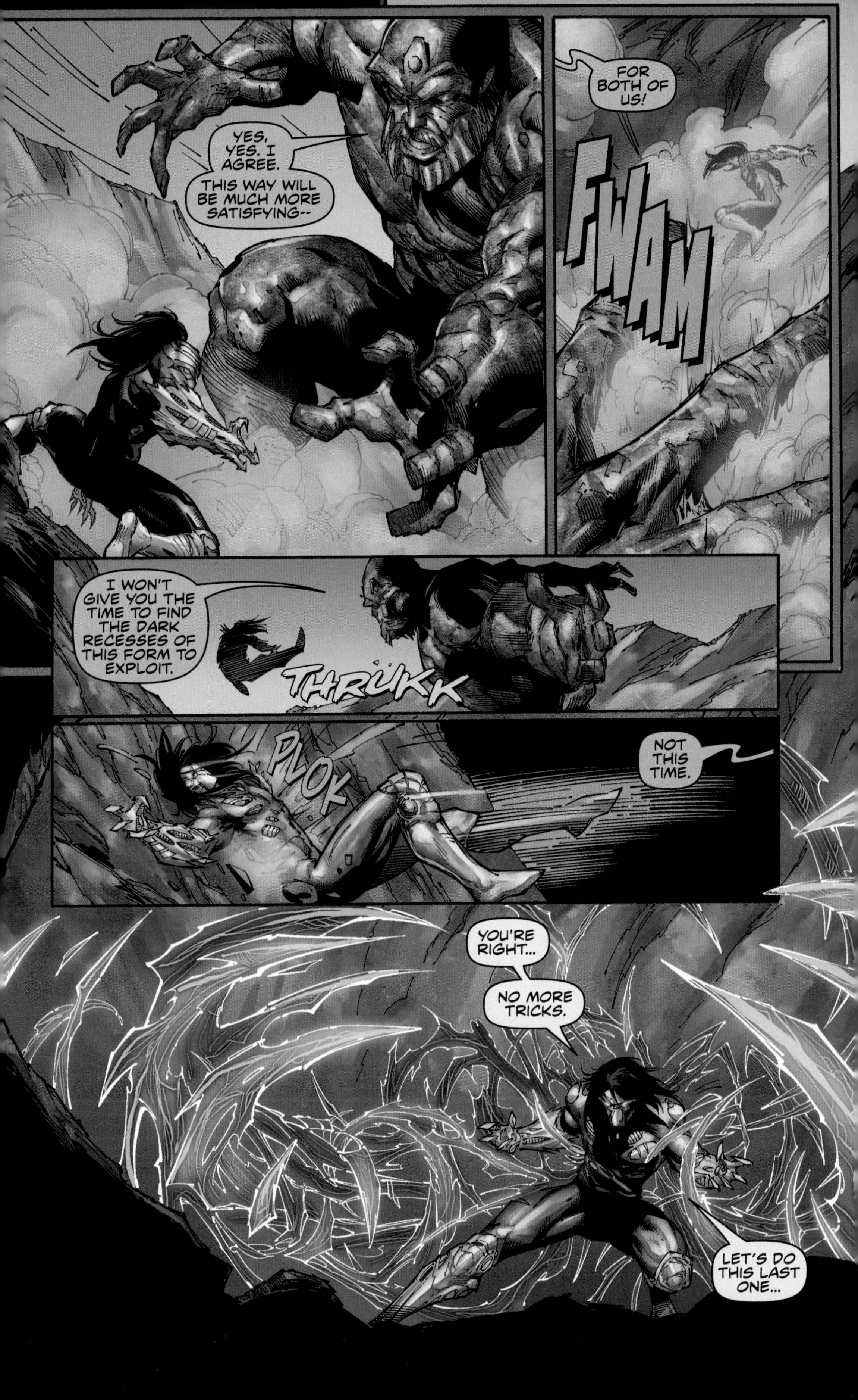
YES, YES. I AGREE.
THIS WAY WILL BE MUCH MORE SATISFYING--
FOR BOTH OF US!
FWAM
I WON'T GIVE YOU THE TIME TO FIND THE DARK RECESSES OF THIS FORM TO EXPLOIT.
THRUKK
PLOK
NOT THIS TIME.
YOU'RE RIGHT...
NO MORE TRICKS.
LET'S DO THIS LAST ONE...

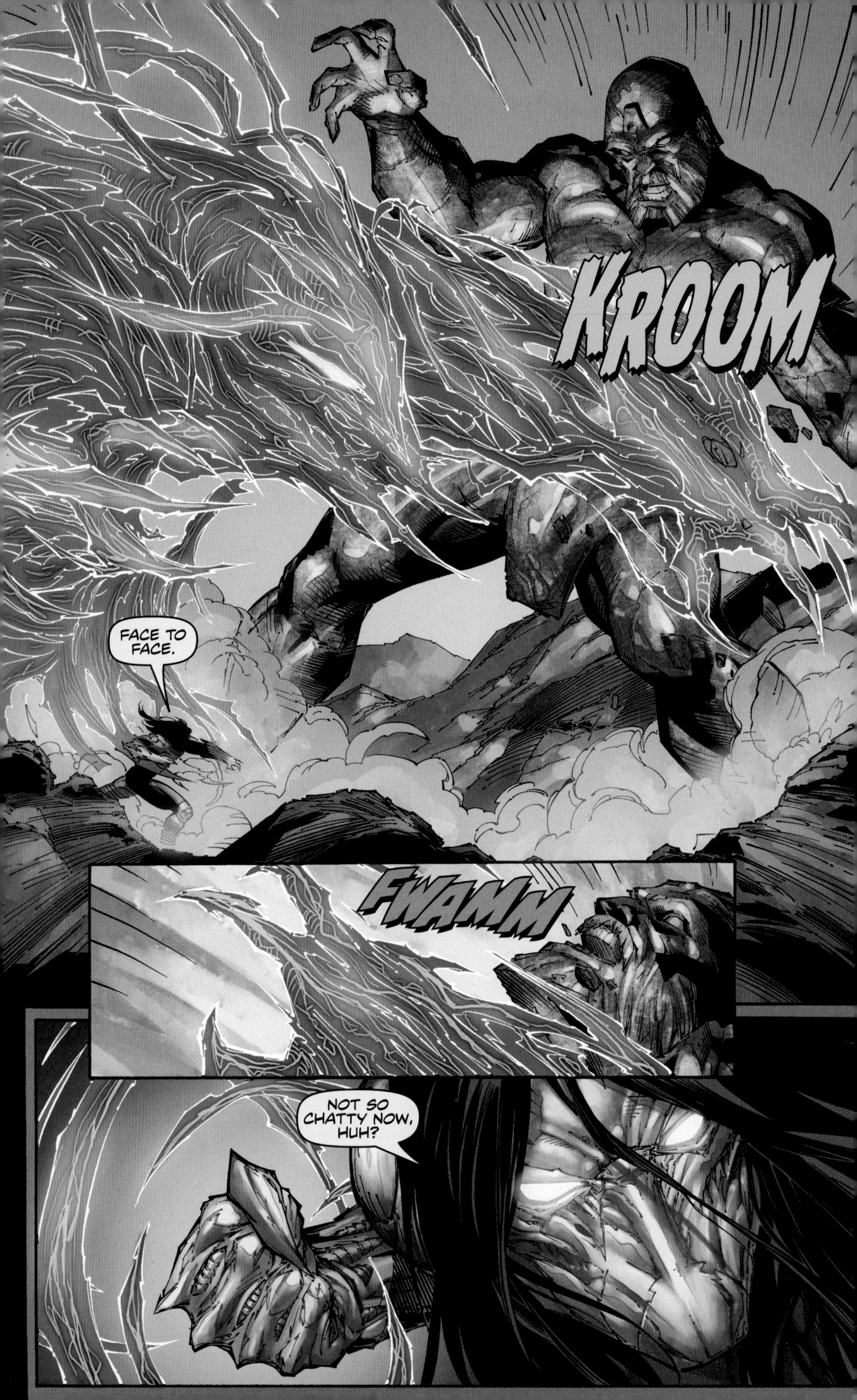
KROOM
FACE TO FACE.
FWAMM
NOT SO CHATTY NOW, HUH?

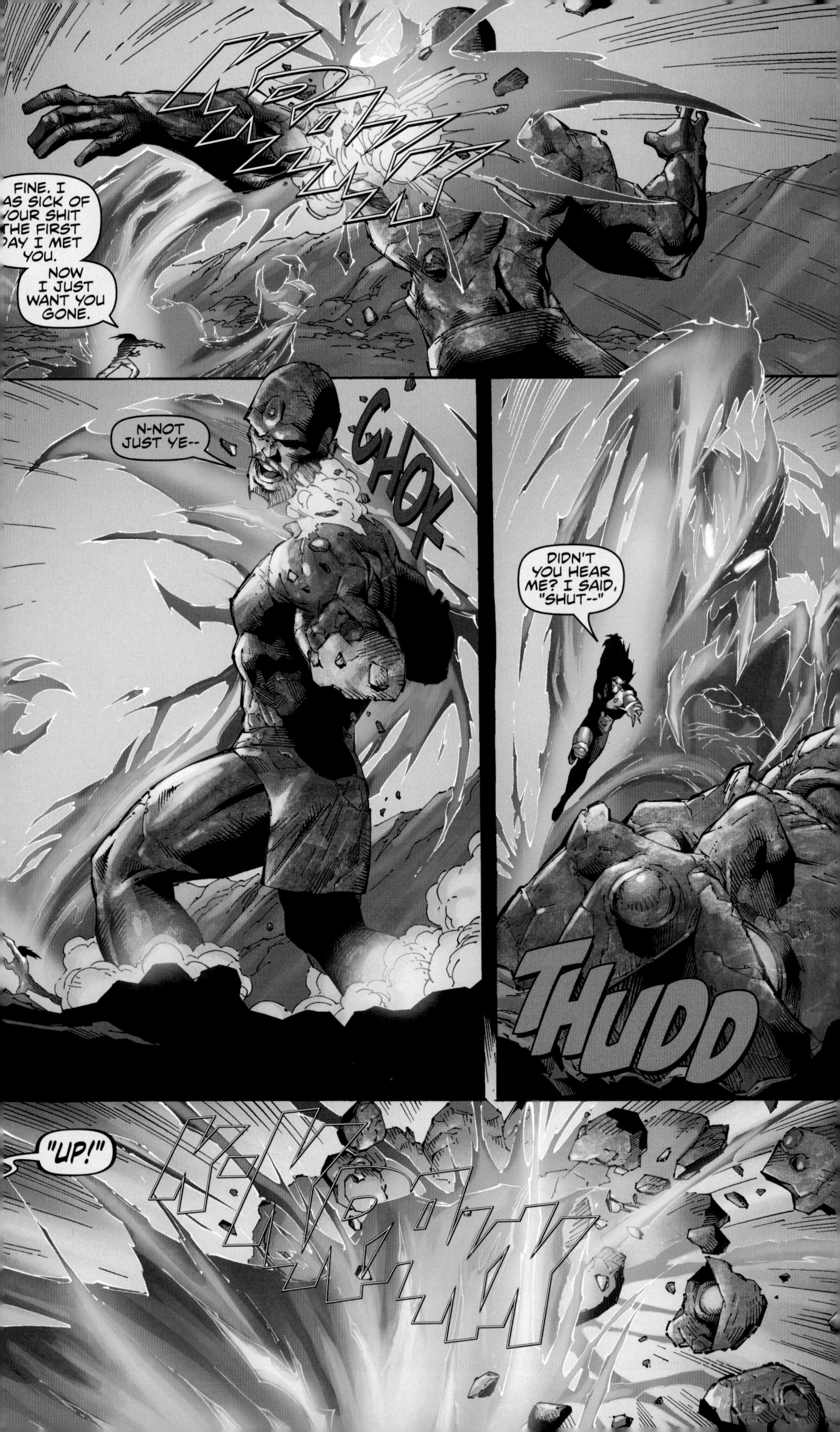
FINE. I AS SICK OF OUR SHIT THE FIRST AY I MET YOU.
NOW I JUST WANT YOU GONE.
N-NOT JUST YE--
CHOK
DIDN'T YOU HEAR ME? I SAID, "SHUT--"
THUDD
"UP!"

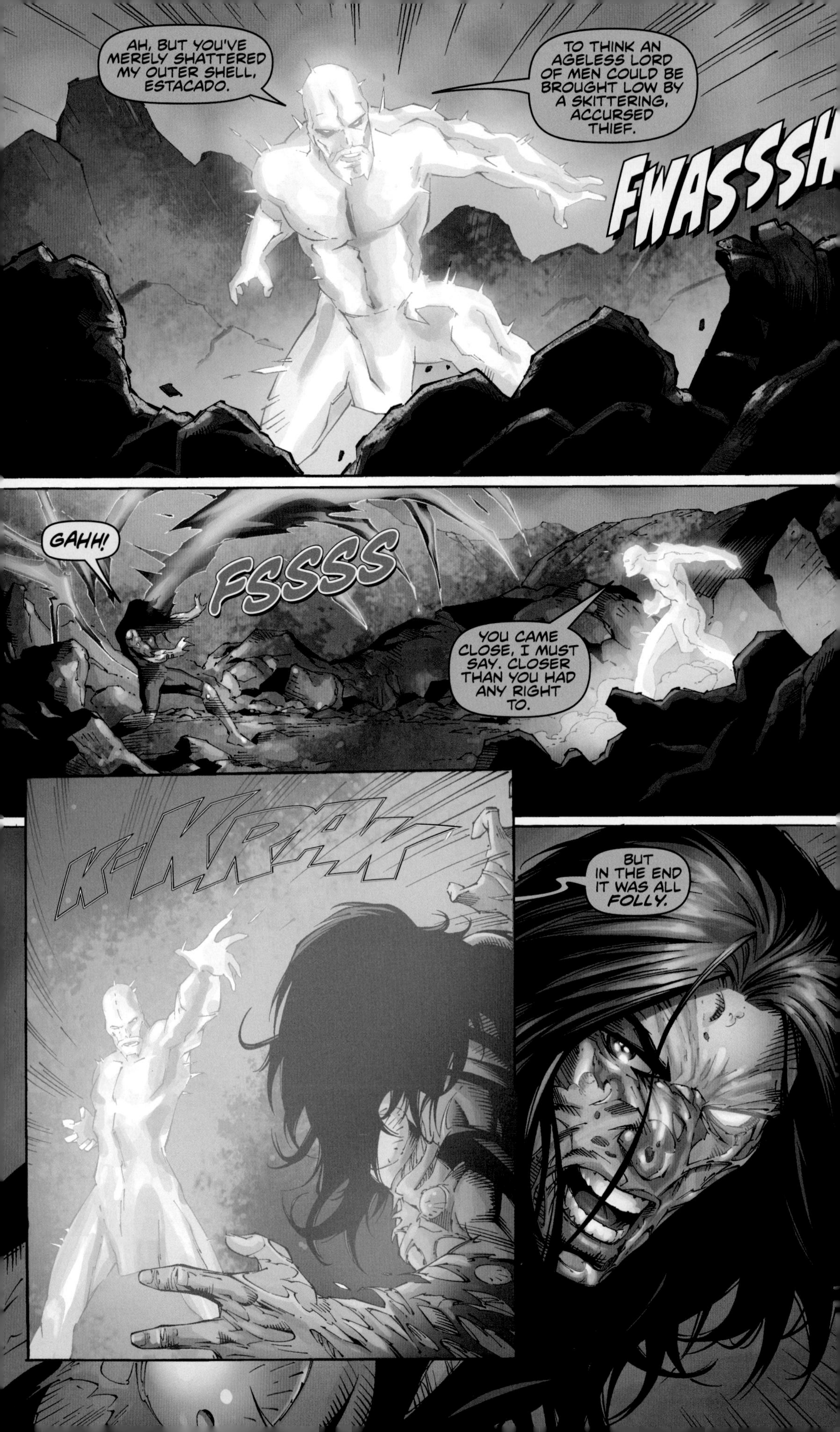
AH, BUT YOU'VE MERELY SHATTERED MY OUTER SHELL, ESTACADO.
TO THINK AN AGELESS LORD OF MEN COULD BE BROUGHT LOW BY A SKITTERING, ACCURSED THIEF.
FWASSSH
GAHH!
FSSSS
YOU CAME CLOSE, I MUST SAY. CLOSER THAN YOU HAD ANY RIGHT TO.
K-KRAK
BUT IN THE END IT WAS ALL FOLLY.

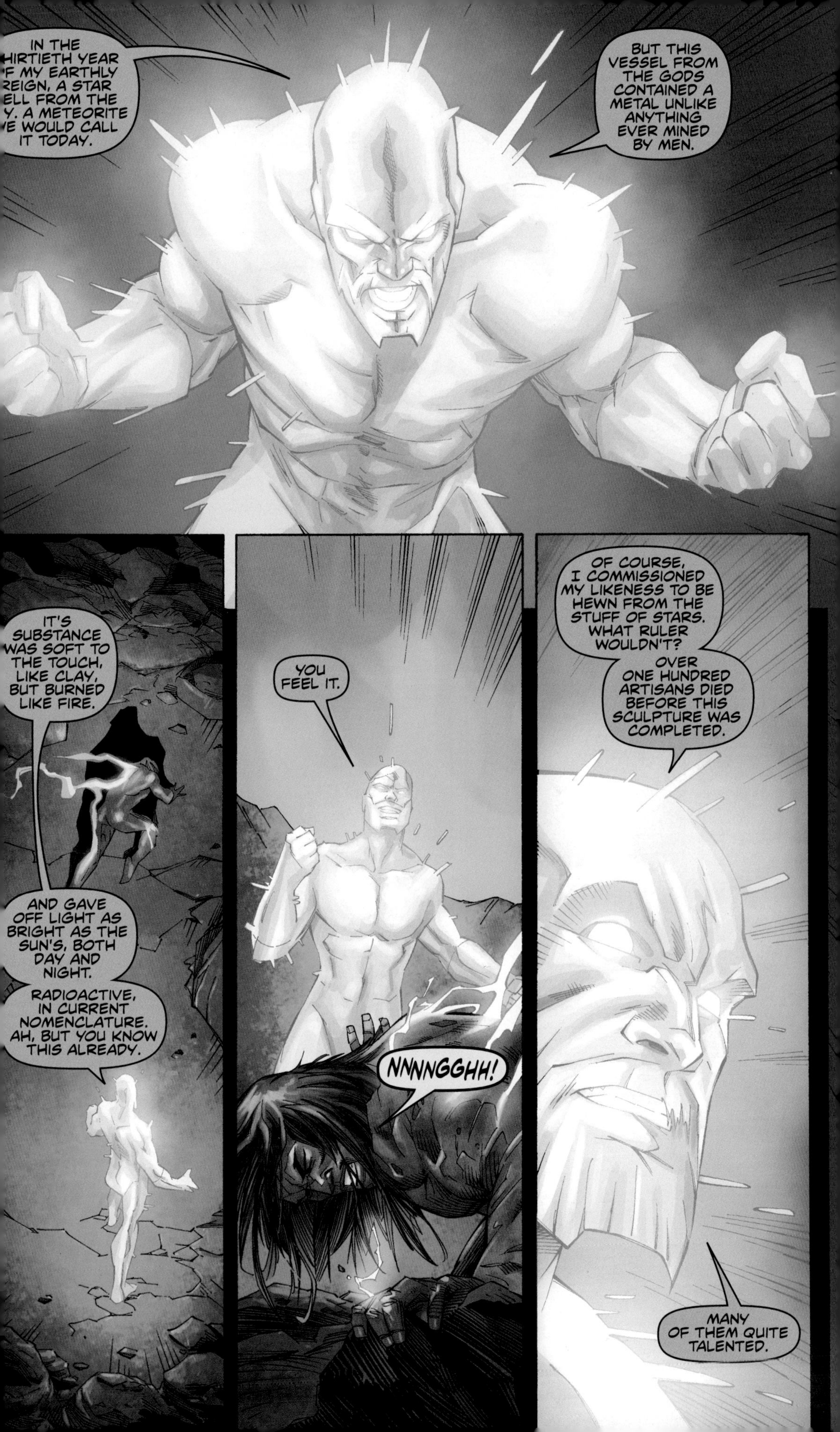
IN THE HIRTIETH YEAR F MY EARTHLY REIGN, A STAR ELL FROM THE Y. A METEORITE E WOULD CALL IT TODAY.
BUT THIS VESSEL FROM THE GODS CONTAINED A METAL UNLIKE ANYTHING EVER MINED BY MEN.
IT'S SUBSTANCE WAS SOFT TO THE TOUCH, LIKE CLAY, BUT BURNED LIKE FIRE.
AND GAVE OFF LIGHT AS BRIGHT AS THE SUN'S, BOTH DAY AND NIGHT.
RADIOACTIVE, IN CURRENT NOMENCLATURE. AH, BUT YOU KNOW THIS ALREADY.
YOU FEEL IT.
NNNNGGHH!
OF COURSE, I COMMISSIONED MY LIKENESS TO BE HEWN FROM THE STUFF OF STARS. WHAT RULER WOULDN'T?
OVER ONE HUNDRED ARTISANS DIED BEFORE THIS SCULPTURE WAS COMPLETED.
MANY OF THEM QUITE TALENTED.

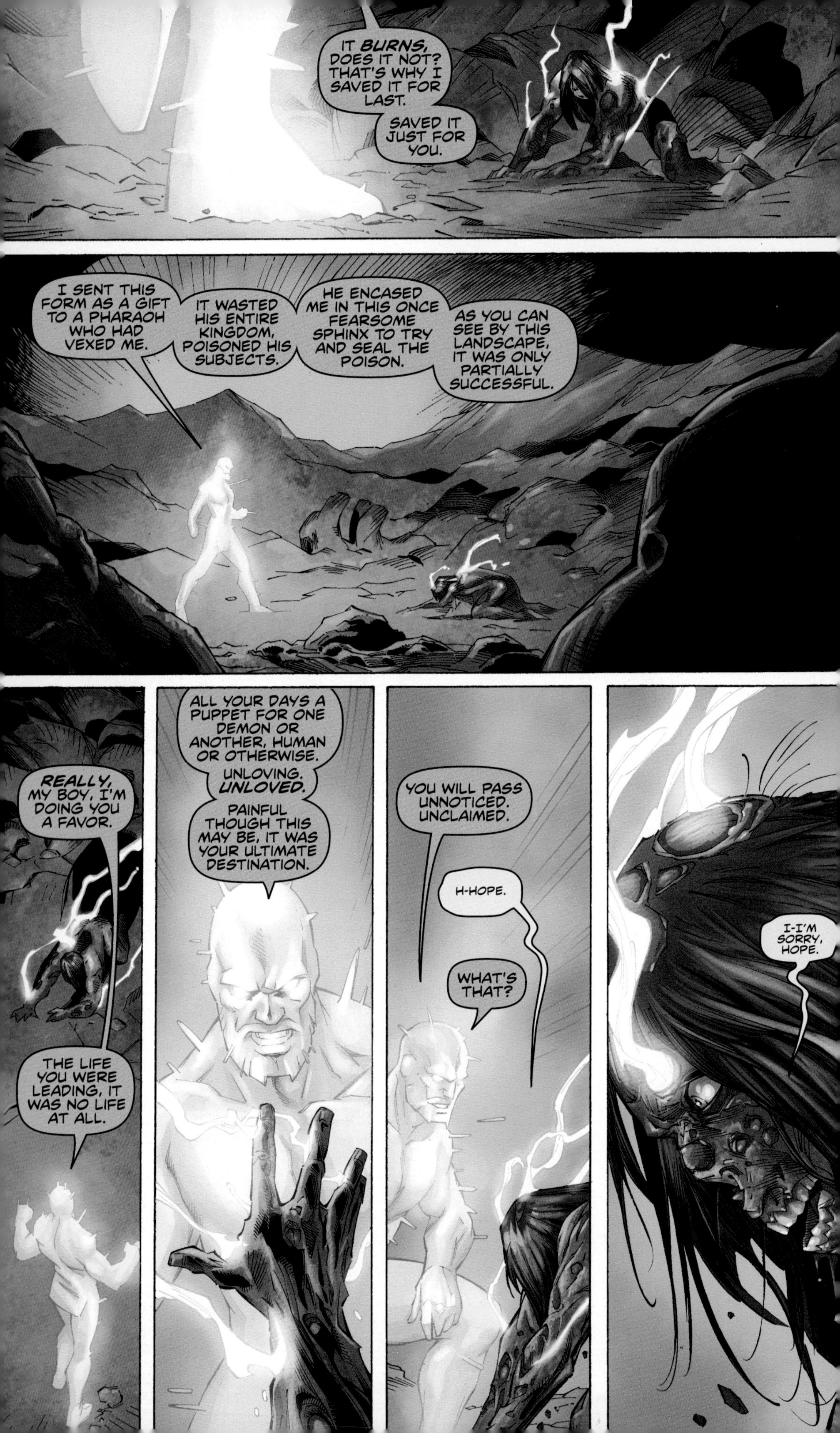
IT *BURNS,* DOES IT NOT? THAT'S WHY I SAVED IT FOR LAST.
SAVED IT JUST FOR YOU.
I SENT THIS FORM AS A GIFT TO A PHARAOH WHO HAD VEXED ME.
IT WASTED HIS ENTIRE KINGDOM, POISONED HIS SUBJECTS.
HE ENCASED ME IN THIS ONCE FEARSOME SPHINX TO TRY AND SEAL THE POISON.
AS YOU CAN SEE BY THIS LANDSCAPE, IT WAS ONLY PARTIALLY SUCCESSFUL.
REALLY, MY BOY, I'M DOING YOU A FAVOR.
THE LIFE YOU WERE LEADING, IT WAS NO LIFE AT ALL.
ALL YOUR DAYS A PUPPET FOR ONE DEMON OR ANOTHER, HUMAN OR OTHERWISE.
UNLOVING. ***UNLOVED.***
PAINFUL THOUGH THIS MAY BE, IT WAS YOUR ULTIMATE DESTINATION.
YOU WILL PASS UNNOTICED. UNCLAIMED.
H-HOPE.
WHAT'S THAT?
I-I'M SORRY, HOPE.

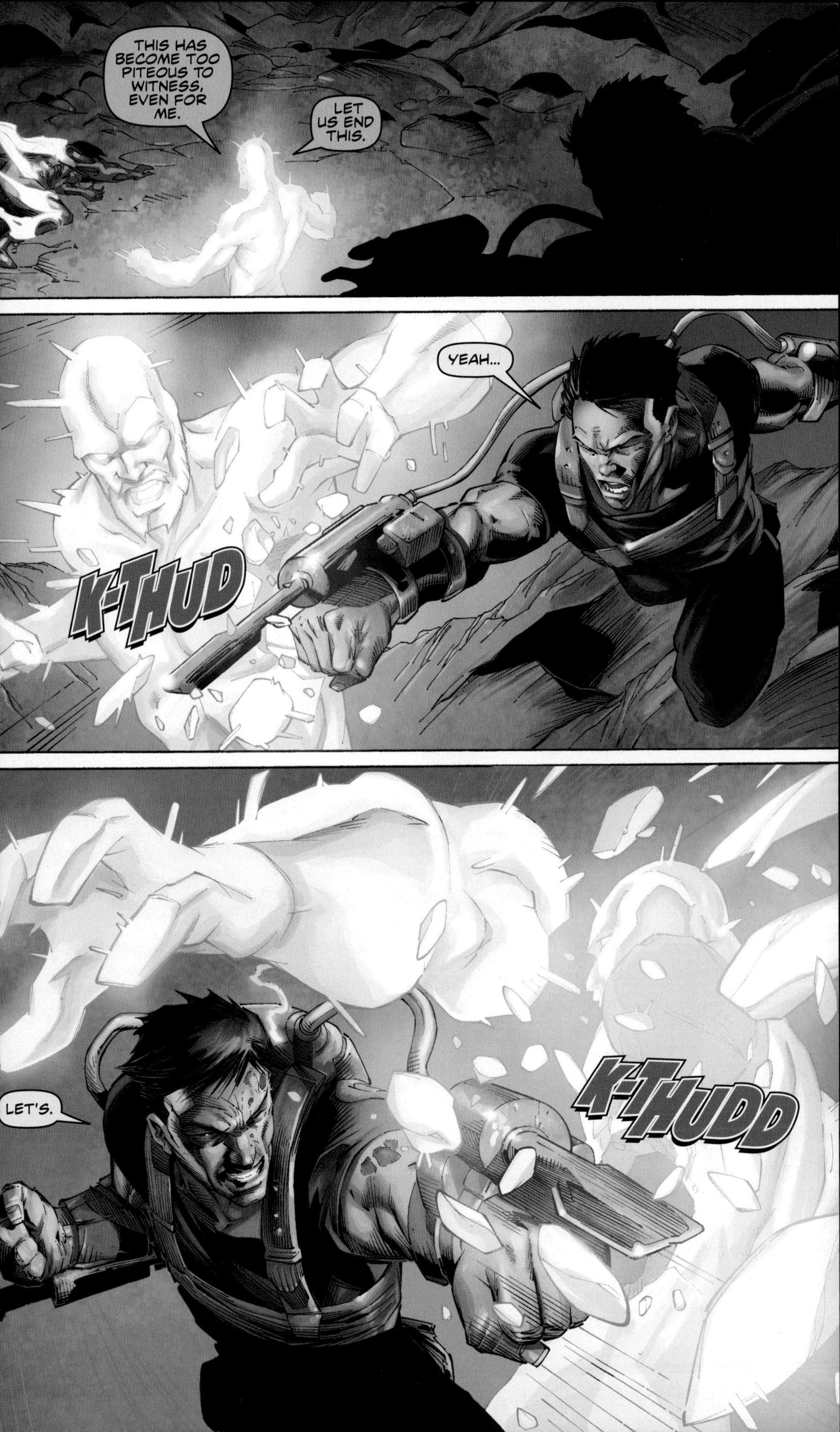
THIS HAS BECOME TOO PITEOUS TO WITNESS, EVEN FOR ME.
LET US END THIS.
YEAH...
K-THUD
LET'S.
K-THUDD

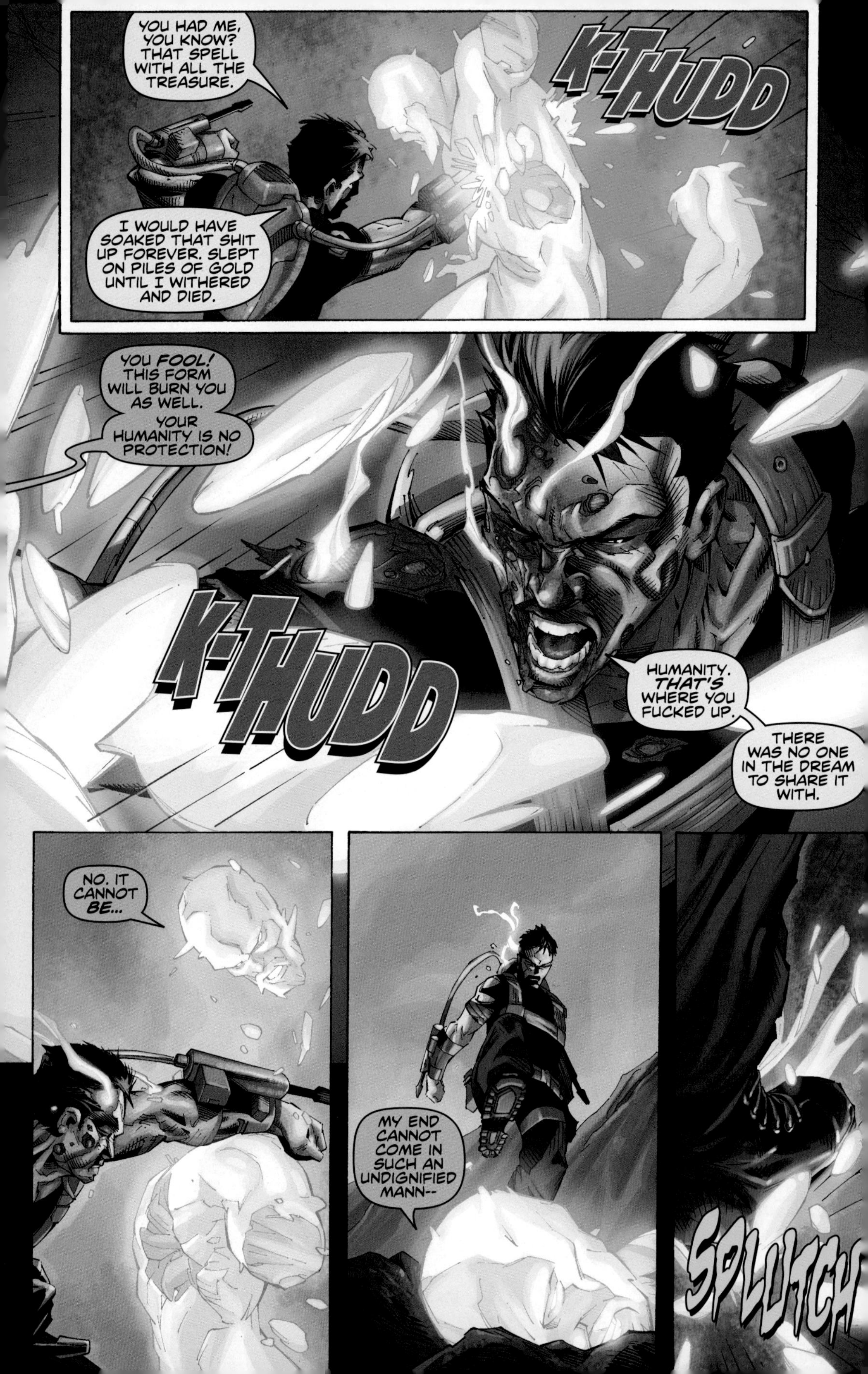
YOU HAD ME, YOU KNOW? THAT SPELL WITH ALL THE TREASURE.
K-THUDD
I WOULD HAVE SOAKED THAT SHIT UP FOREVER. SLEPT ON PILES OF GOLD UNTIL I WITHERED AND DIED.
YOU *FOOL!* THIS FORM WILL BURN YOU AS WELL.
YOUR HUMANITY IS NO PROTECTION!
K-THUDD
HUMANITY. *THAT'S* WHERE YOU FUCKED UP.
THERE WAS NO ONE IN THE DREAM TO SHARE IT WITH.
NO. IT CANNOT *BE*...
MY END CANNOT COME IN SUCH AN UNDIGNIFIED MANN--
SPLUTCH

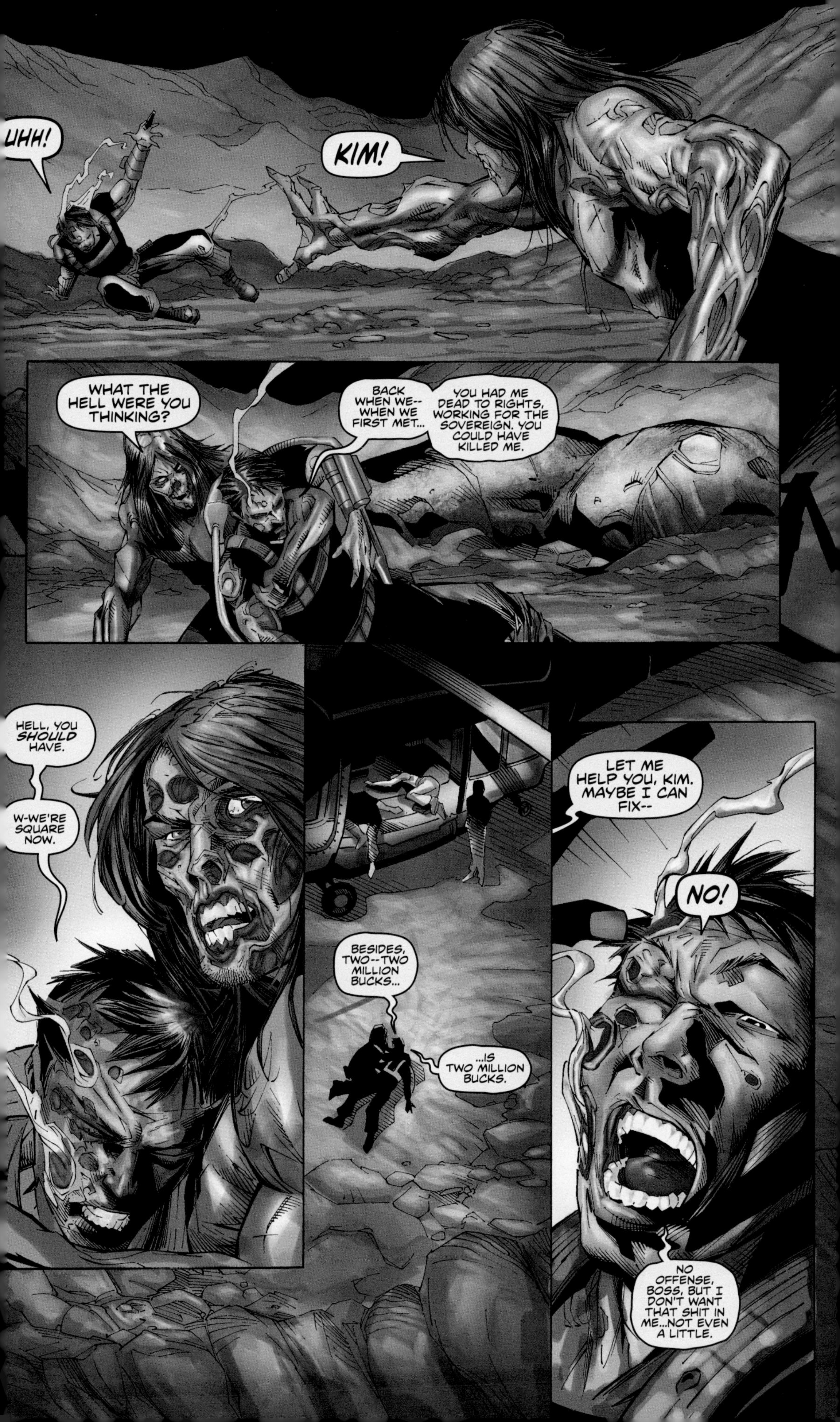
UHH!
KIM!
WHAT THE HELL WERE YOU THINKING?
BACK WHEN WE-- WHEN WE FIRST MET...
YOU HAD ME DEAD TO RIGHTS, WORKING FOR THE SOVEREIGN. YOU COULD HAVE KILLED ME.
HELL, YOU SHOULD HAVE.
W-WE'RE SQUARE NOW.
BESIDES, TWO--TWO MILLION BUCKS...
...IS TWO MILLION BUCKS.
LET ME HELP YOU, KIM. MAYBE I CAN FIX--
NO!
NO OFFENSE, BOSS, BUT I DON'T WANT THAT SHIT IN ME...NOT EVEN A LITTLE.

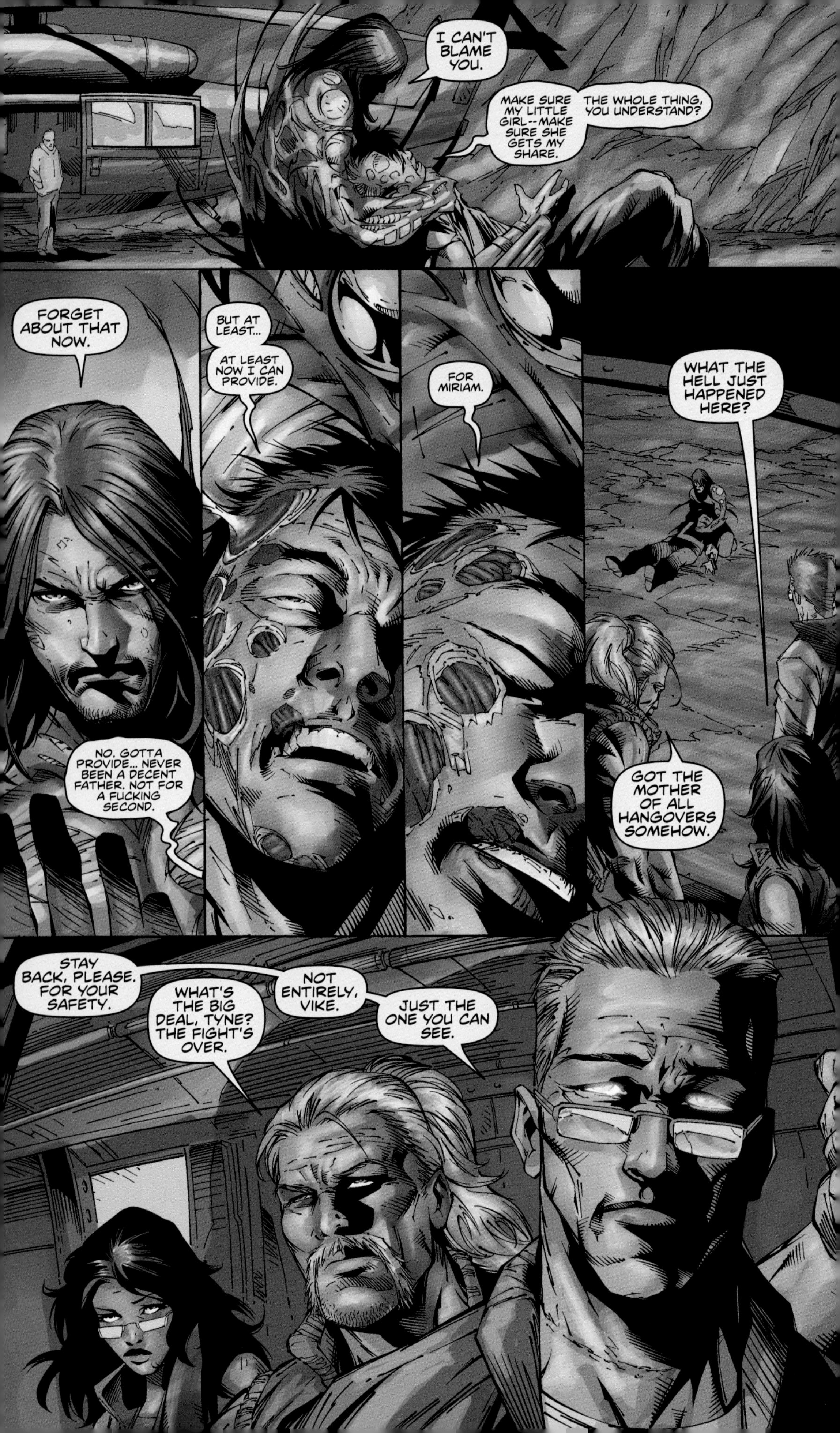
I CAN'T BLAME YOU.
MAKE SURE MY LITTLE GIRL--MAKE SURE SHE GETS MY SHARE.
THE WHOLE THING, YOU UNDERSTAND?
FORGET ABOUT THAT NOW.
NO. GOTTA PROVIDE... NEVER BEEN A DECENT FATHER. NOT FOR A FUCKING SECOND.
BUT AT LEAST...
AT LEAST NOW I CAN PROVIDE.
FOR MIRIAM.
WHAT THE HELL JUST HAPPENED HERE?
GOT THE MOTHER OF ALL HANGOVERS SOMEHOW.
STAY BACK, PLEASE. FOR YOUR SAFETY.
WHAT'S THE BIG DEAL, TYNE? THE FIGHT'S OVER.
NOT ENTIRELY, VIKE.
JUST THE ONE YOU CAN SEE.

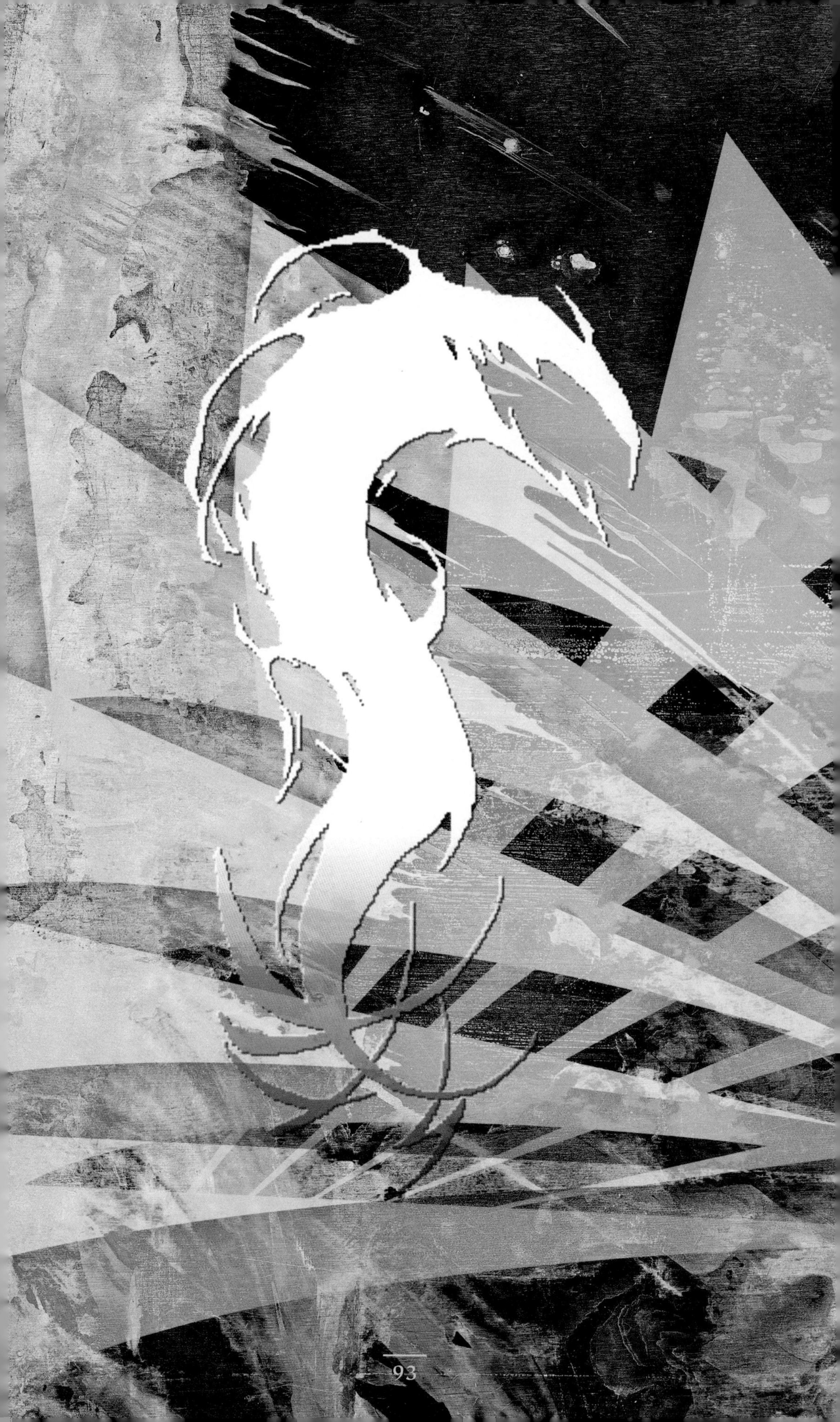

The Darkness®

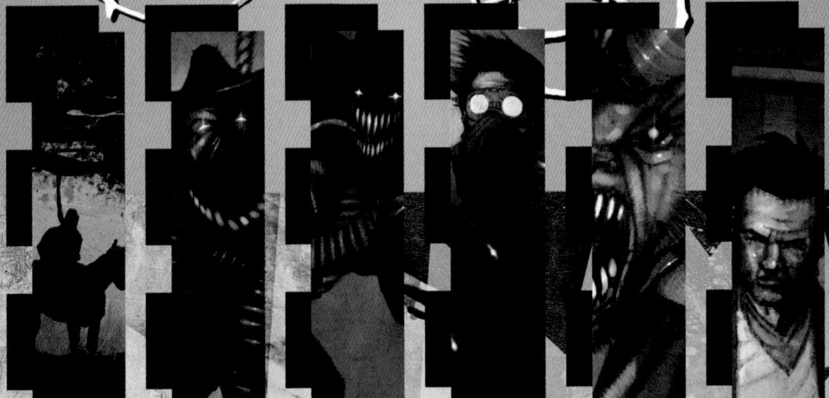

High Noon

written by: Joshua Hale Fialkov
art by: Matt Timson
letters by: Troy Peteri

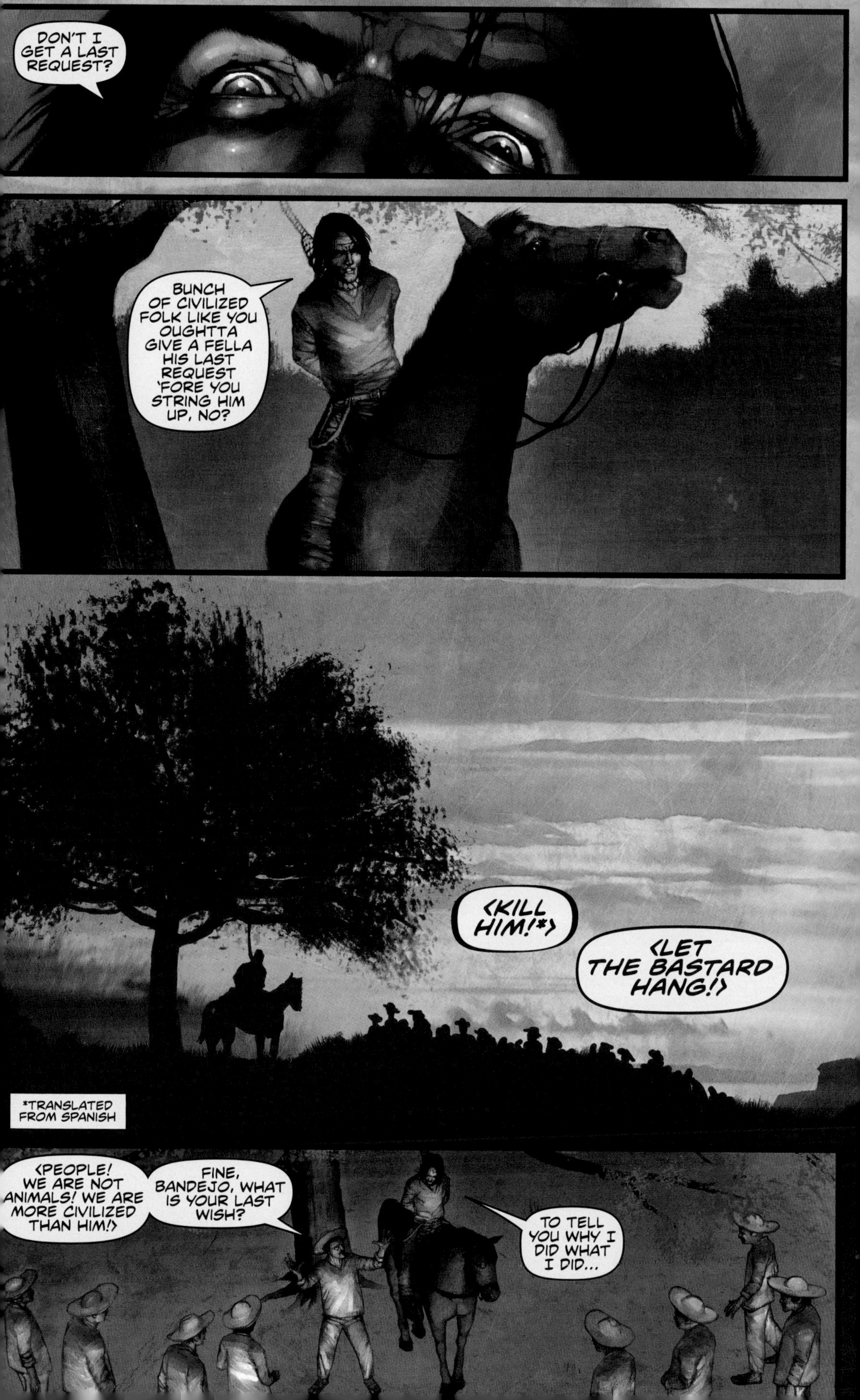
DON'T I GET A LAST REQUEST?
BUNCH OF CIVILIZED FOLK LIKE YOU OUGHTTA GIVE A FELLA HIS LAST REQUEST 'FORE YOU STRING HIM UP, NO?
<KILL HIM!*>
<LET THE BASTARD HANG!>
*TRANSLATED FROM SPANISH
<PEOPLE! WE ARE NOT ANIMALS! WE ARE MORE CIVILIZED THAN HIM!>
FINE, BANDEJO, WHAT IS YOUR LAST WISH?
TO TELL YOU WHY I DID WHAT I DID...

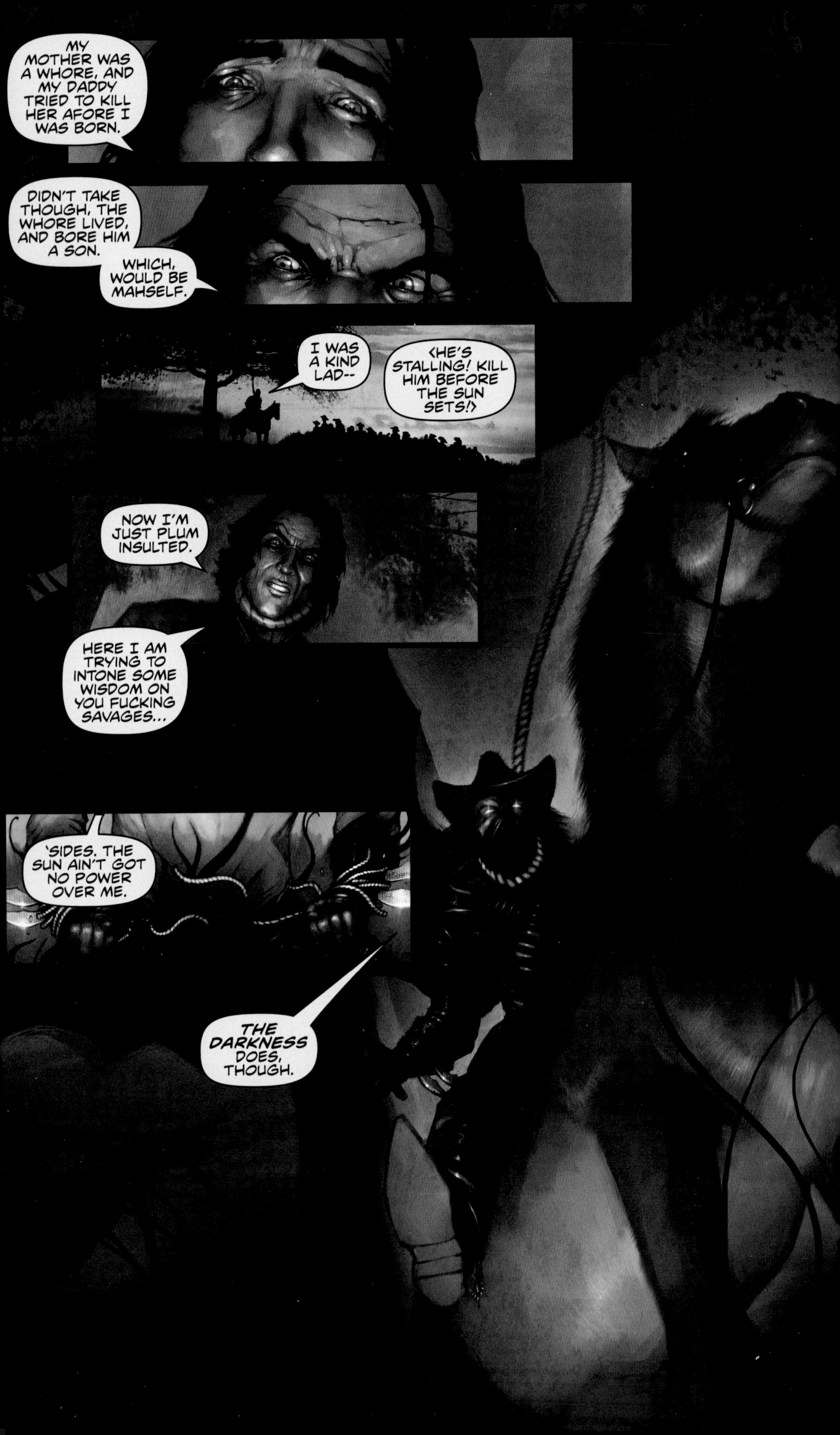
MY MOTHER WAS A WHORE, AND MY DADDY TRIED TO KILL HER AFORE I WAS BORN.
DIDN'T TAKE THOUGH, THE WHORE LIVED, AND BORE HIM A SON.
WHICH, WOULD BE MAHSELF.
I WAS A KIND LAD--
<HE'S STALLING! KILL HIM BEFORE THE SUN SETS!>
NOW I'M JUST PLUM INSULTED.
HERE I AM TRYING TO INTONE SOME WISDOM ON YOU FUCKING SAVAGES...
'SIDES. THE SUN AIN'T GOT NO POWER OVER ME.
THE DARKNESS DOES, THOUGH.

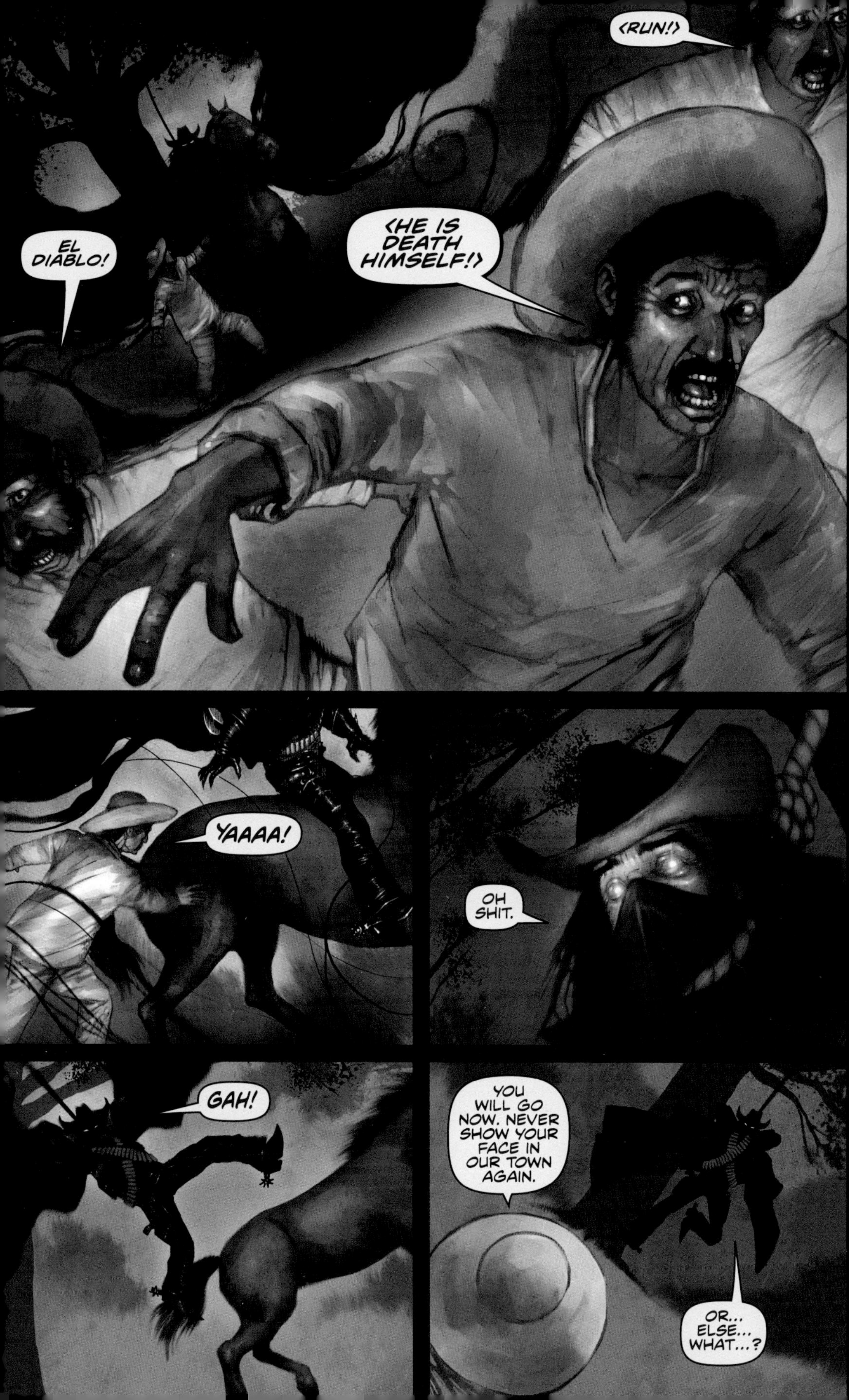
<RUN!>
EL DIABLO!
<HE IS DEATH HIMSELF!>
YAAAA!
OH SHIT.
GAH!
YOU WILL GO NOW. NEVER SHOW YOUR FACE IN OUR TOWN AGAIN.
OR... ELSE... WHAT...?

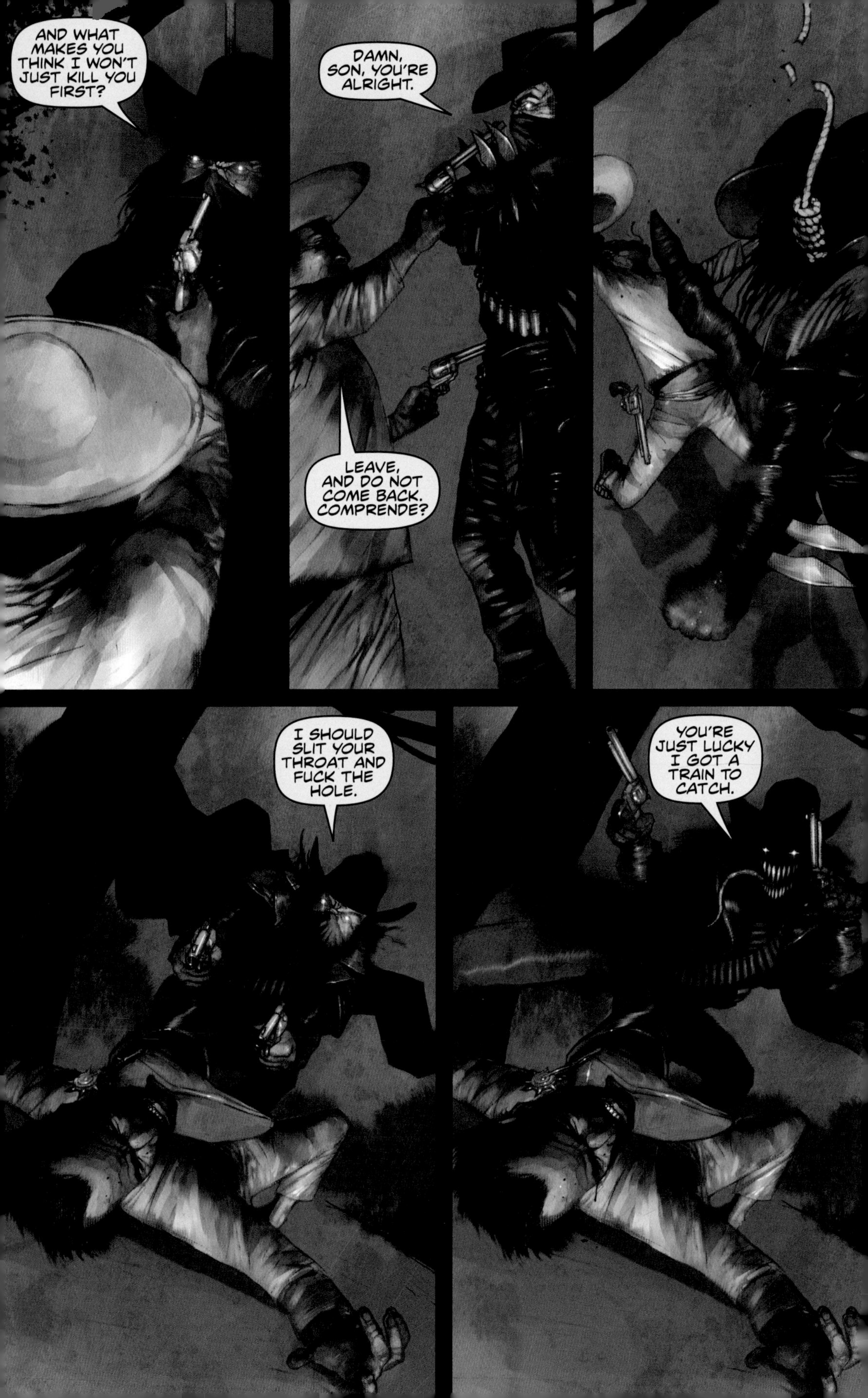
AND WHAT MAKES YOU THINK I WON'T JUST KILL YOU FIRST?
DAMN, SON, YOU'RE ALRIGHT.
LEAVE, AND DO NOT COME BACK. COMPRENDE?
I SHOULD SLIT YOUR THROAT AND FUCK THE HOLE.
YOU'RE JUST LUCKY I GOT A TRAIN TO CATCH.

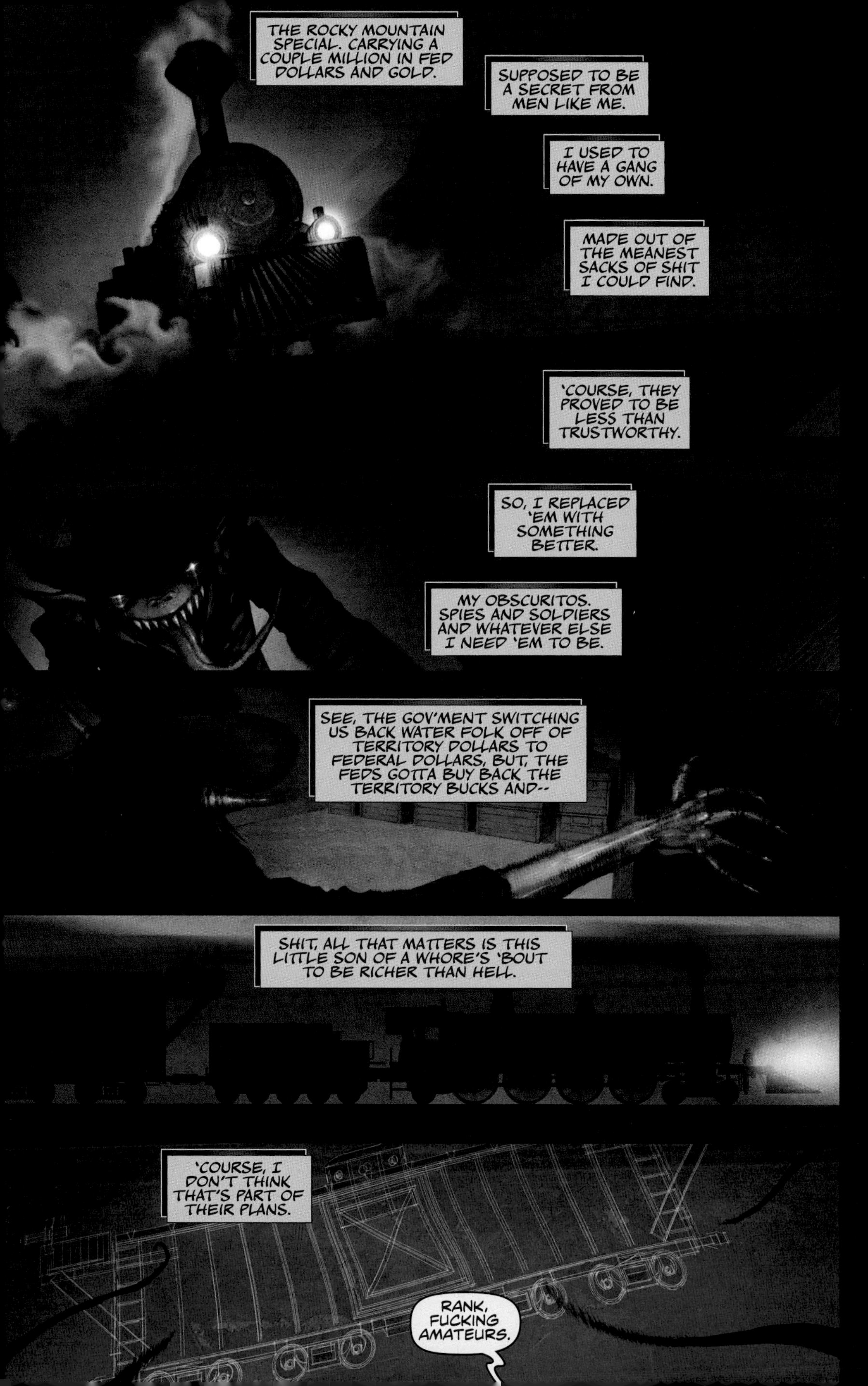

THE ROCKY MOUNTAIN SPECIAL. CARRYING A COUPLE MILLION IN FED DOLLARS AND GOLD.
SUPPOSED TO BE A SECRET FROM MEN LIKE ME.
I USED TO HAVE A GANG OF MY OWN.
MADE OUT OF THE MEANEST SACKS OF SHIT I COULD FIND.
'COURSE, THEY PROVED TO BE LESS THAN TRUSTWORTHY.
SO, I REPLACED 'EM WITH SOMETHING BETTER.
MY OBSCURITOS. SPIES AND SOLDIERS AND WHATEVER ELSE I NEED 'EM TO BE.
SEE, THE GOV'MENT SWITCHING US BACK WATER FOLK OFF OF TERRITORY DOLLARS TO FEDERAL DOLLARS, BUT, THE FEDS GOTTA BUY BACK THE TERRITORY BUCKS AND--
SHIT, ALL THAT MATTERS IS THIS LITTLE SON OF A WHORE'S 'BOUT TO BE RICHER THAN HELL.
'COURSE, I DON'T THINK THAT'S PART OF THEIR PLANS.
RANK, FUCKING AMATEURS.

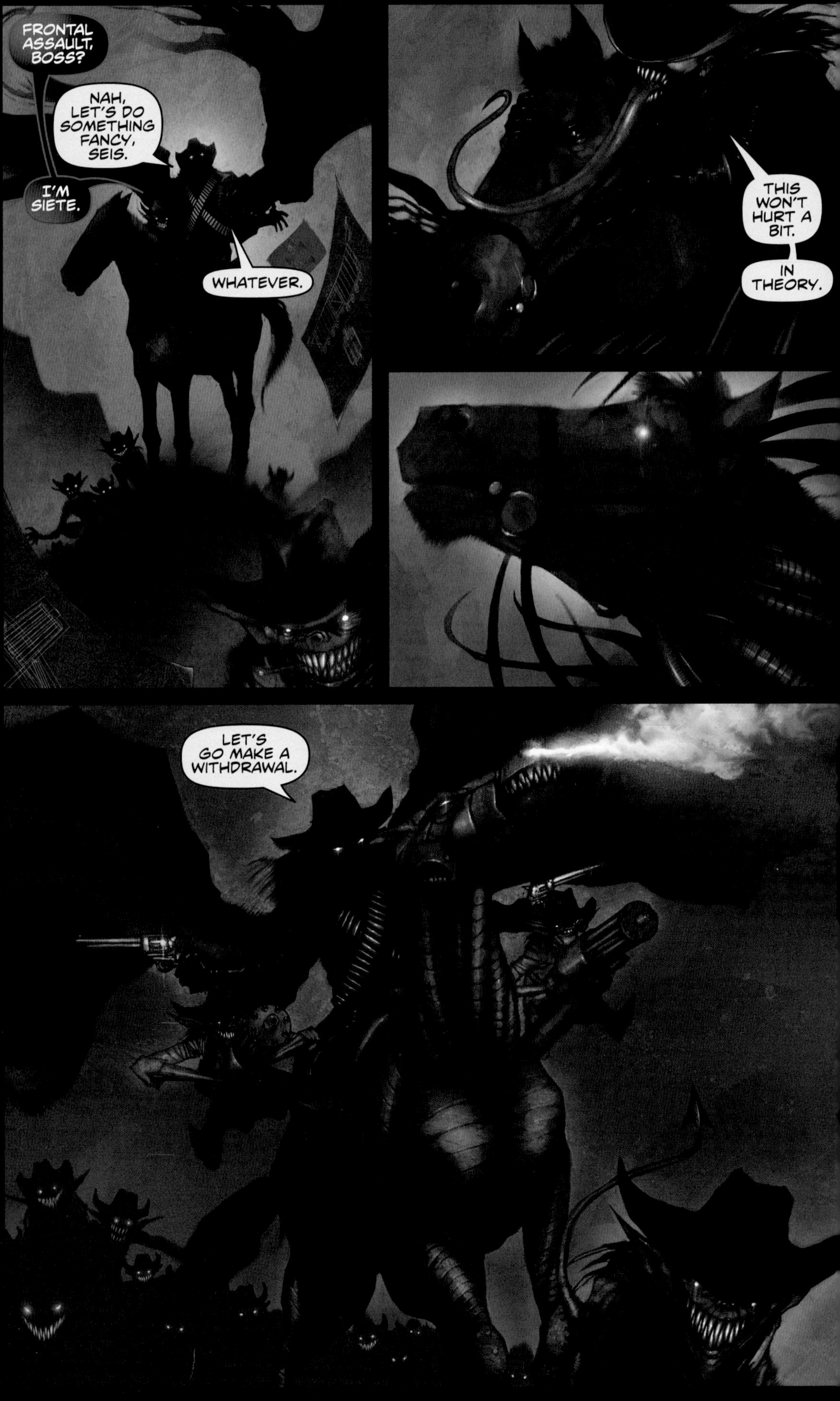
FRONTAL ASSAULT, BOSS?
NAH, LET'S DO SOMETHING FANCY, SEIS.
I'M SIETE.
WHATEVER.
THIS WON'T HURT A BIT.
IN THEORY.
LET'S GO MAKE A WITHDRAWAL.

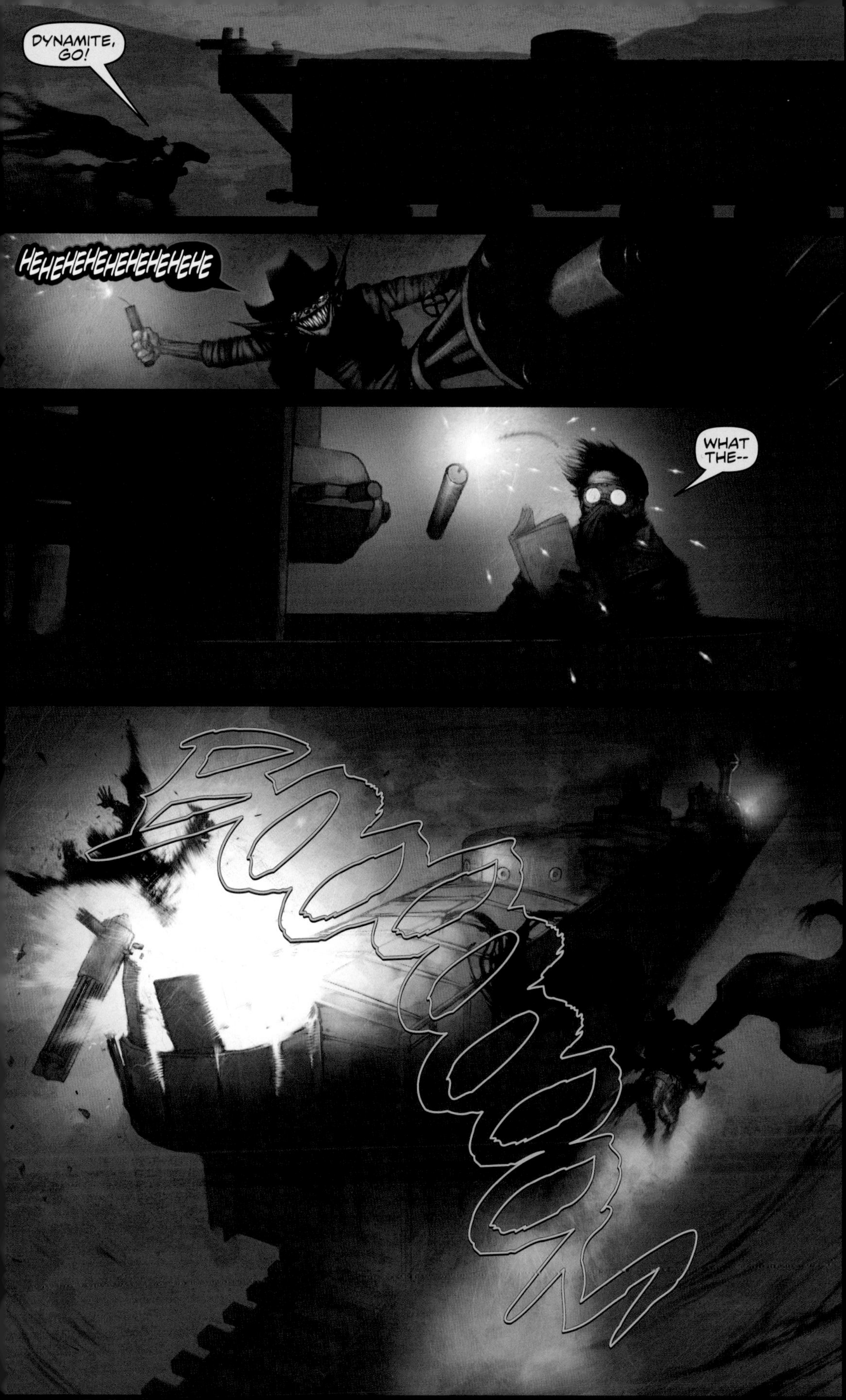
DYNAMITE, GO!
HEHEHEHEHEHEHEHEHEHE
WHAT THE--
BOOOOOOOM

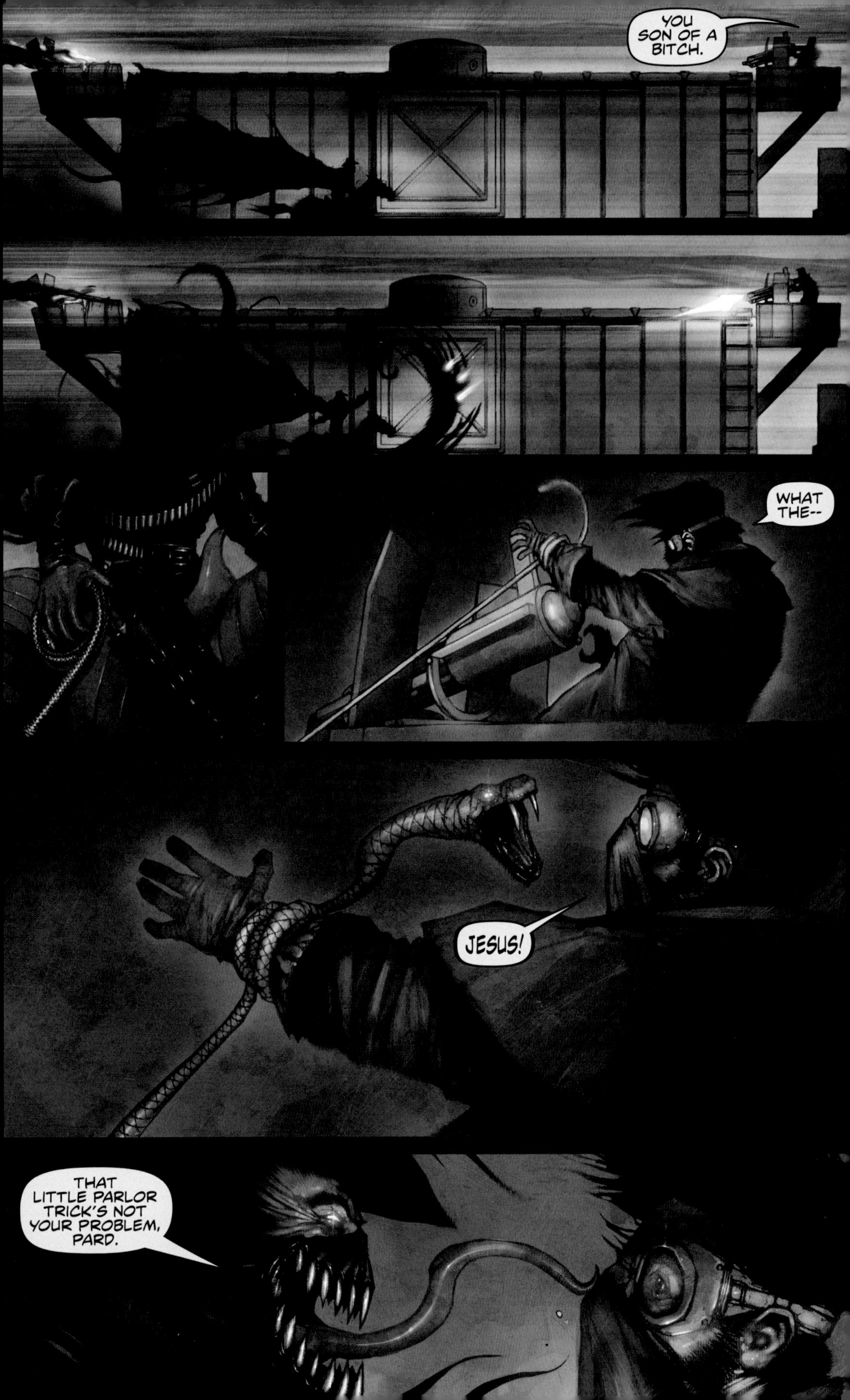
YOU SON OF A BITCH.
WHAT THE--
JESUS!
THAT LITTLE PARLOR TRICK'S NOT YOUR PROBLEM, PARD.

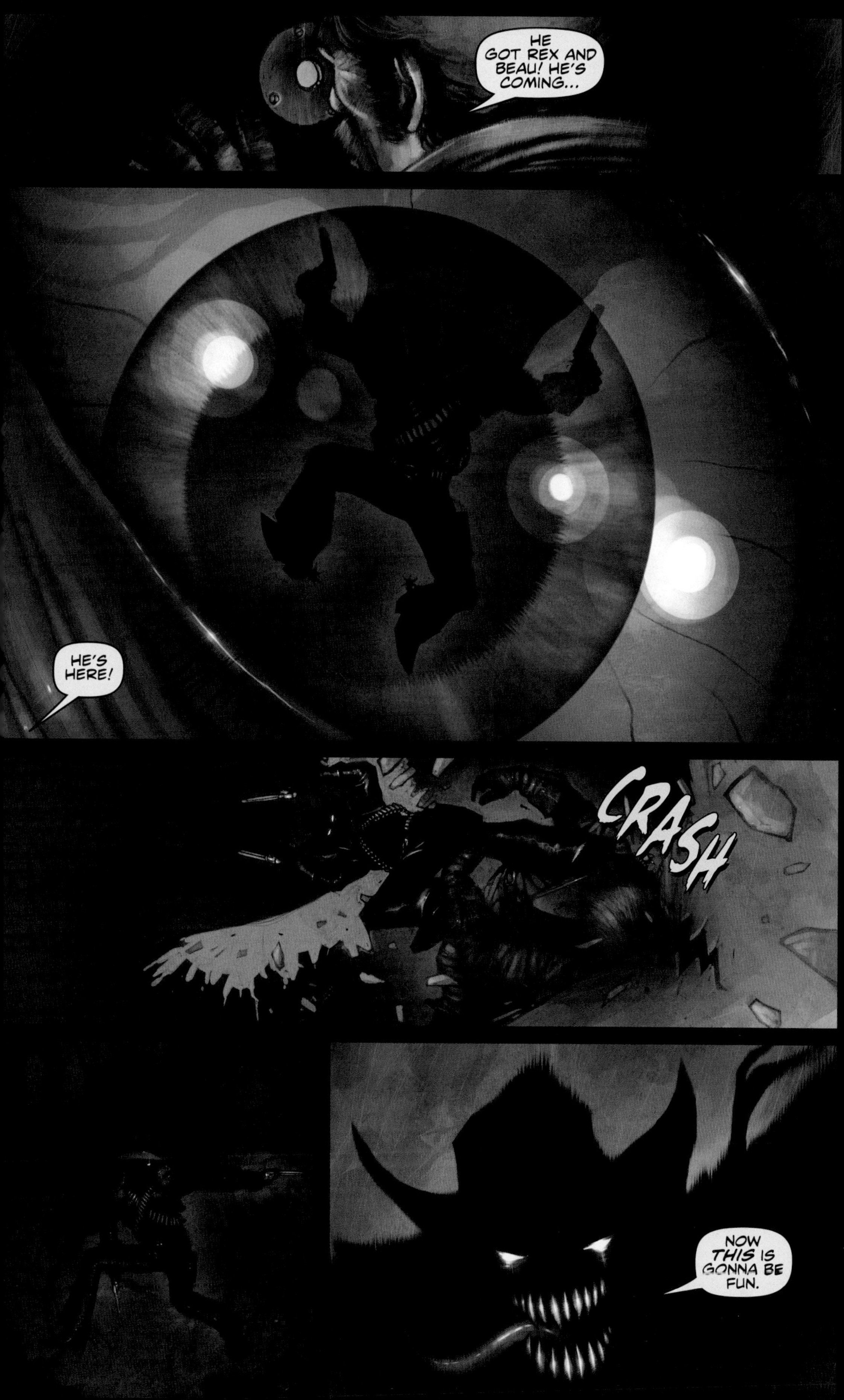
HE GOT REX AND BEAU! HE'S COMING...
HE'S HERE!
CRASH
NOW THIS IS GONNA BE FUN.

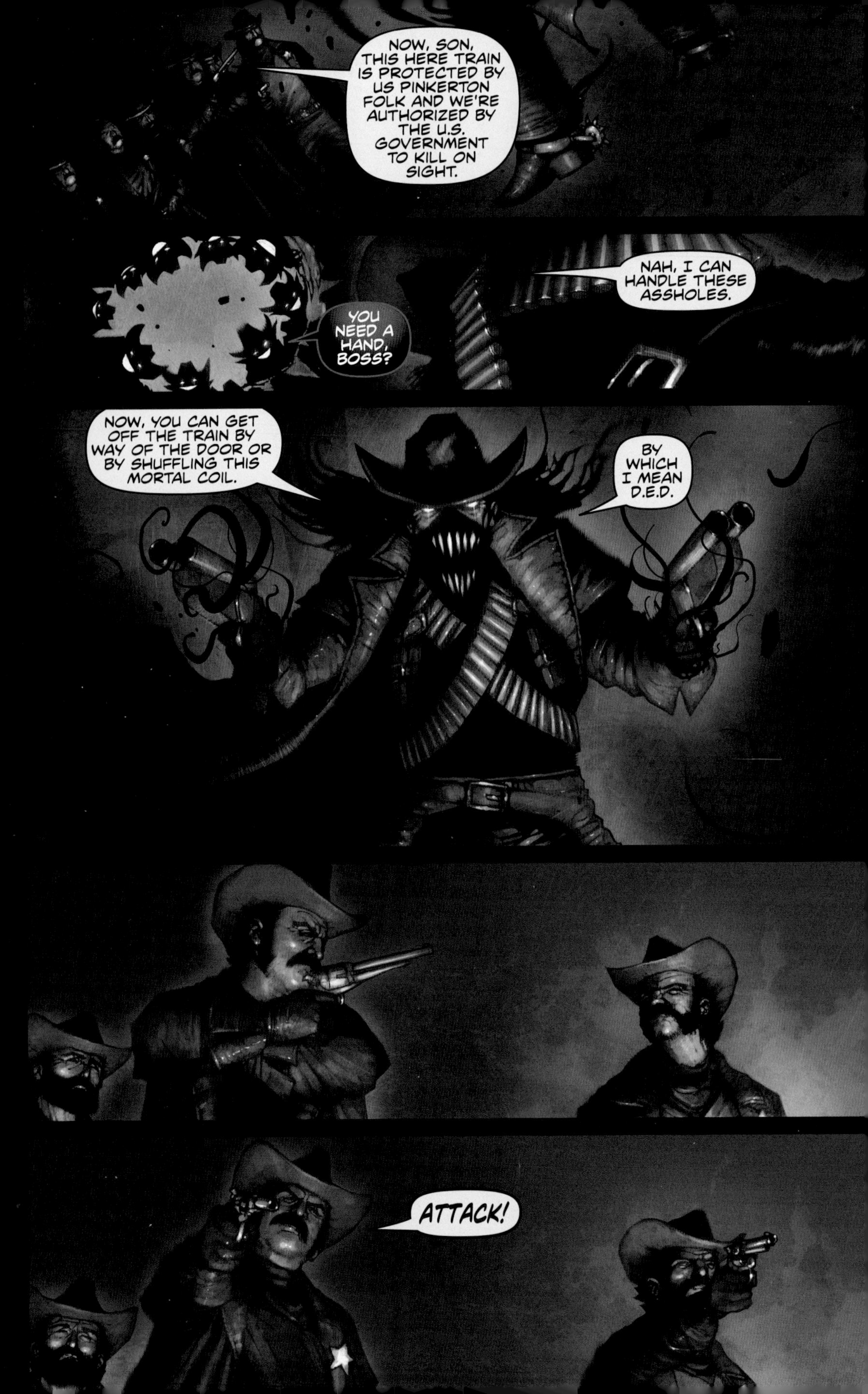
NOW, SON, THIS HERE TRAIN IS PROTECTED BY US PINKERTON FOLK AND WE'RE AUTHORIZED BY THE U.S. GOVERNMENT TO KILL ON SIGHT.
YOU NEED A HAND, BOSS?
NAH, I CAN HANDLE THESE ASSHOLES.
NOW, YOU CAN GET OFF THE TRAIN BY WAY OF THE DOOR OR BY SHUFFLING THIS MORTAL COIL.
BY WHICH I MEAN D.E.D.
ATTACK!

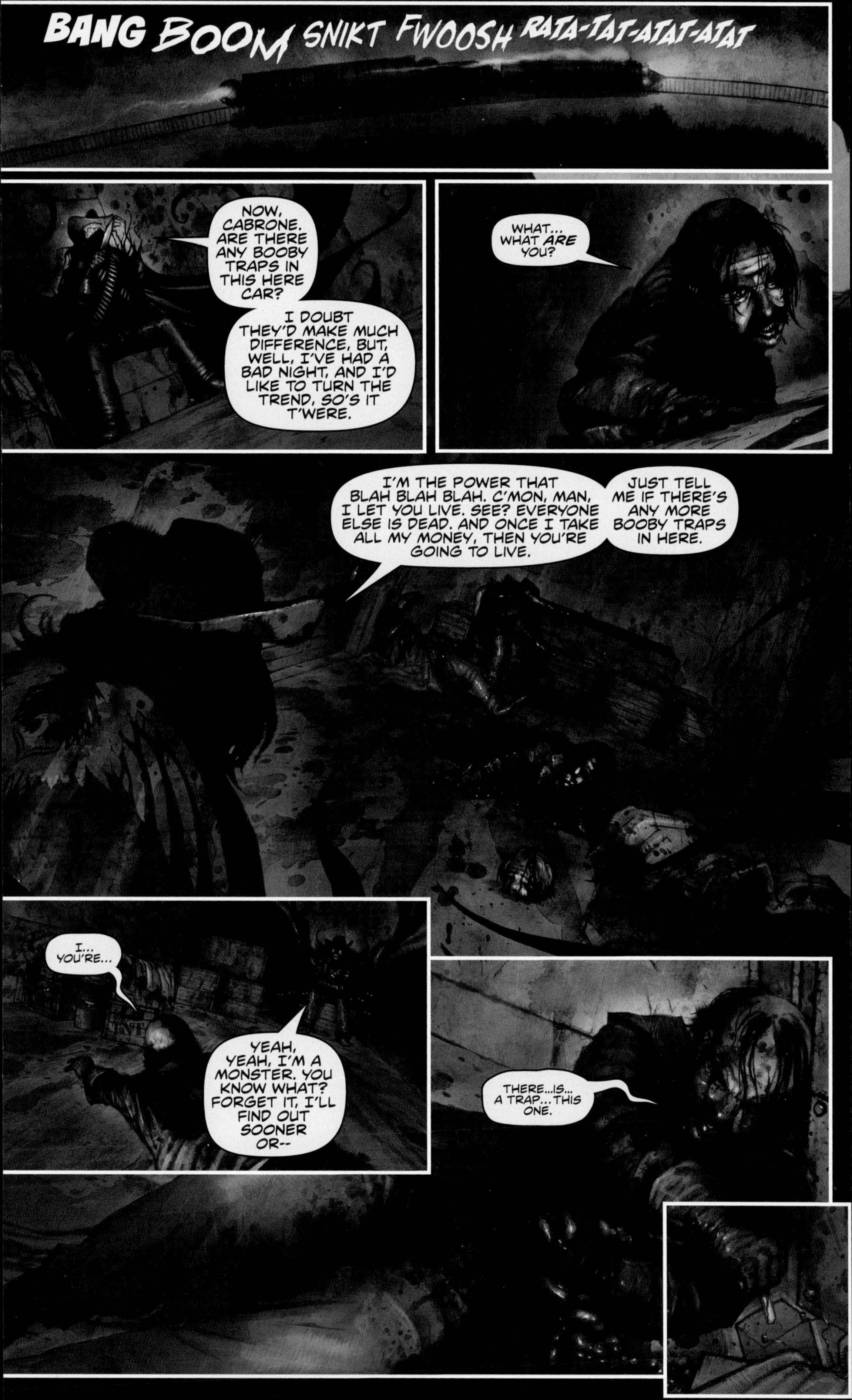
BANG BOOM SNIKT FWOOSH RATA-TAT-ATAT-ATAT
NOW, CABRONE. ARE THERE ANY BOOBY TRAPS IN THIS HERE CAR?
I DOUBT THEY'D MAKE MUCH DIFFERENCE, BUT, WELL, I'VE HAD A BAD NIGHT, AND I'D LIKE TO TURN THE TREND, SO'S IT T'WERE.
WHAT... WHAT ARE YOU?
I'M THE POWER THAT BLAH BLAH BLAH. C'MON, MAN, I LET YOU LIVE. SEE? EVERYONE ELSE IS DEAD. AND ONCE I TAKE ALL MY MONEY, THEN YOU'RE GOING TO LIVE.
JUST TELL ME IF THERE'S ANY MORE BOOBY TRAPS IN HERE.
I... YOU'RE...
YEAH, YEAH, I'M A MONSTER. YOU KNOW WHAT? FORGET IT, I'LL FIND OUT SOONER OR--
THERE...IS... A TRAP... THIS ONE.

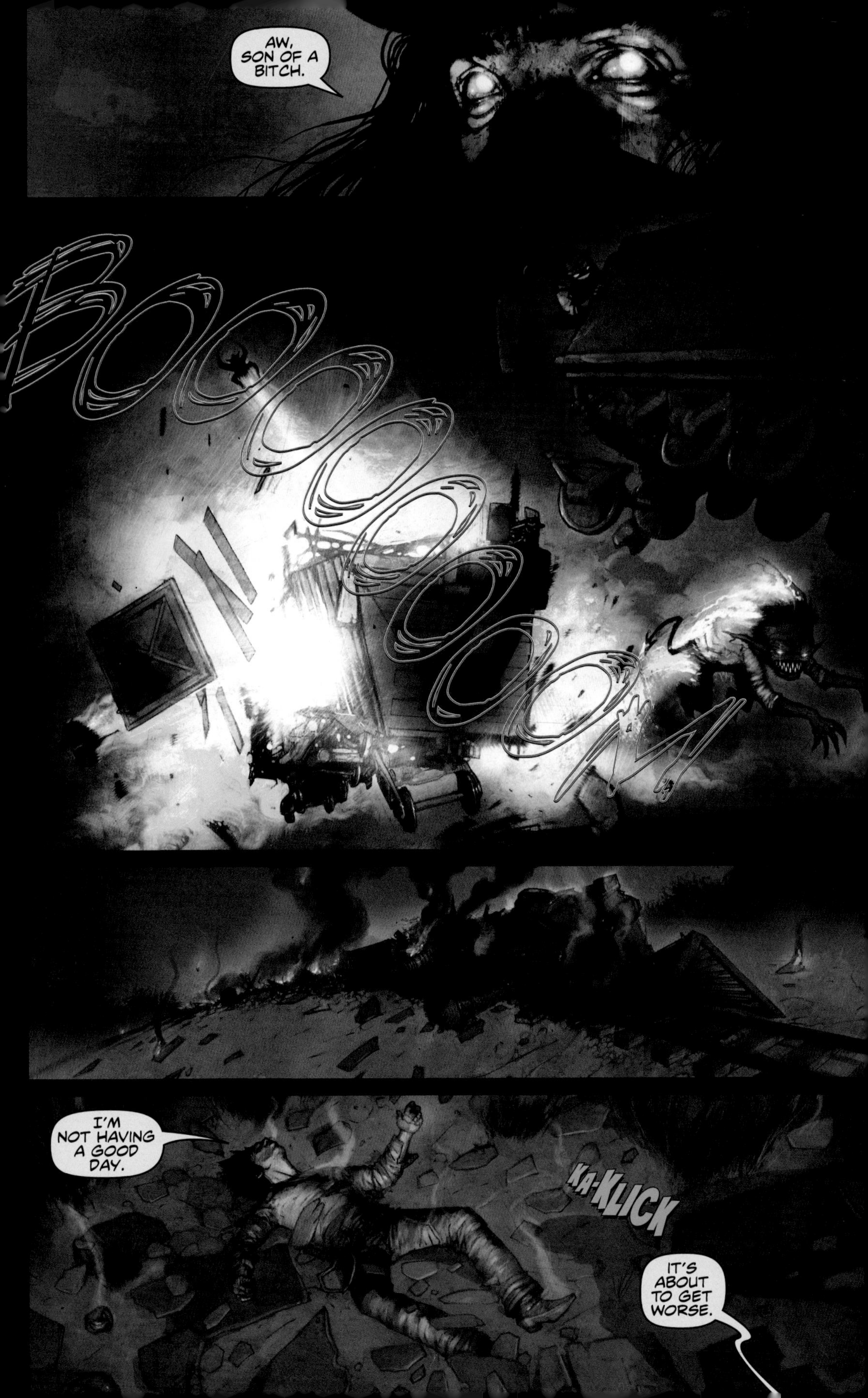
AW, SON OF A BITCH.
BOOOOOOOOOM
I'M NOT HAVING A GOOD DAY.
KA-KLICK
IT'S ABOUT TO GET WORSE.

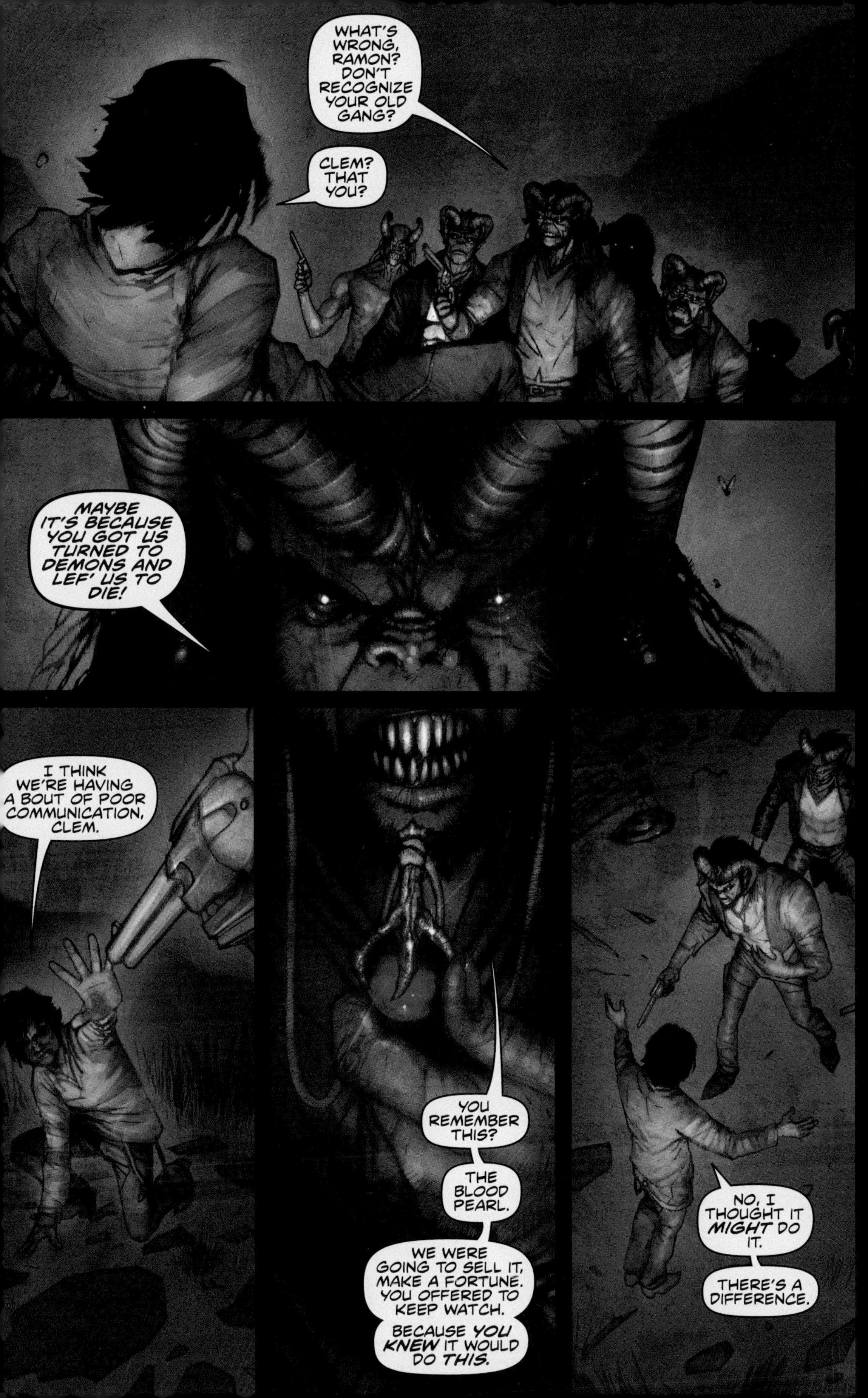
WHAT'S WRONG, RAMON? DON'T RECOGNIZE YOUR OLD GANG?
CLEM? THAT YOU?
MAYBE IT'S BECAUSE YOU GOT US TURNED TO DEMONS AND LEF' US TO DIE!
I THINK WE'RE HAVING A BOUT OF POOR COMMUNICATION, CLEM.
YOU REMEMBER THIS?
THE BLOOD PEARL.
WE WERE GOING TO SELL IT, MAKE A FORTUNE. YOU OFFERED TO KEEP WATCH.
BECAUSE *YOU KNEW* IT WOULD DO *THIS*.
NO, I THOUGHT IT *MIGHT* DO IT.
THERE'S A DIFFERENCE.

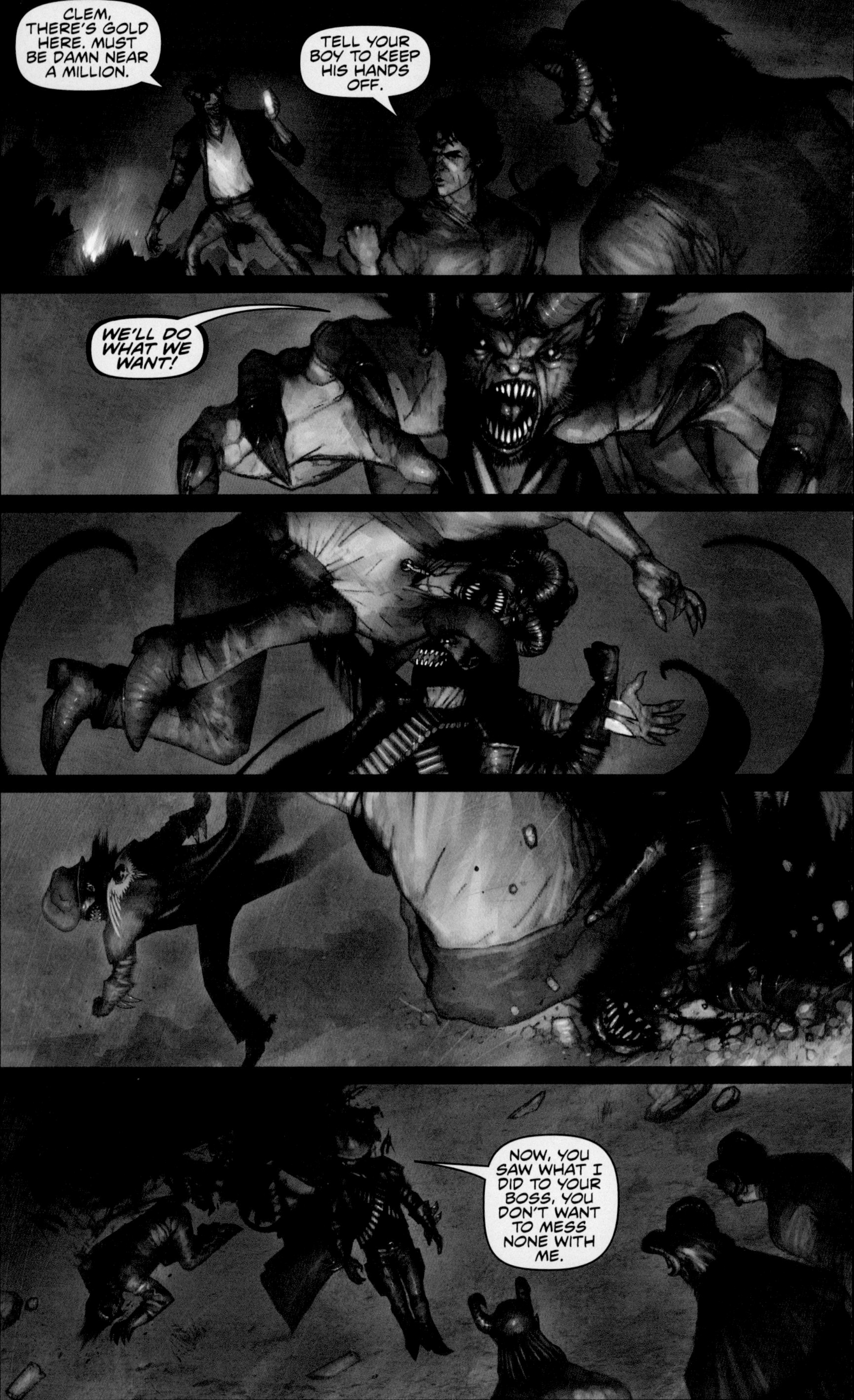
CLEM, THERE'S GOLD HERE. MUST BE DAMN NEAR A MILLION.
TELL YOUR BOY TO KEEP HIS HANDS OFF.
WE'LL DO WHAT WE WANT!
NOW, YOU SAW WHAT I DID TO YOUR BOSS, YOU DON'T WANT TO MESS NONE WITH ME.

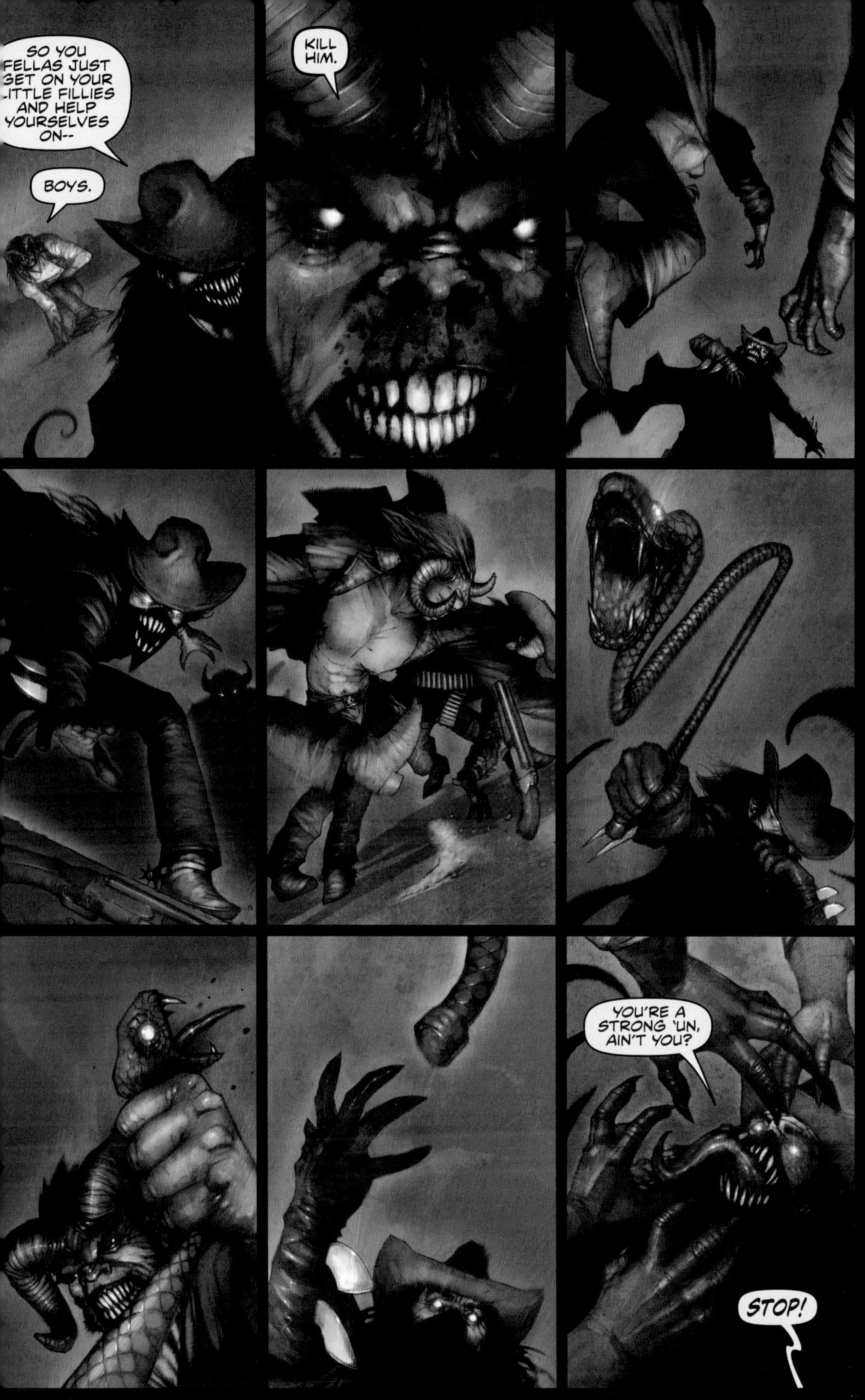
SO YOU FELLAS JUST GET ON YOUR LITTLE FILLIES AND HELP YOURSELVES ON--
BOYS.
KILL HIM.
YOU'RE A STRONG 'UN, AIN'T YOU?
STOP!

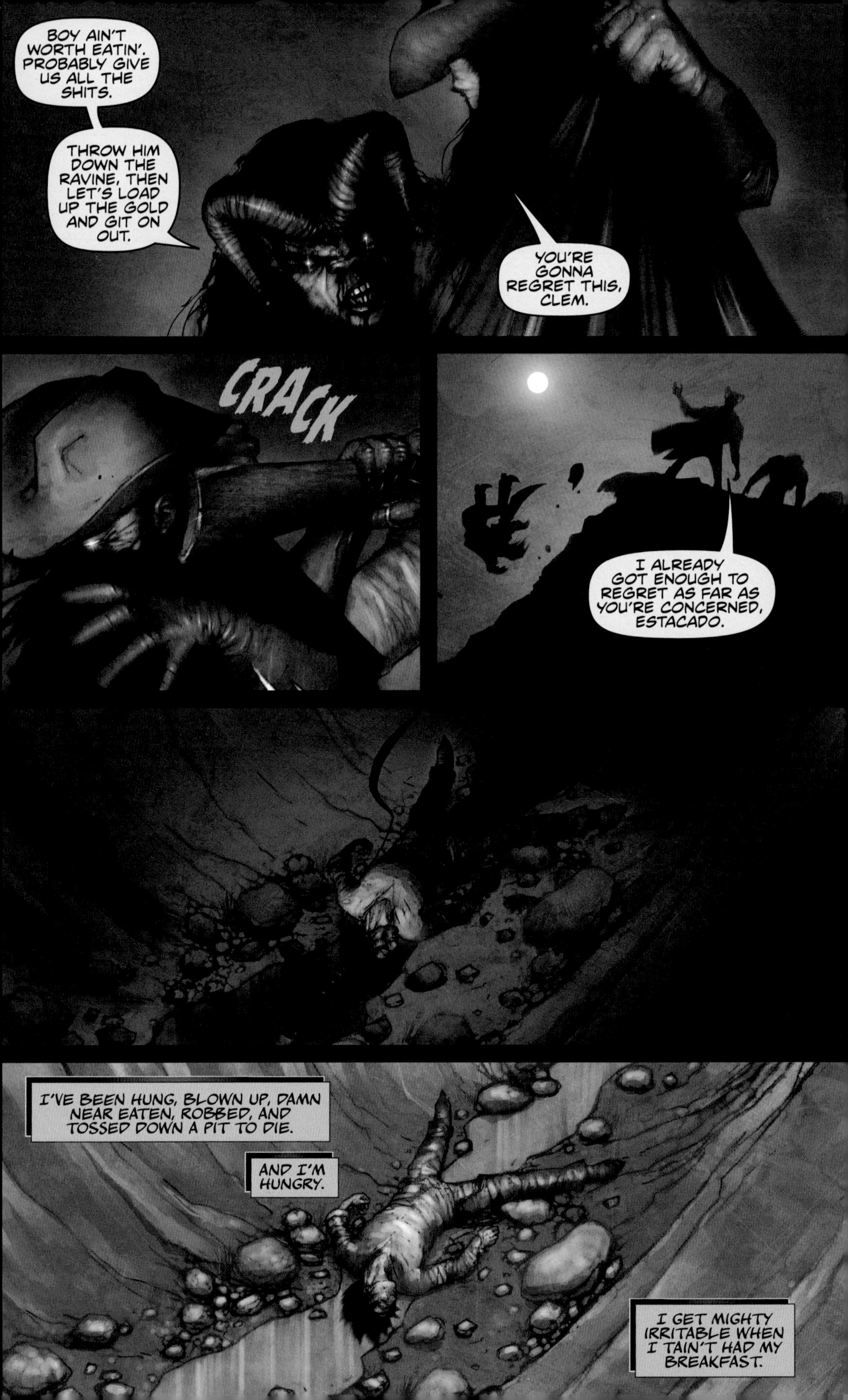
BOY AIN'T WORTH EATIN'. PROBABLY GIVE US ALL THE SHITS.
THROW HIM DOWN THE RAVINE, THEN LET'S LOAD UP THE GOLD AND GIT ON OUT.
YOU'RE GONNA REGRET THIS, CLEM.
CRACK
I ALREADY GOT ENOUGH TO REGRET AS FAR AS YOU'RE CONCERNED, ESTACADO.
I'VE BEEN HUNG, BLOWN UP, DAMN NEAR EATEN, ROBBED, AND TOSSED DOWN A PIT TO DIE.
AND I'M HUNGRY.
I GET MIGHTY IRRITABLE WHEN I TAIN'T HAD MY BREAKFAST.

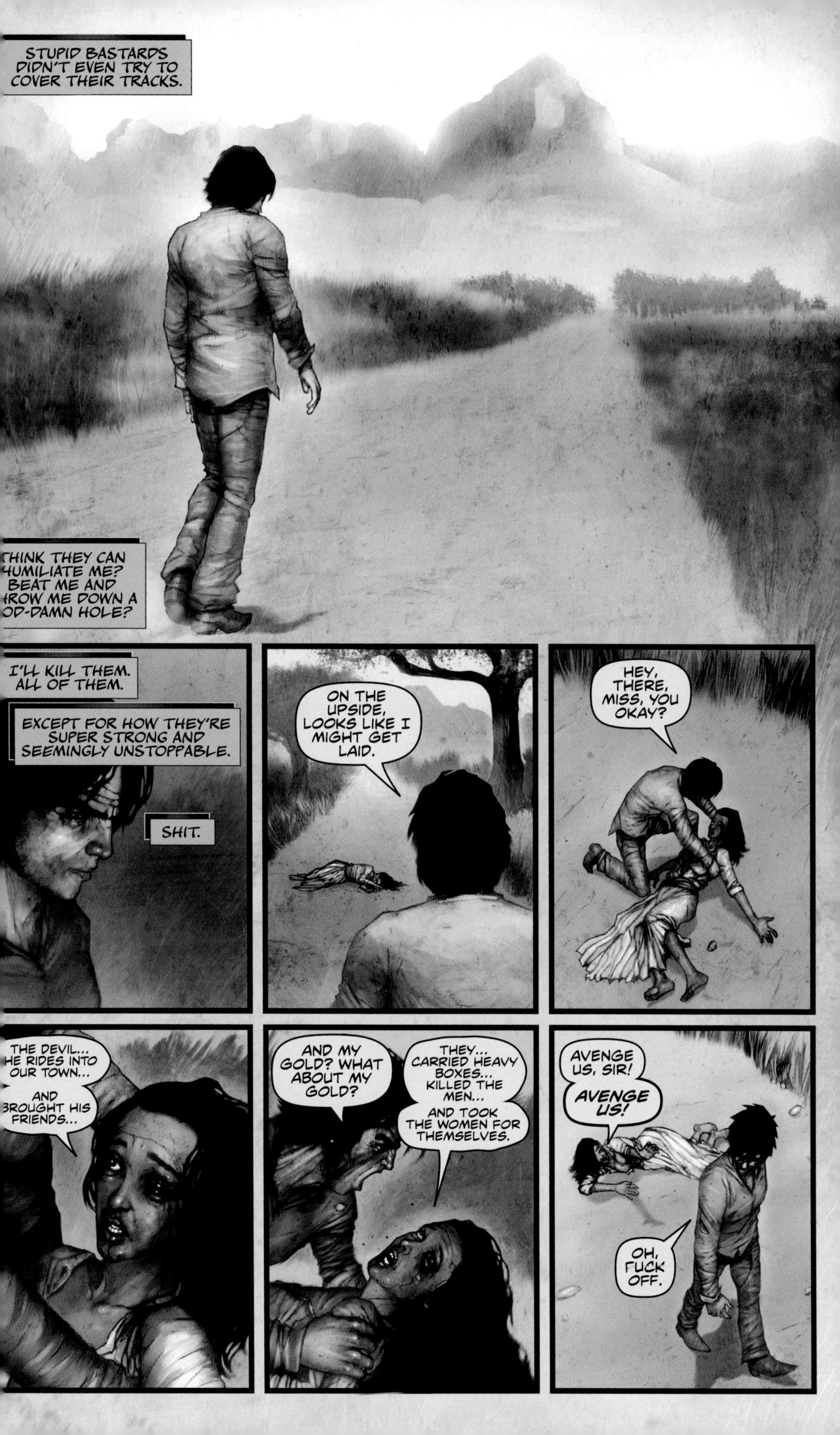
STUPID BASTARDS DIDN'T EVEN TRY TO COVER THEIR TRACKS.
THINK THEY CAN HUMILIATE ME? BEAT ME AND THROW ME DOWN A GOD-DAMN HOLE?
I'LL KILL THEM. ALL OF THEM.
EXCEPT FOR HOW THEY'RE SUPER STRONG AND SEEMINGLY UNSTOPPABLE.
SHIT.
ON THE UPSIDE, LOOKS LIKE I MIGHT GET LAID.
HEY, THERE, MISS, YOU OKAY?
THE DEVIL... HE RIDES INTO OUR TOWN...
AND BROUGHT HIS FRIENDS...
AND MY GOLD? WHAT ABOUT MY GOLD?
THEY... CARRIED HEAVY BOXES... KILLED THE MEN...
AND TOOK THE WOMEN FOR THEMSELVES.
AVENGE US, SIR!
AVENGE US!
OH, FUCK OFF.

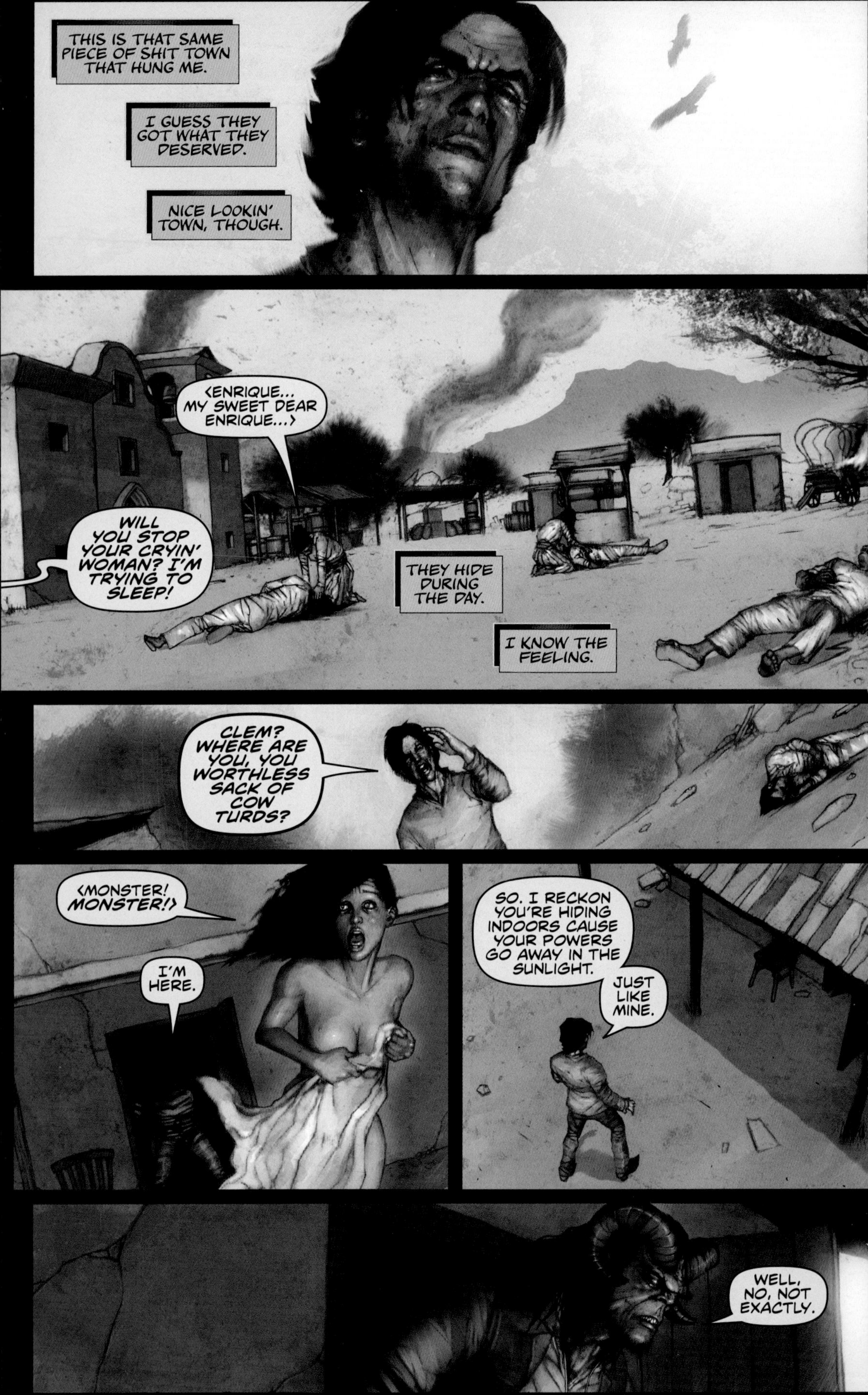
THIS IS THAT SAME PIECE OF SHIT TOWN THAT HUNG ME.
I GUESS THEY GOT WHAT THEY DESERVED.
NICE LOOKIN' TOWN, THOUGH.
<ENRIQUE... MY SWEET DEAR ENRIQUE...>
WILL YOU STOP YOUR CRYIN' WOMAN? I'M TRYING TO SLEEP!
THEY HIDE DURING THE DAY.
I KNOW THE FEELING.
CLEM? WHERE ARE YOU, YOU WORTHLESS SACK OF COW TURDS?
<MONSTER! MONSTER!>
I'M HERE.
SO. I RECKON YOU'RE HIDING INDOORS CAUSE YOUR POWERS GO AWAY IN THE SUNLIGHT.
JUST LIKE MINE.
WELL, NO, NOT EXACTLY.

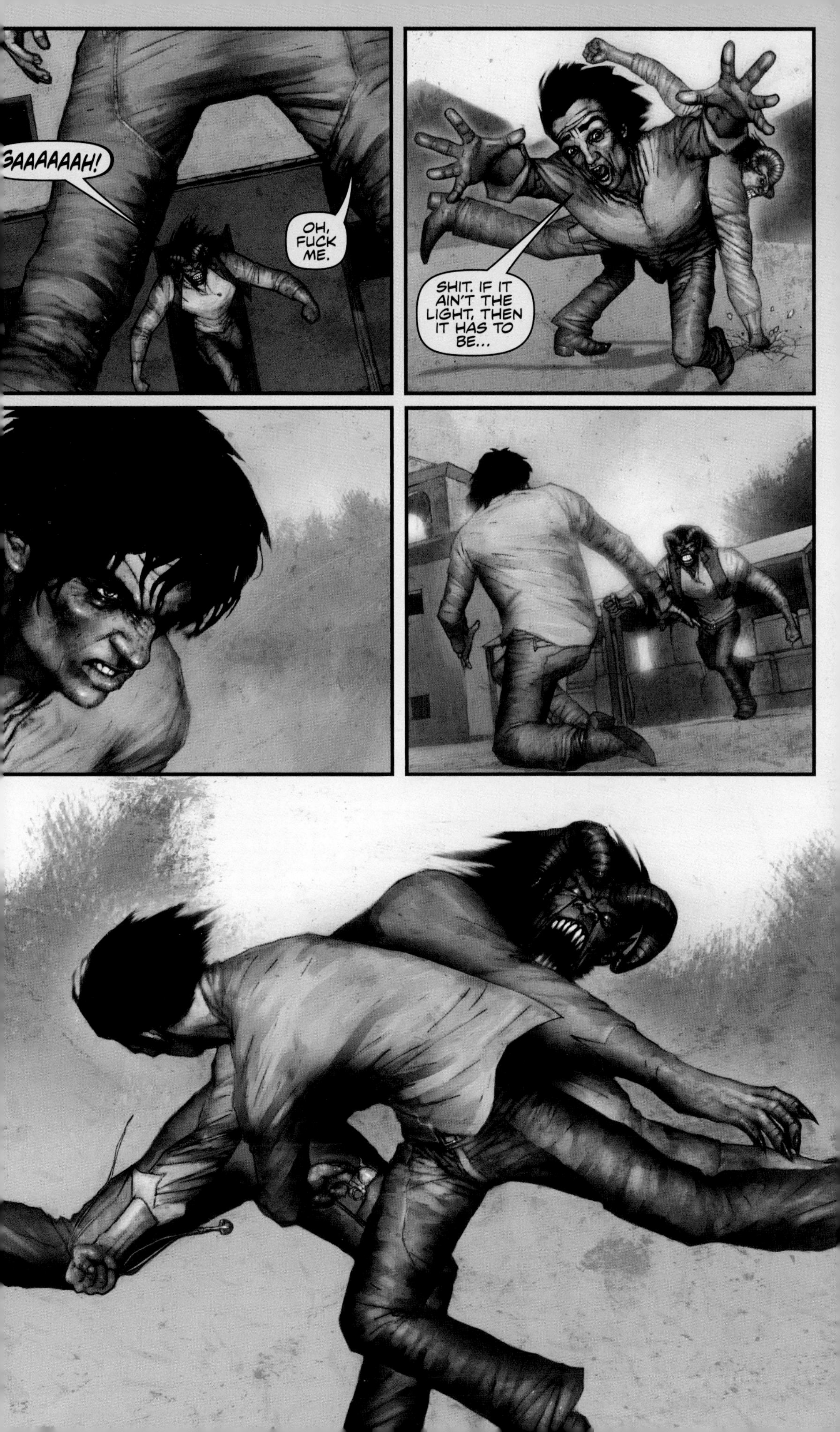
GAAAAAAH!
OH, FUCK ME.
SHIT. IF IT AIN'T THE LIGHT, THEN IT HAS TO BE...

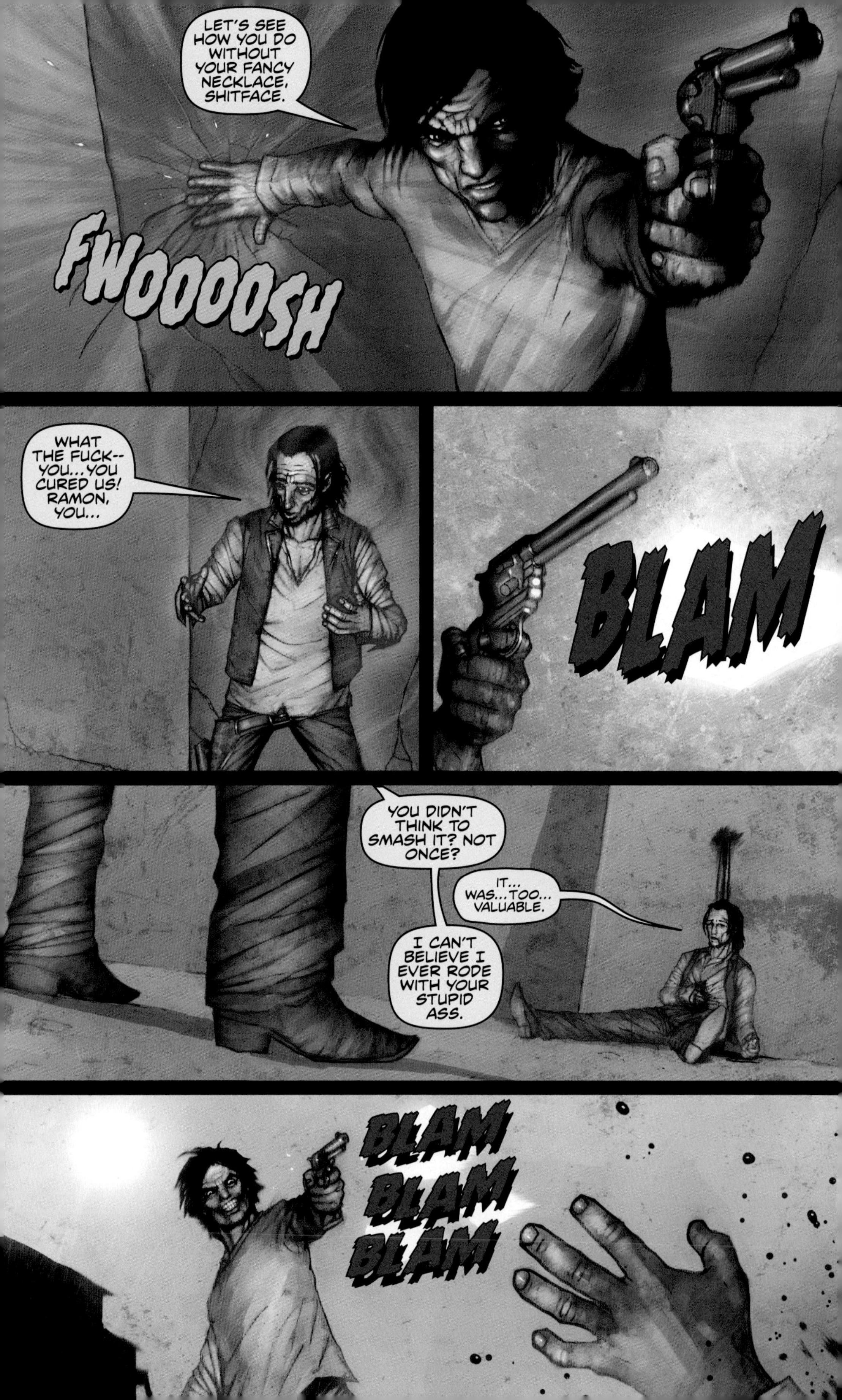
LET'S SEE HOW YOU DO WITHOUT YOUR FANCY NECKLACE, SHITFACE.
FWOOOOSH
WHAT THE FUCK-- YOU...YOU CURED US! RAMON, YOU...
BLAM
YOU DIDN'T THINK TO SMASH IT? NOT ONCE?
IT... WAS...TOO... VALUABLE.
I CAN'T BELIEVE I EVER RODE WITH YOUR STUPID ASS.
BLAM
BLAM
BLAM

GRACIAS, GRACIAS, SEÑOR...!

YEAH, YEAH.

BOYS!

NOW, I CAN KILL YOU, OR YOU CAN WORK FOR ME.

EITHER WAY, *ALL* OF THAT GOLD FROM LAST NIGHT IS MINE.

THAT AIN'T FAIR--

GAH!

KA-BLAM

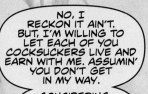

NO, I RECKON IT AIN'T. BUT, I'M WILLING TO LET EACH OF YOU COCKSUCKERS LIVE AND EARN WITH ME. ASSUMIN' YOU DON'T GET IN MY WAY.

CONSIDERING YOU THREW ME OFF A CLIFF, I THINK THAT'S MIGHTY GENEROUS OF ME.

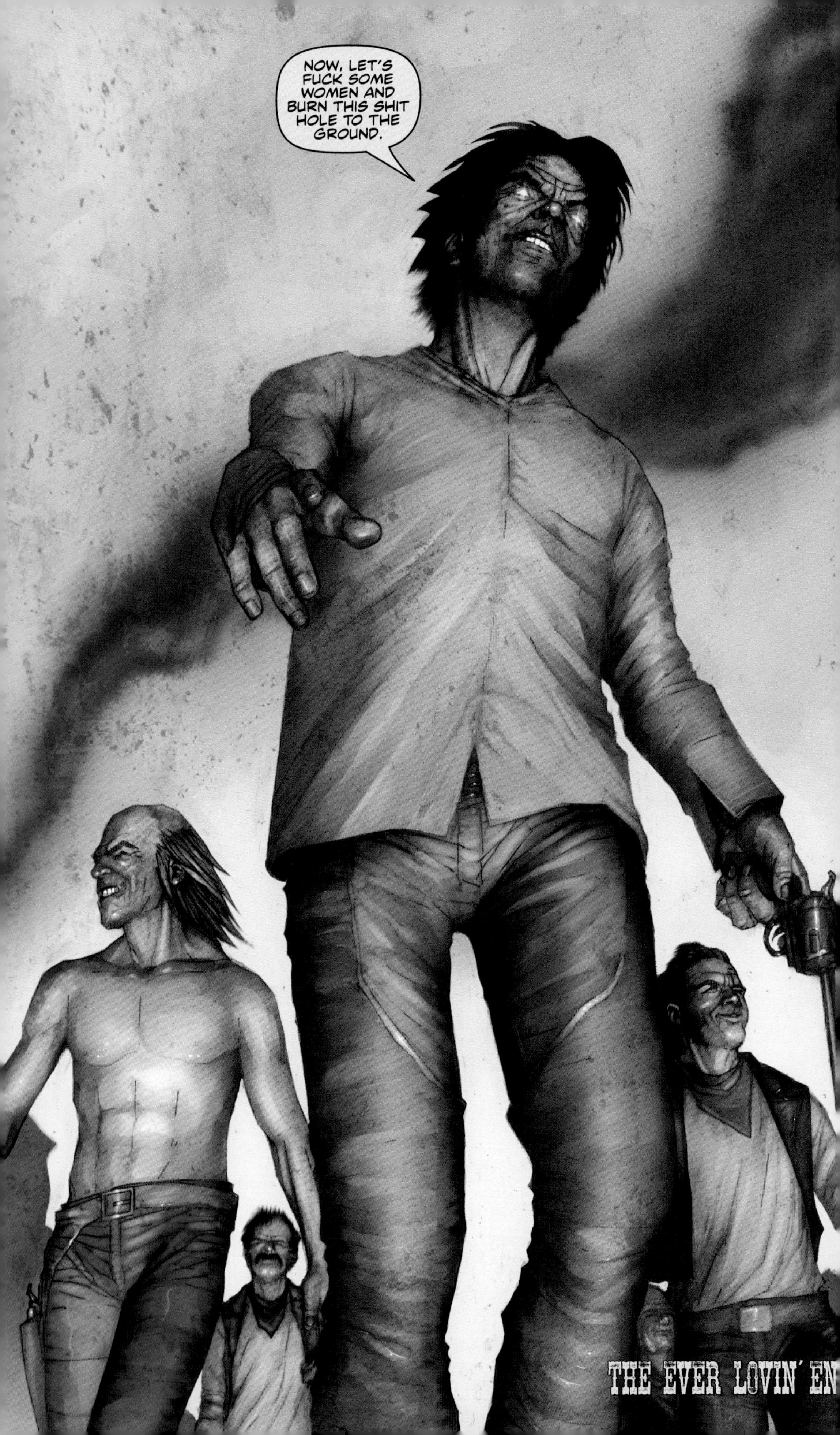
NOW, LET'S FUCK SOME WOMEN AND BURN THIS SHIT HOLE TO THE GROUND.
THE EVER LOVIN' EN

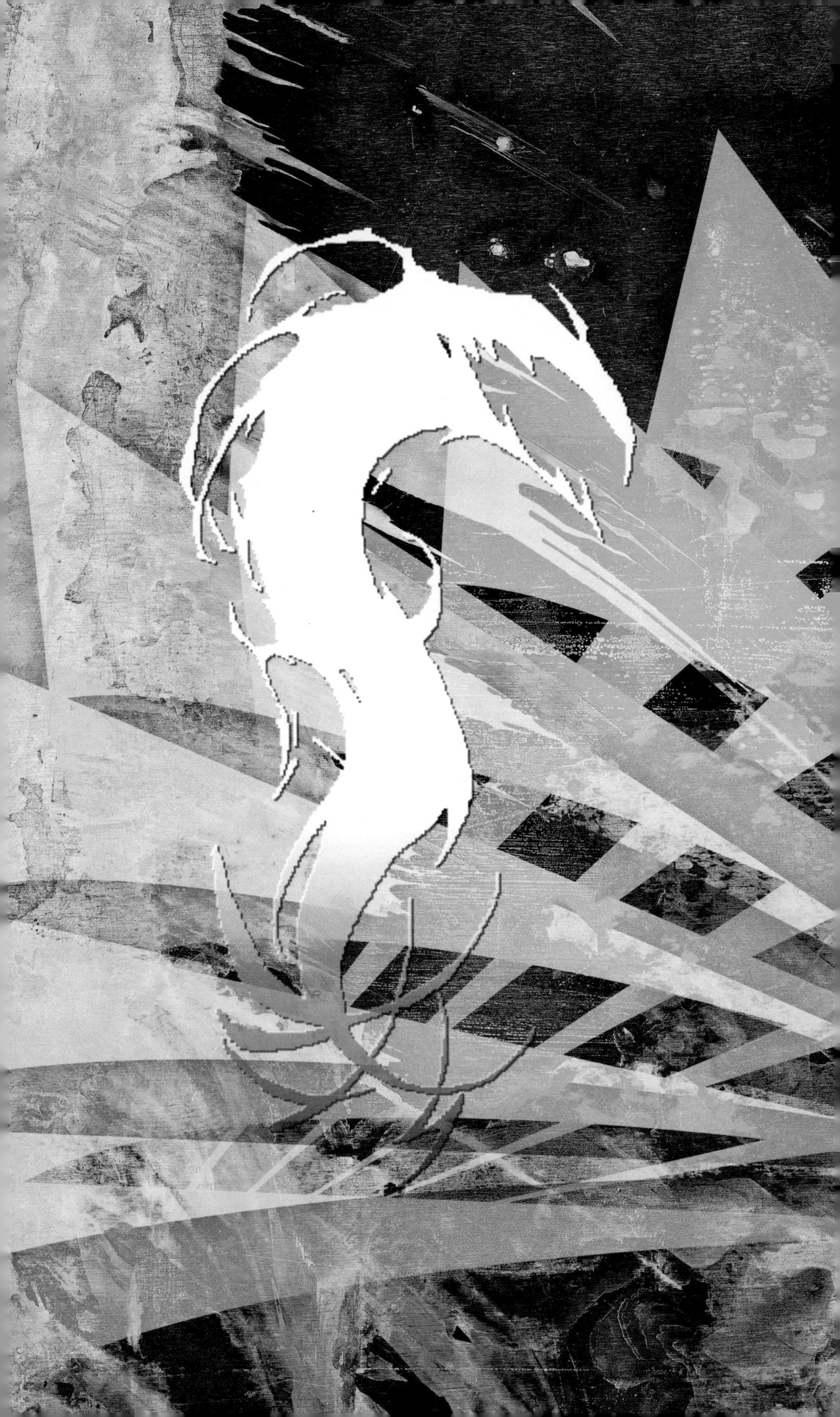

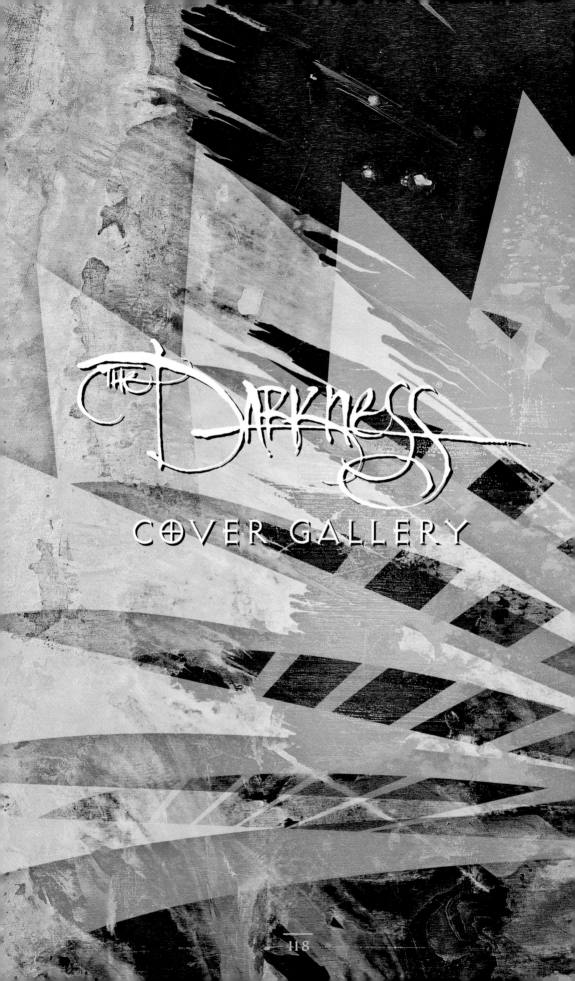

THE DARKNESS

COVER GALLERY

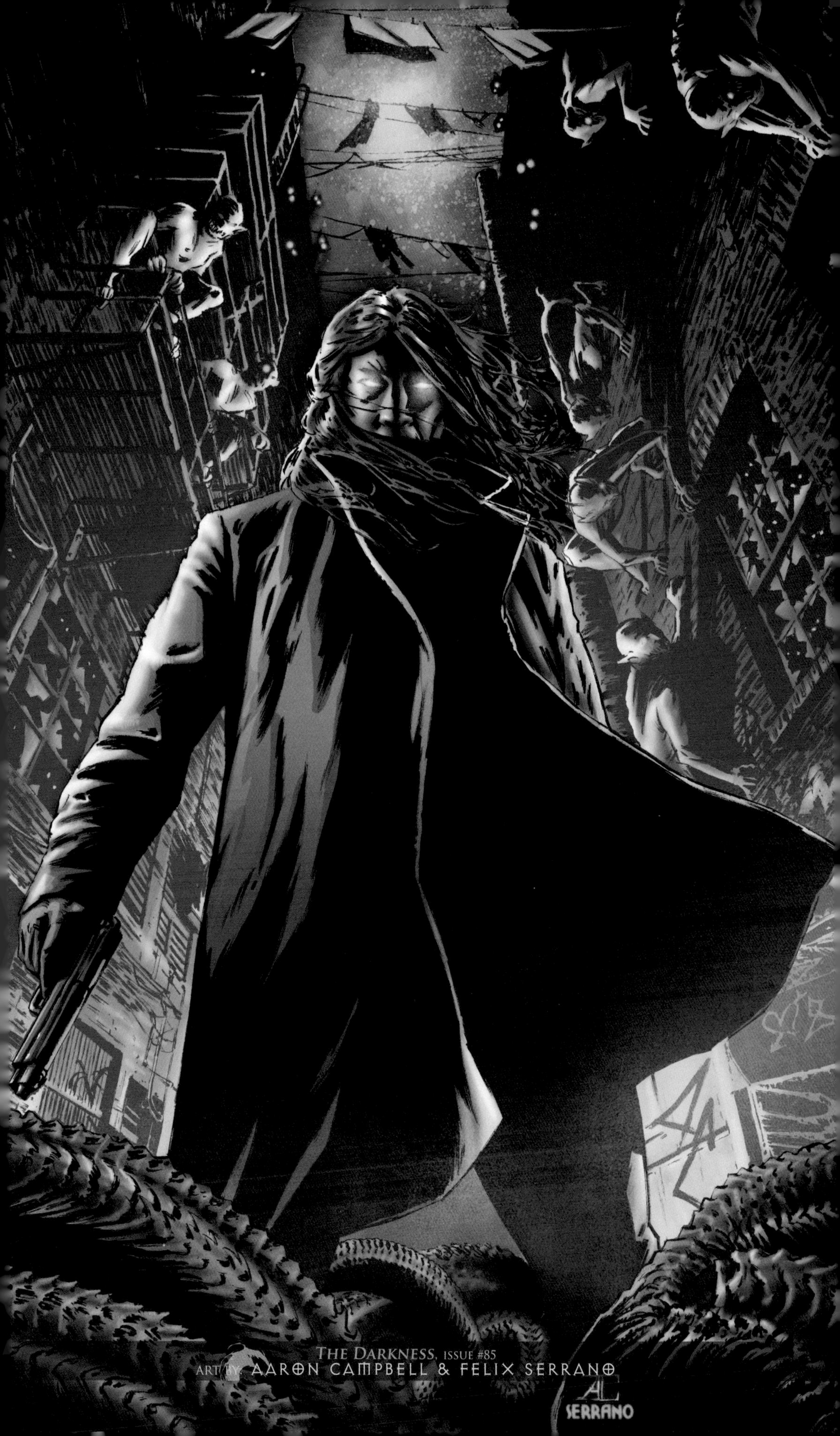
SERRANO

THE DARKNESS, ISSUE #85
ART BY: AARON CAMPBELL & FELIX SERRANO

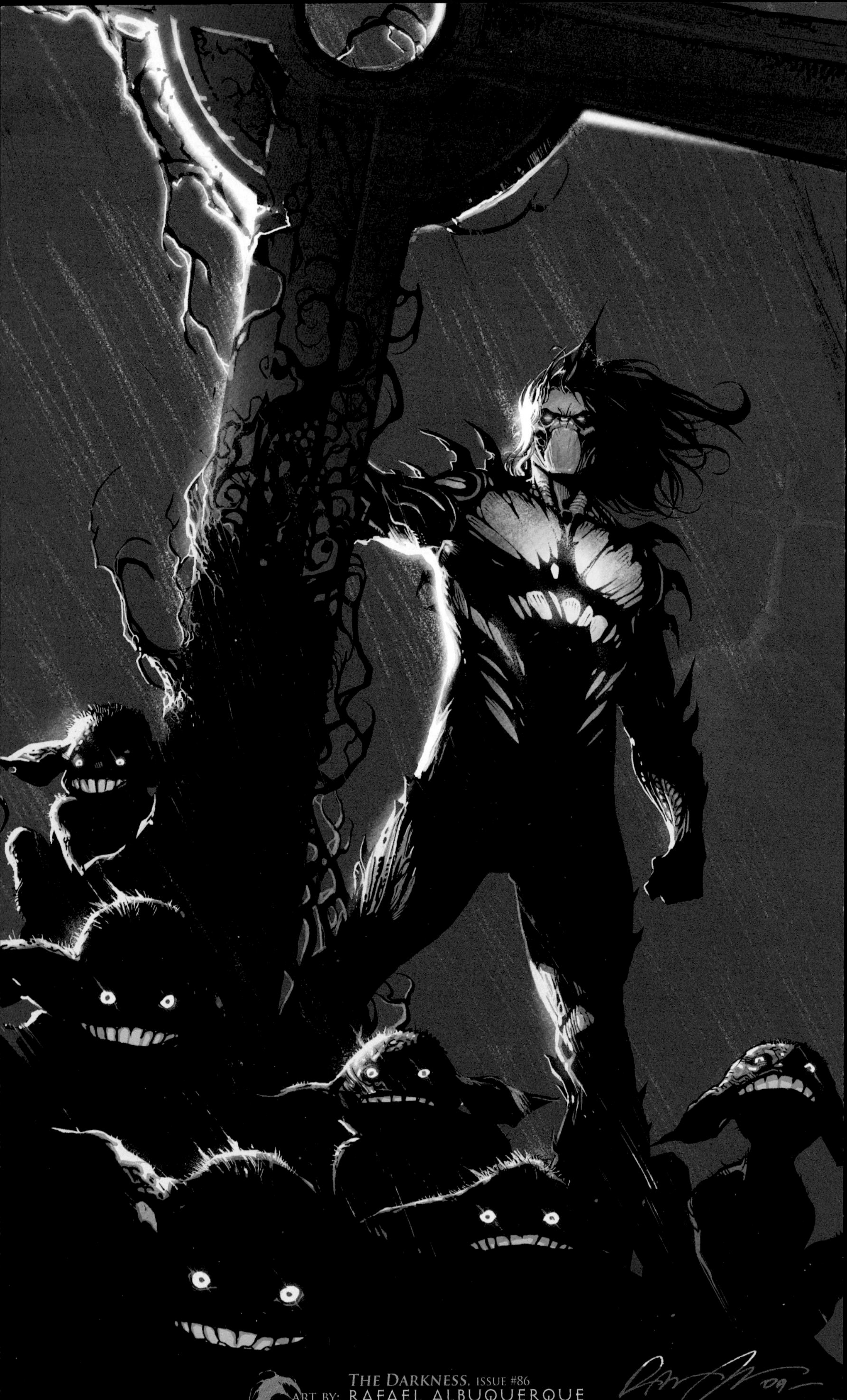

THE DARKNESS, ISSUE #86
ART BY: RAFAEL ALBUQUERQUE

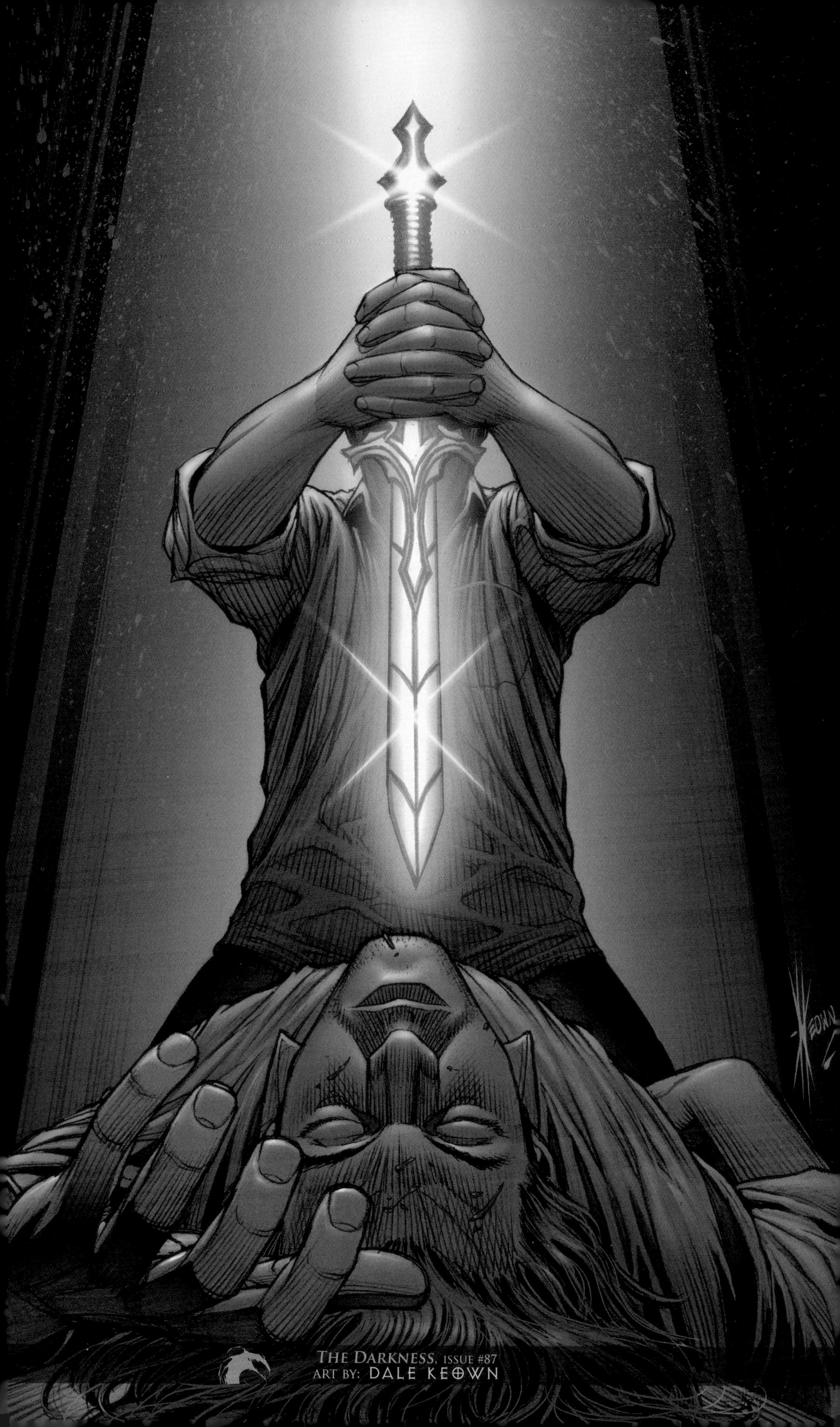

THE DARKNESS, ISSUE #87
ART BY: DALE KEOWN

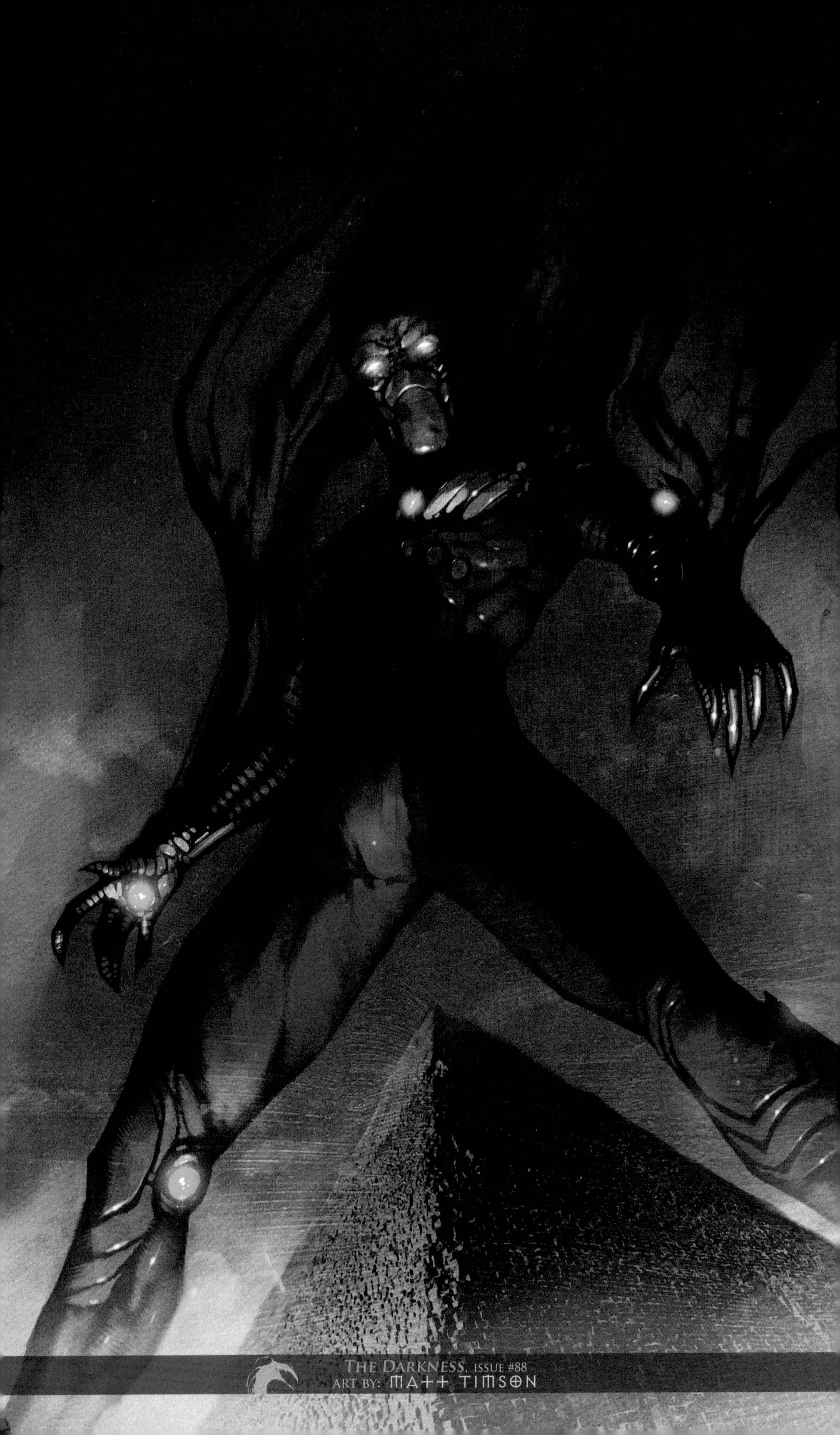

The Darkness, issue #88
Art by: Matt Timson

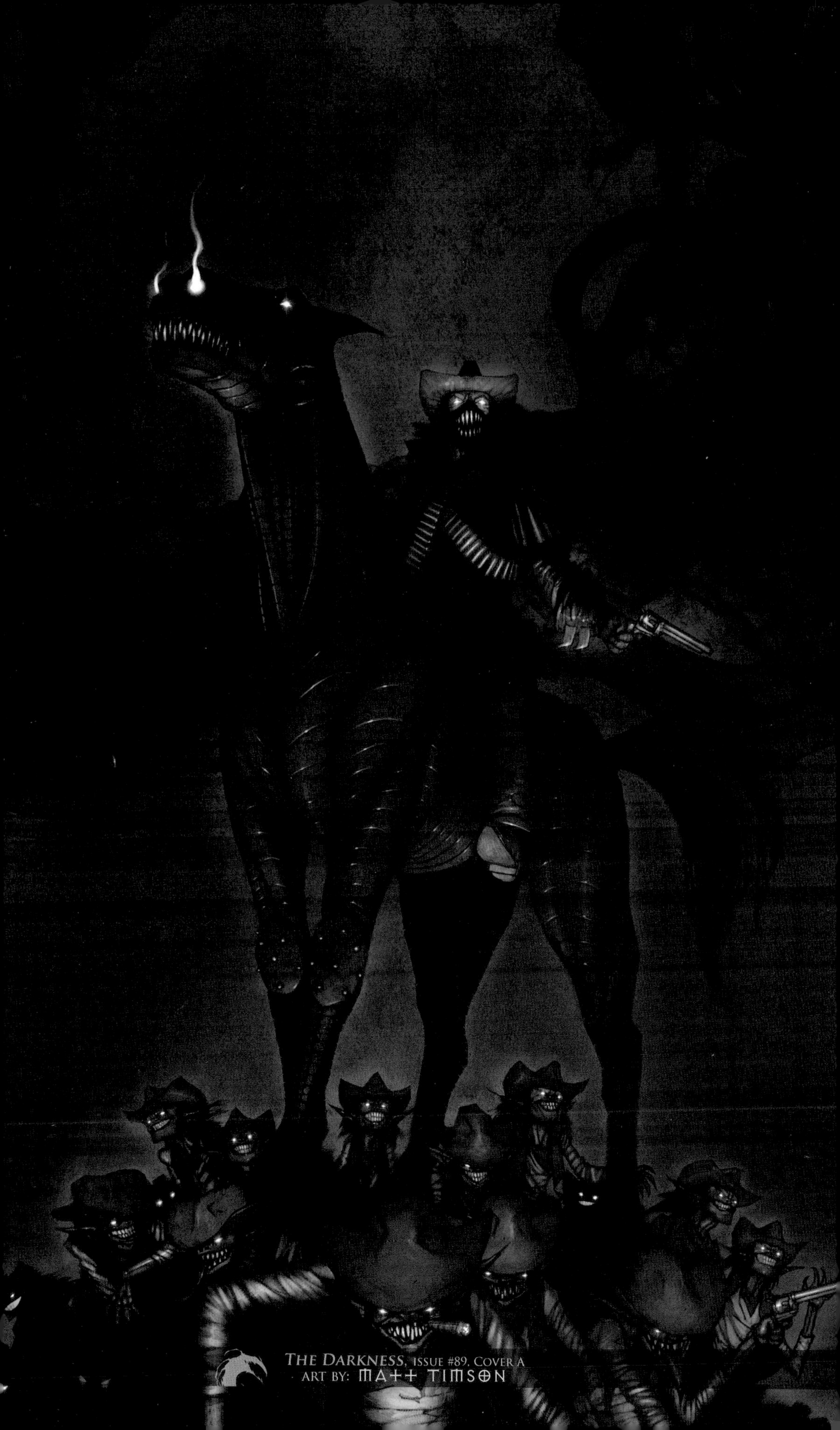

THE DARKNESS, ISSUE #89, COVER A
ART BY: MATT TIMSON

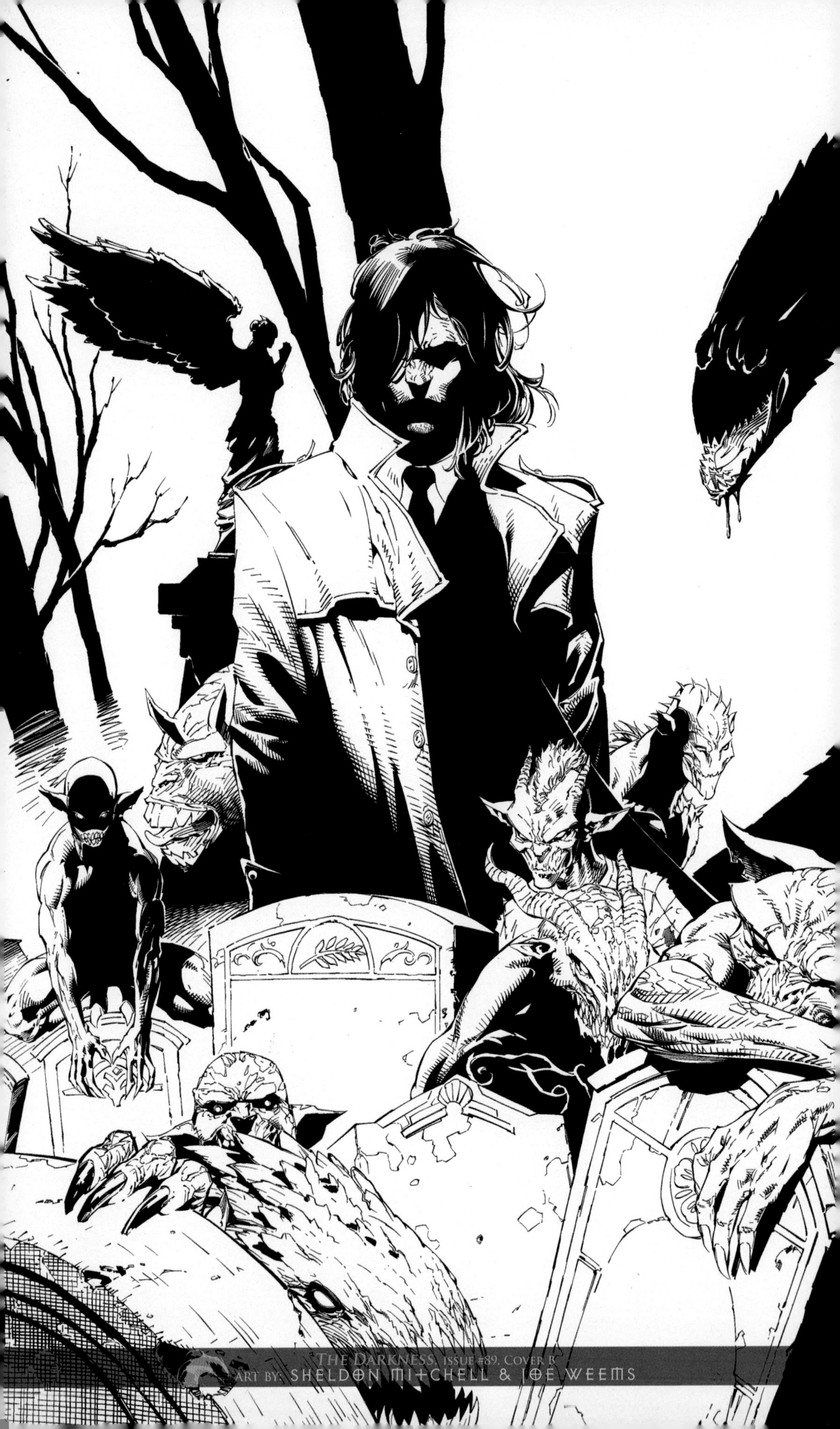

The Darkness, Issue #89, Cover B
Art by: Sheldon Mitchell & Joe Weems

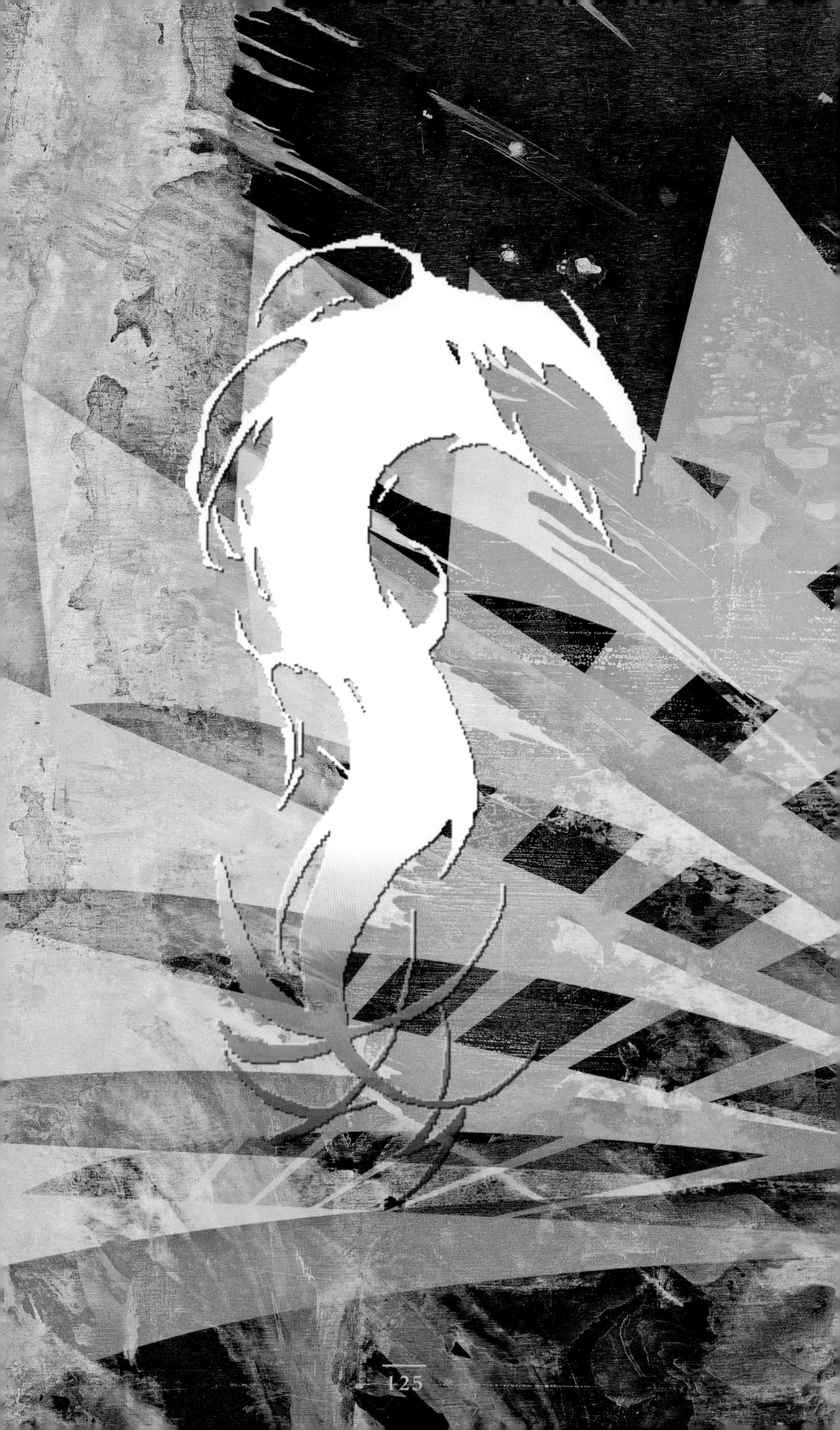

THE DARKNESS

SKETCH GALLERY

Artist Aaron Campbell was asked to provide an iconic image of Jackie Estacado for **The Darkness #85** cover. Included below are four layouts he submitted for consideration.

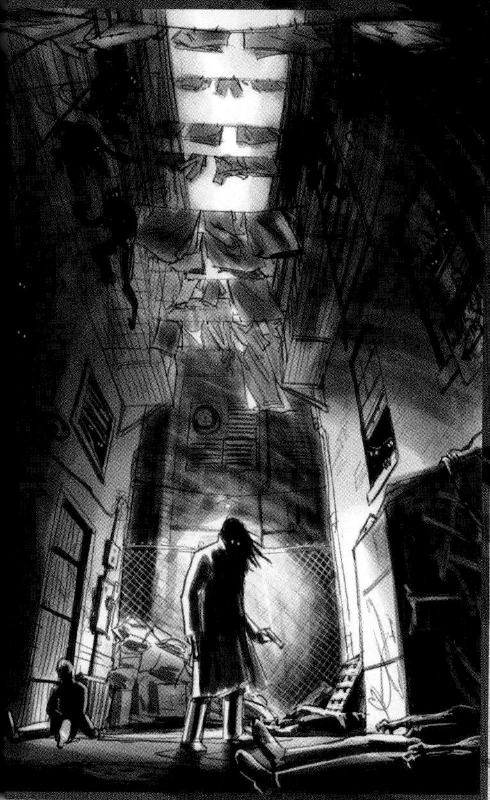

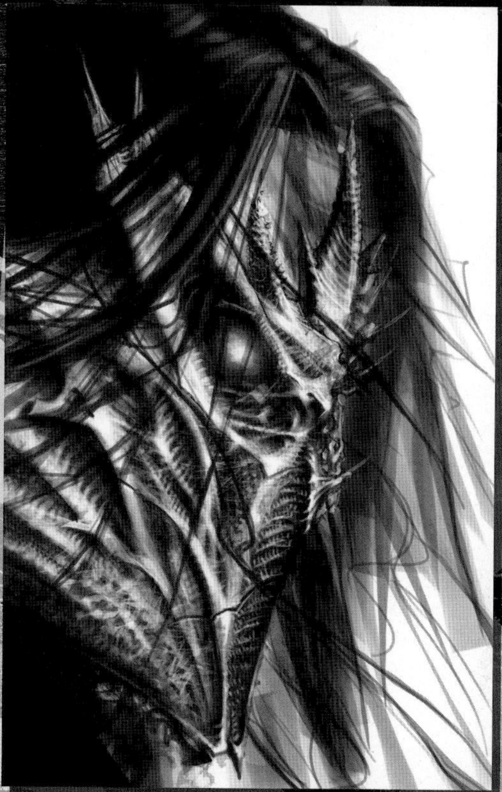

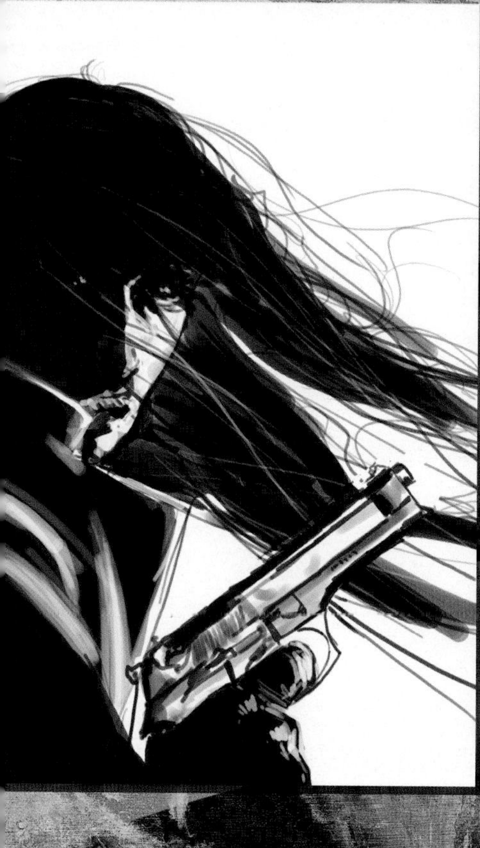

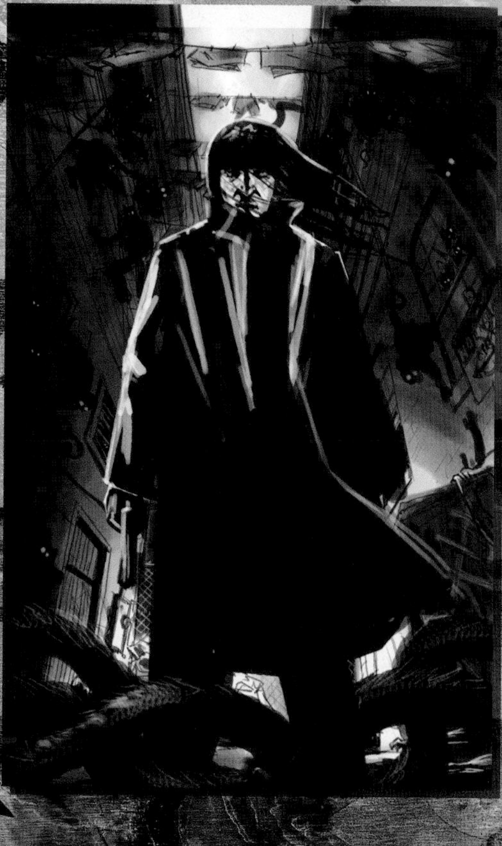

Artist Matt Timson was the first artist to envision The Darknes in the Wild West and generated the designs below for Ramon Estacado and his former gang member, Clem.

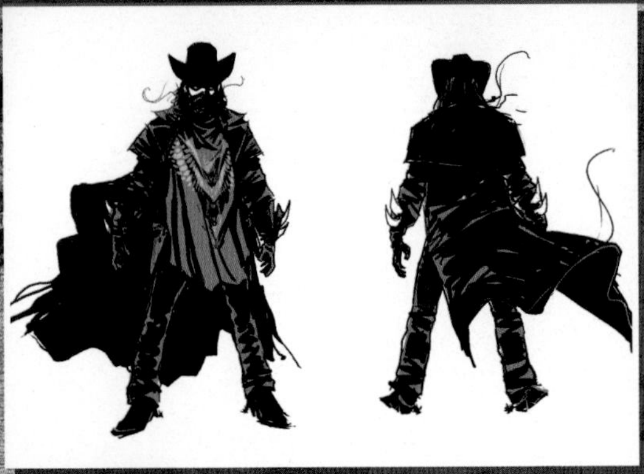

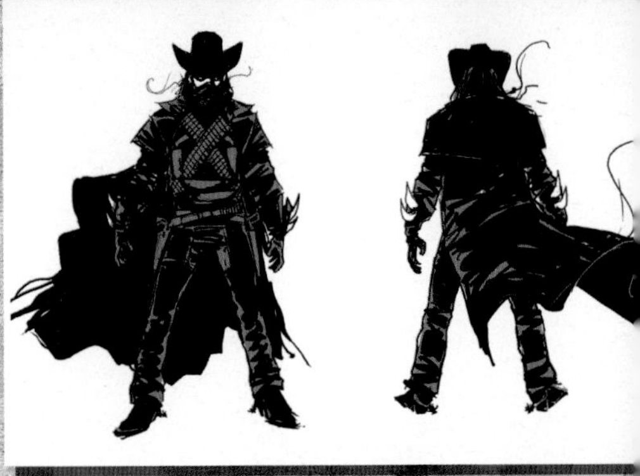

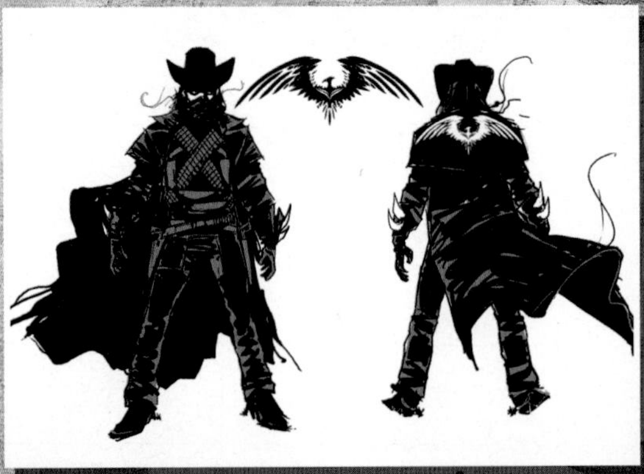

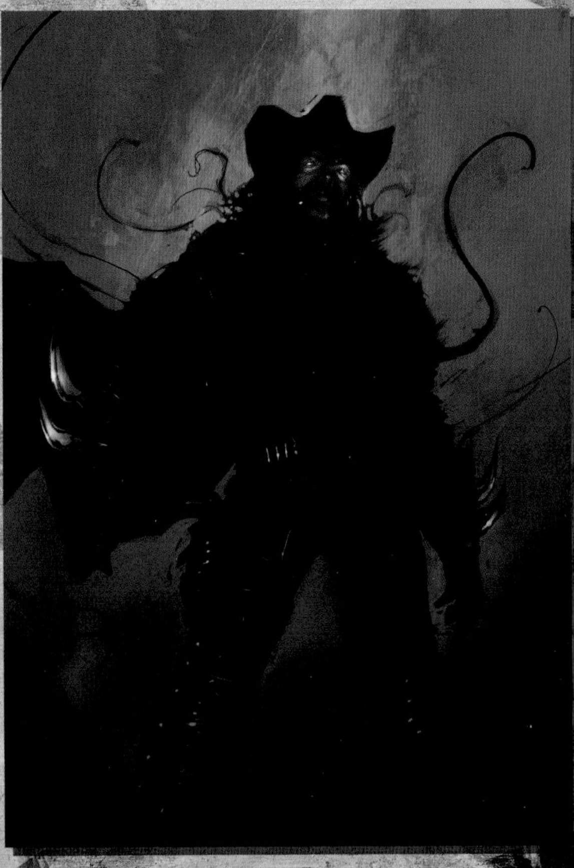

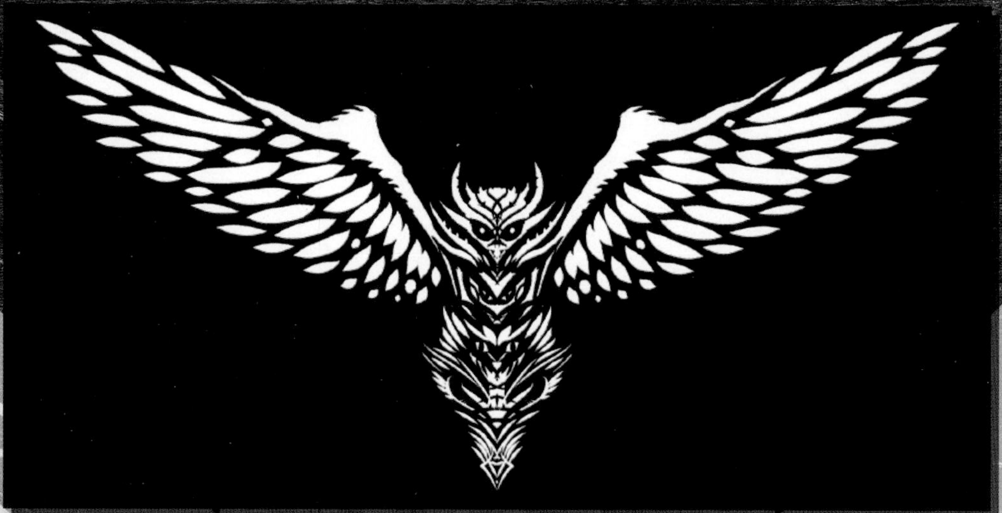

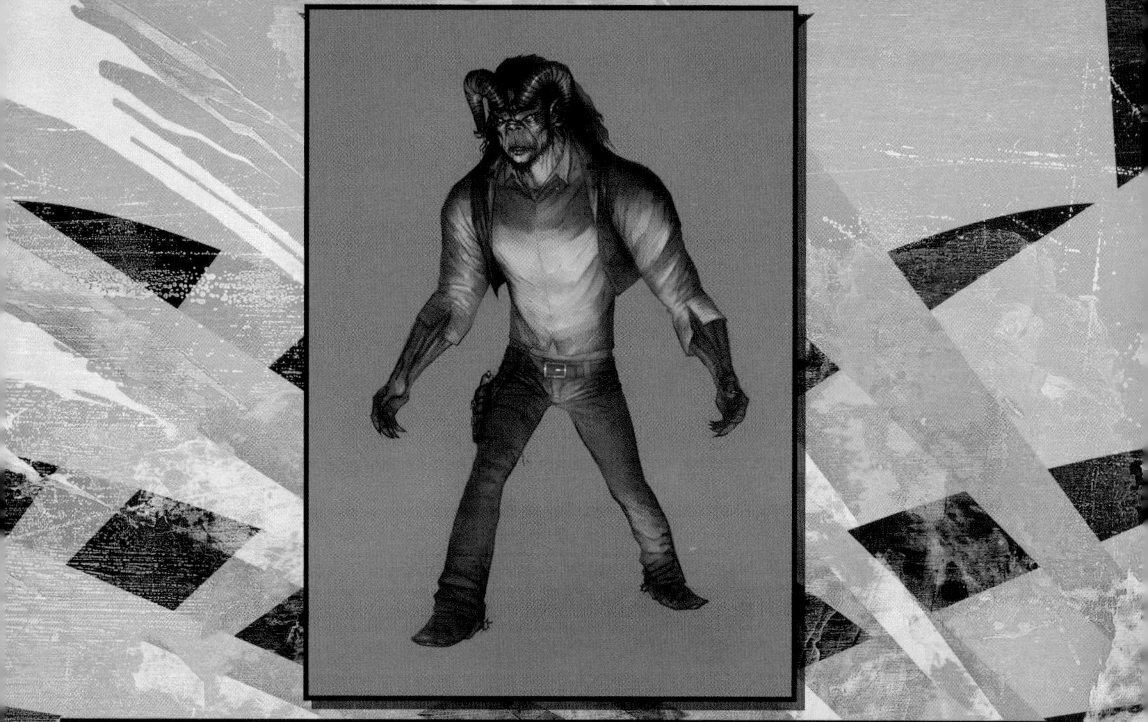

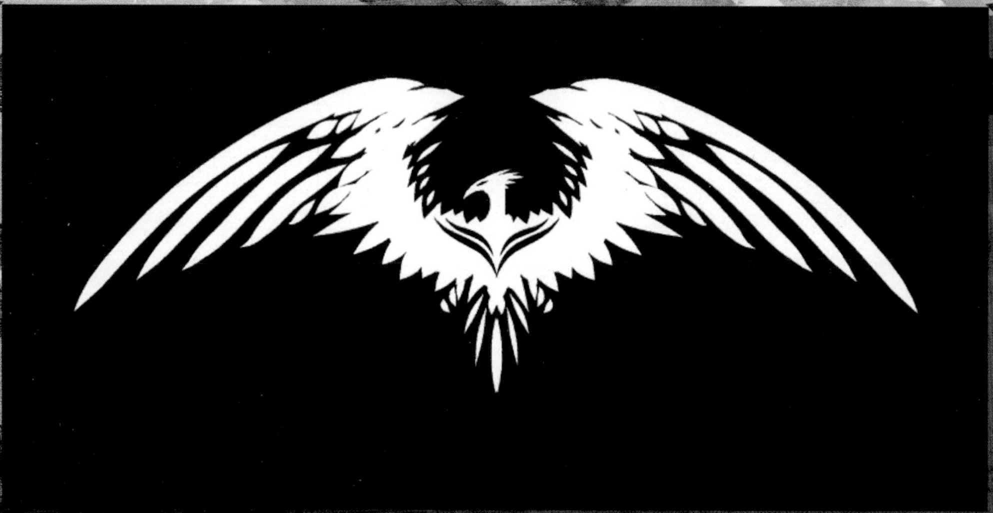

THE DARKNESS

SCRIPTBOOK

On the following pages take a look at the script for The Darkness issue #88 written by Phil Hester along with pencils by artist Romano Molenaar from the production process.

DARKNESS #88 PAGE 2
We start with a prologue focusing on Kim's estranged ex-wife and daughter. They are in dire straits, avoiding the landlord as a bleak Christmas approaches. Miriam (Kim's daughter) begs to see the tree lit, and when she does discovers a large box under the tree full of one hundred dollar bills.

CAP: PROLOGUE

CAP: Gary, Indiana. Now.

MIRIAM: I want the Christmas lights on. I want to see my presents.

MOM: Not now, honey. Not much to see this year anyway.

MIRIAM: I want to see the tree.

MOM: In the morning, baby.

MIRIAM: It's prettier at night. Everyone knows that.

MOM: I know, but if we turn on the lights...

MOM: Well, Mommy doesn't want to talk to the landlord right now, and if he knows we're home-

MIRIAM: That's why I had to watch Rudolph under the covers.

MOM: Yes, sweetie. The tree can be your surprise in the morning.

MIRIAM: But, Mama, it's Christmas Eve.

MOM: M- Maybe just for a second. I'll count to twenty.

MIRIAM: I heard Santa and everything. I think he left me something good.

MOM: Baby, I'm not sure Santa's going to make it this-

TAG: To: Miriam Kim From: Dad

MOM: Now, how did that get here?

MIRIAM: Awww, I thought it was going to be Koo-Koo Pets Zoo.

MIRIAM: But it's just stupid money all the way to the bottom.

CAP: 11 kilometers west of Bahariya Oasis, Egypt. Two weeks earlier.

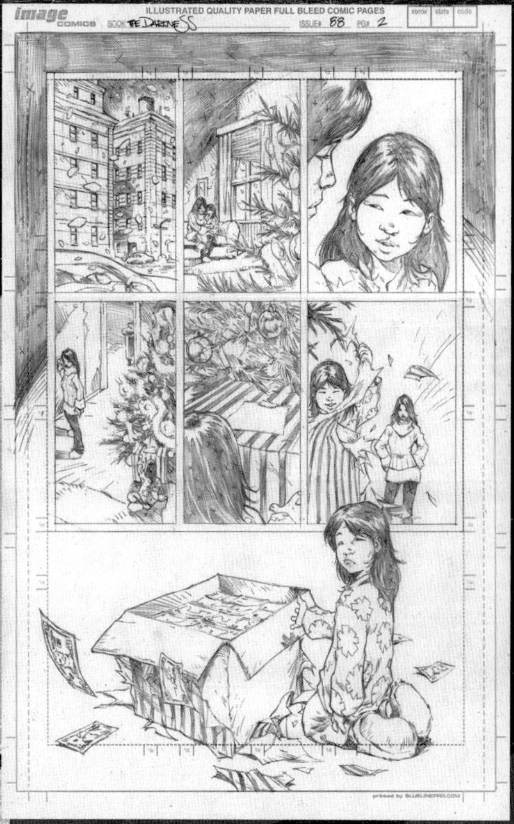
image COMICS
ILLUSTRATED QUALITY PAPER FULL BLEED COMIC PAGES
BOOK THE DARKNESS ISSUE# 88 PG# 2
xerox stats code
printed by BLUELINEPRO.COM

DARKNESS #88 PAGE 3
Cut to a crude outpost set in the middle of the desert, just some tin buildings and beat up jeeps. The base has been blasted, smoking ruins. Jackie's team: Vike, Kim, & Kash stand in the center of a bunch of dead Egyptians, their assault rifles smoking. All have small Bluetooth earpieces to communicate with Tyne and Jackie, who are in a large helicopter over the dunes. The sun is beginning to set.

TITLE: Regicide: Terminus
Credits

KIM: Well, that was fun.

VIKE: Not that I'm complaining--

VIKE: But tell me again why we had to risk our asses in a firefight with these broke-dick Al Qaeda rejects...

VIKE: When our boss coulda swooped in here solo and ate 'em up in his sleep.

KIM: We're trying to conserve Mr. Estacado's operating time.

KIM: He's on the clock once the sun goes down and there's a lot heavier stuff coming down the pike.

TYNE (radio): Recent intelligence told us the Sovereign would have conventional forces as a first line of defense around his last headquarters.

TYNE (radio): We assumed you could handle it.

VIKE: Oh, I handled.

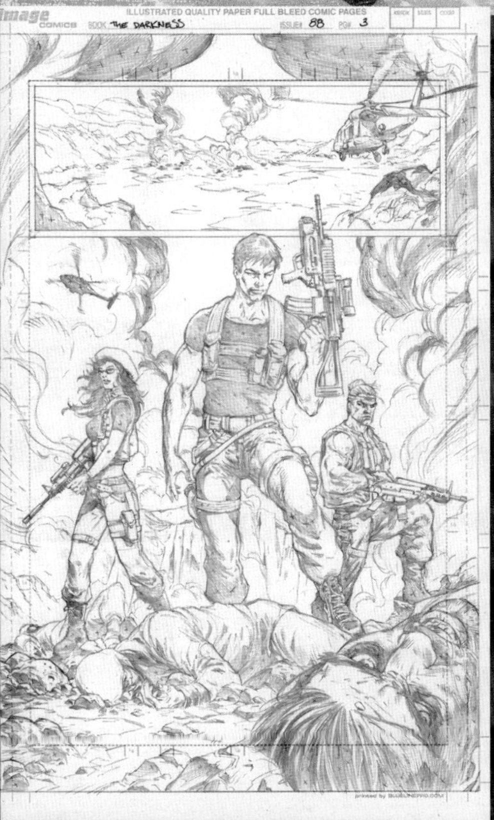
image COMICS
ILLUSTRATED QUALITY PAPER FULL BLEED COMIC PAGES
BOOK THE DARKNESS ISSUE# 88 PG# 3
xerox stats code
printed by BLUELINEPRO.COM

DARKNESS #88 PAGE 4
The assault team suits up with pneumatic back packs that run to small jackhammers slung under their forearms. Vike has a huge set under both arms, while Kim & Kash have small ones under one arm. They all still hold huge rifles. They converse with Tyne and Jackie in the chopper, where they hold one of the army of sculptors who once worked in the cave compound buried in the sand.

TYNE: Listen up. The Sovereign is spooked.

TYNE: He's got an army of sculptors banging out new bodies for him in there. Crude, ugly forms, but functional.

TYNE: He knows we're closing in on his last body and he's building lifeboats. Hundreds of them.

VIKE: Hence the strap-on jackhammers?

TYNE (radio): Yeah. Kim and Kash will have long range concussive rounds, but we imagine a few Sovereign statues will get close enough for hand to hand.

TYNE (radio): That's when your pneumatic hammers go to work on their stone asses.

SFX: K-Thud! K-Thud! Pssshh!

VIKE: Hey, boss-- I get to keep these bad boys, you can tear up my paycheck.

KIM: Outside of these guards, this cave entrance seems to be pretty much disused.

KIM: You sure this is the one?

TYNE: Yeah, our intel is pretty fresh.

JACKIE: Right, Michelangelo?

SCULPTOR: I- I sculpt. I know nothing. I only sculpt.

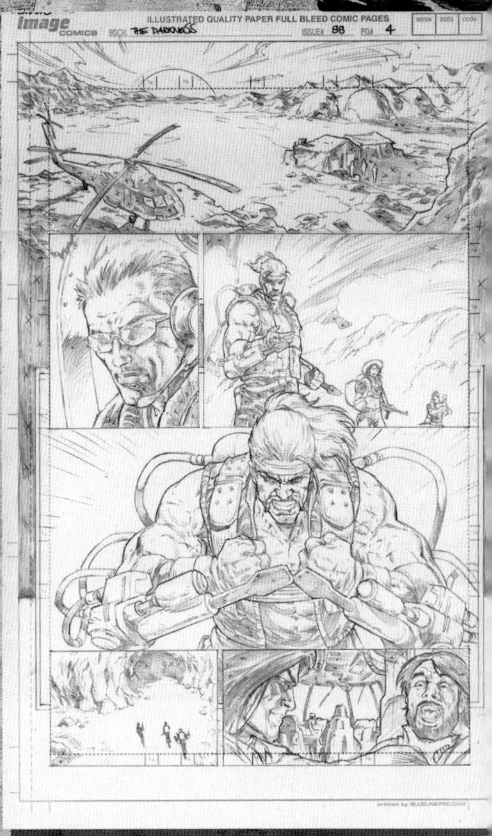

image COMICS
ILLUSTRATED QUALITY PAPER FULL BLEED COMIC PAGES
BOOK THE DARKNESS
ISSUE# 88 PG# 4

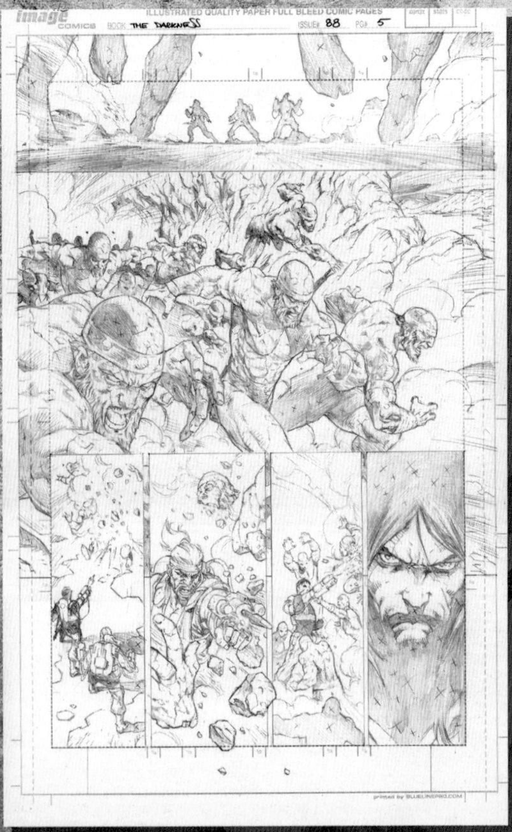

image COMICS
ILLUSTRATED QUALITY PAPER FULL BLEED COMIC PAGES
BOOK THE DARKNESS
ISSUE# 88 PG# 5

DARKNESS #88 PAGE 5
Suddenly, a sea of crude, stone Sovereign statues pour from the mouth of a rocky cave (actually a bit of the giant Sov statue poking above the dunes). The team battles them with rifles and pneumatic hammers, but are slowly overwhelmed. As the sun sets, Jackie swoops into the cave.

KIM: You know what? Forget that last question.

KIM: Pretty sure we're in the right place.

SOVEREIGN: Brazen little fools, coming into my home like this.

SOVEREIGN: My...

HOME!

KASH: Jesus, there are hundreds of them.

VIKE: Get behind me, kid. Start up your thumper.

VIKE: Strictly hand to hand now.

KIM: Getting crowded in here, boss.

KIM: Boss?

KIM: Boss, you hear me?

JACKIE: I hear you.

DARKNESS #88 PAGE 6

With a simple gesture, Jackie causes Darkness matter to erupt from the stone statues, disintegrating them. Dust fills the air, choking the human team in the cave. Kim staggers, choking on the fumes. It's more than dust!

JACKIE: You might want to duck.

JACKIE: My arch-enemy's about to become little flying pieces of arch-enemy.

KIM: So... that's it?

KASH: Didn't you ever play video games, Kim? There'll be an end boss.

KASH: There's always an end boss.

JACKIE: Last one. Last place for that son of a bitch to hide.

KASH: Damn, this dust is brutal.

VIKE: Some noxious shit right there.

KIM: Man, I don't feel so...

KIM: The hell?

DARKNESS #88 PAGE 7

Kim falls to the ground, but when he looks up from the cave floor he finds all his team gone and a landscape of gold and treasure that would make Scrooge McDuck blush. The luster of the gold lights his smiling face from below (this is an illusion).

DISEMBODIED SOVEREIGN VOICE: It's yours, Kim. Enough wealth to buy a country all your own.

DISEMBODIED SOVEREIGN VOICE: Enough riches to right every wrong in your path, afore and behind.

DISEMBODIED SOVEREIGN VOICE: Enough to last you the rest of your life...

DISEMBODIED SOVEREIGN VOICE: And beyond.

DARKNESS #88 PAGE 9
Kash also undergoes the illusion. She is lifted out of the cave on a column of earth. An lush oasis spreads out before her. It's idyllic, a place of complete isolation and safety.

KASH: Guys?

KASH: Guys, what's wro-

SFX: KKrrrummmmbbblee–Ppsshhhh!

DISEMBODIED SOVEREIGN VOICE: You're free to go, Kashine. Truly free.

DISEMBODIED SOVEREIGN VOICE: This place is yours.

DISEMBODIED SOVEREIGN VOICE: No one can find you here.

DISEMBODIED SOVEREIGN VOICE: No one will remember you ever lived.

DISEMBODIED SOVEREIGN VOICE: Drink of these waters, sleep under the trees, eat their fruit.

DISEMBODIED SOVEREIGN VOICE: Tread the warm grass and cool clay.

DISEMBODIED SOVEREIGN VOICE: The entirety of this world is your home.

DISEMBODIED SOVEREIGN VOICE: And your home alone.

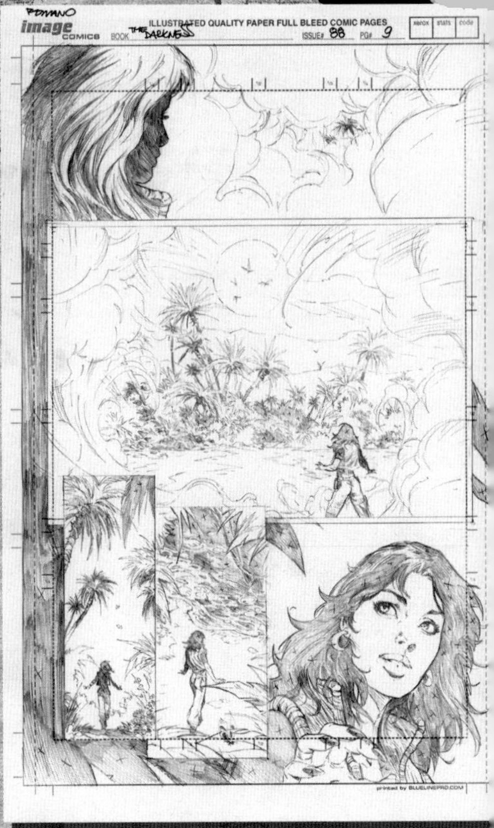
ILLUSTRATED QUALITY PAPER FULL BLEED COMIC PAGES
ISSUE# 88 PG# 9

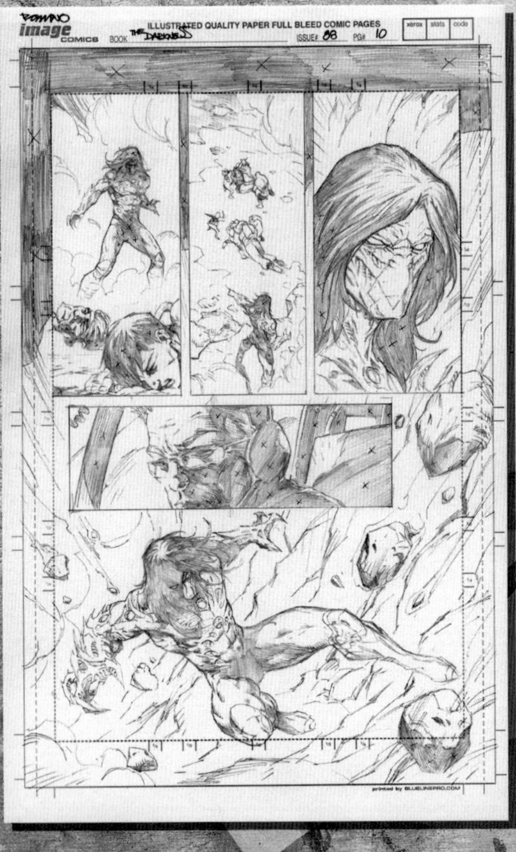
ILLUSTRATED QUALITY PAPER FULL BLEED COMIC PAGES
ISSUE# 88 PG# 10

DARKNESS #88 PAGE 10
Jackie, upon seeing his team fall into a stupor, calls up Darklings to drag them away. Now that the cave is lit only by dim torchlight, he doesn't need human help anymore. He's in his element. He converse with Tyne about the whereabouts of the last statue when the walls of the cave shudder.

JACKIE: Okay, I get it.

JACKIE: You want to keep this one on one. Fine by me.

JACKIE: Take 'em outside. Tyne will get 'em into the chopper.

JACKIE: You hear that, Tyne?

TYNE (radio): Of course.

JACKIE: What's the story? I thought the last statue was supposed to be huge, imposing.

JACKIE: I don't see anything like that here. A whole lot of nothing.

TYNE: Well, we're relying on texts that are thousands of years old.

TYNE: They tell of a colossal monument to a king of a sunken isle raised by a rival Pharaoh as reparations for some conflict.

TYNE: It could all be myth, mind you, but assuming it's true, it should be right in front of you.

TYNE (radio): Really, it should be impossible to miss.

JACKIE: Yeah, well, maybe we should have Google mapped it befo-

SFX; Rrrmmmblll

JACKIE: Whoa!

TYNE: Uh, you're not in front of it, Jackie.

DARKNESS #88 PAGE 11
Cut to outside with Tyne and the kayoed crew. Tyne looks up in astonishment as the giant Sovereign rises from the sand. It gloats, but Jackie bursts from its chest.

TYNE: You're in it!

SOVEREIGN: Hurrrhh.

SOVEREIGN: Yes, what should I do with you now, bothersome gnat?

SOVEREIGN: Chew you to pieces? Grind you to dust in my guts?

SFX: K-choom!

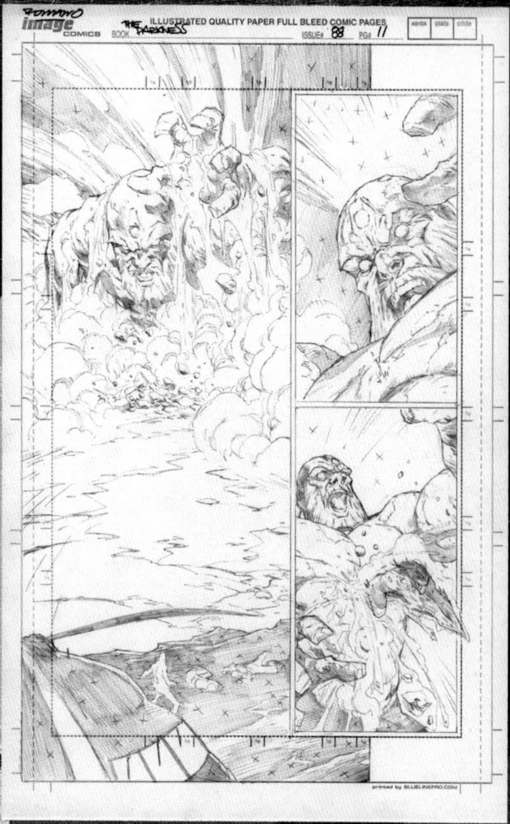
image COMICS
ILLUSTRATED QUALITY PAPER FULL BLEED COMIC PAGES
BOOK THE DARKNESS
ISSUE# 88 PG# 11

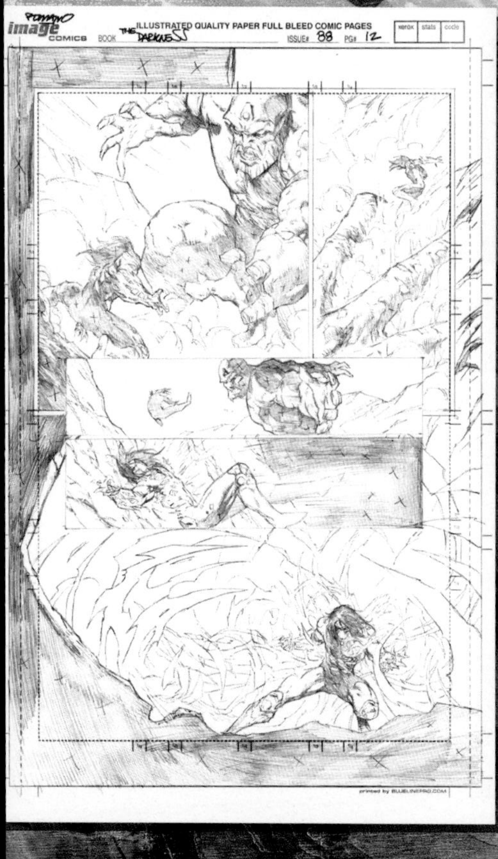
image COMICS
ILLUSTRATED QUALITY PAPER FULL BLEED COMIC PAGES
BOOK THE DARKNESS
ISSUE# 88 PG# 12

DARKNESS #88 PAGE 12
The giant Sovereign swats at Jackie, knocking him to and fro. Jackie begins to grow, his armor bulging like a warping berserker from a Simon Bisley comic.

SOVEREIGN: Yes, yes. I agree.

SOVEREIGN: This way will be much more satisfying–

SOVEREIGN: For both of us!

SFX: Fwam!

SOVEREIGN: I won't give you the time to find the dark recesses of this form to exploit.

SFX: Thrukk!

SOVEREIGN: Not this time.

SFX: Plok!

JACKIE: You're right...

JACKIE: No more tricks.

JACKIE: Lets' do this last one...

DARKNESS #88 PAGE 13
Splashy page. Jackie is surrounded by a swirling mass of Darkness energy that coalesces around him like an energy armor that's just as tall as The Sovereign. Like a giant mecha made of swirling tornadoes of Darkness energy. They duke it out like Gargantuas.

JACKIE: Face to face.

SFX: Kroom!

SFX: Fwamm!

JACKIE: Not so chatty now, huh?

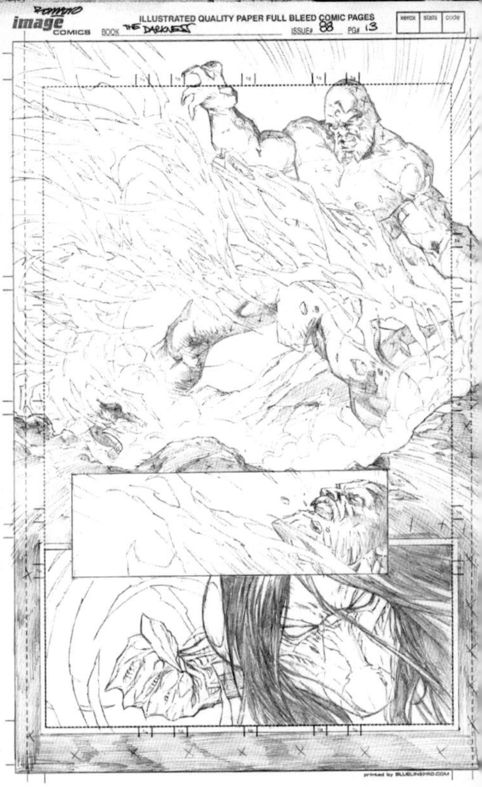
image COMICS
ILLUSTRATED QUALITY PAPER FULL BLEED COMIC PAGES
BOOK THE DARKNESS ISSUE# 88 PG# 13
xerox stats code
printed by BLUELINEPRO.COM

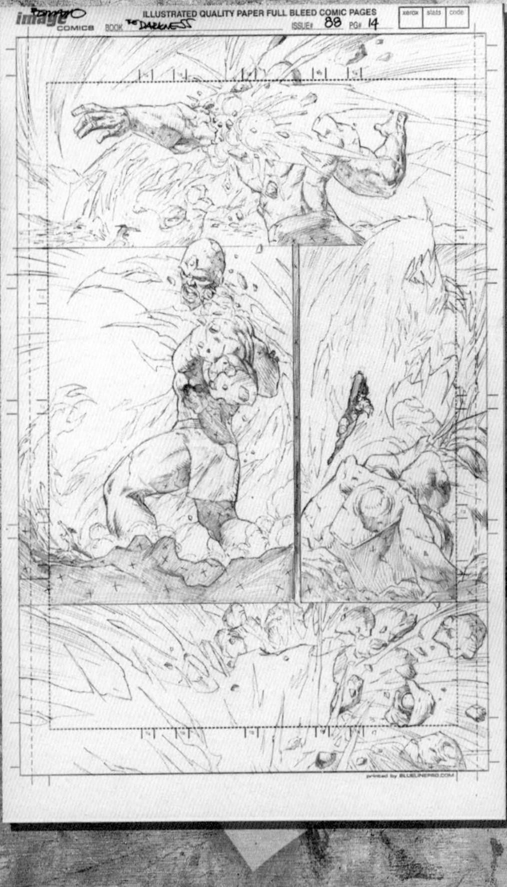
image COMICS
ILLUSTRATED QUALITY PAPER FULL BLEED COMIC PAGES
BOOK THE DARKNESS ISSUE# 88 PG# 14
xerox stats code
printed by BLUELINEPRO.COM

DARKNESS #88 PAGE 14
Jackie pummels the stone Sovereign into bits until only the skull is whole. Jackie stomps it into dust, but like cracking a shell, reveals a blinding light from within.

JACKIE: Fine. I was sick of your shit the first day I met you.

JACKIE: Now I just want you gone.

SOVEREIGN: N- Not just ye–

JACKIE: Didn't you hear me? I said, "Shut-"

JACKIE: "Up!"

SFX: K-krakk!

DARKNESS #88 PAGE 15
Unearthly, intense light pours from the Sovereign's smaller, radioactive body. It melts Jackie's Darkness armor away, causing him to fall to the ground. The Sovereign presses his attack, knocking the light-weakened Jackie around like a rag doll.

JACKIE: Gahh!

SFX: Fwasssh!

SOVEREIGN: To think an ageless lord of men could be brought low by a skittering, accursed thief.

SFX: Fssss!

SOVEREIGN: You came close, I must say. Closer than you had any right to.

SFX: K-krrakkk!

SOVEREIGN: But in the end it was all folly.

image COMICS
ILLUSTRATED QUALITY PAPER FULL BLEED COMIC PAGES
THE DARKNESS
ISSUE# 88 PG# 15
xerox stats code
printed by BLUELINEPRO.COM

image COMICS
ILLUSTRATED QUALITY PAPER FULL BLEED COMIC PAGES
THE DARKNESS
ISSUE# 88 PG# 16
xerox stats code
printed by BLUELINEPRO.COM

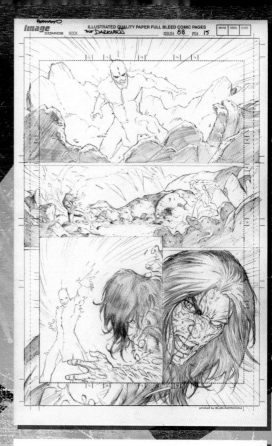

DARKNESS #88 PAGE 16
Radioactive Sov's mere presence subjects Jackie to intense, blistering burns. His armor melts away like wax. Jackie summons one last act of defiance, attempting to choke The Sov, but is rebuffed.

SOVEREIGN: In the thirtieth year of my earthly reign, a star fell from the sky. A meteorite we would call it today.

SOVEREIGN: But this vessel from the gods contained a metal unlike anything ever mined by men.

SOVEREIGN: Its substance was soft to the touch, like clay, but burned like fire.

SOVEREIGN: And gave off light as bright as the sun's, both day and night.

SOVEREIGN: Radioactive, in current nomenclature. Ah, but you know this already.

SOVEREIGN: You feel it.

JACKIE: Nnnngghh!

SOVEREIGN: Of course, I commissioned my likeness to be hewn from the stuff of stars. What ruler wouldn't?

SOVEREIGN: Over one hundred artisans died before this sculpture was completed.

SOVEREIGN: SOVEREIGN: Many of them quite talented.

JACKIE: L- Let me try!

JACKIE: Graah!

DARKNESS #88 PAGE 17
The Sov gloats, his energy roasting Jackie's flesh right off of his bones. Jackie is near death.

SOVEREIGN: It burns, does it not? That's why I saved it for last.

SOVEREIGN: Saved it just for you.

SOVEREIGN: I sent this form as a gift to a Pharaoh who had vexed me.

SOVEREIGN: It wasted his entire kingdom, poisoned his subjects.

SOVEREIGN: He encased me in this once fearsome sphinx to try and seal the poison.

SOVEREIGN: As you can see by this landscape, it was only partially successful.

SOVEREIGN: Now where are you going?

SOVEREIGN: Really, my boy, I'm doing you a favor.

SOVEREIGN: The life you were leading, it was no life at all.

SOVEREIGN: All your days a puppet for one demon or another, human or otherwise.

SOVEREIGN: Unloving. Unloved.

SOVEREIGN: Painful though this may be, it was your ultimate destination.

SOVEREIGN: You will pass unnoticed. Unclaimed.

JACKIE (weakly): H- Hope.

SOVEREIGN: What's that?

JACKIE (weakly): I- I'm sorry, Hope.

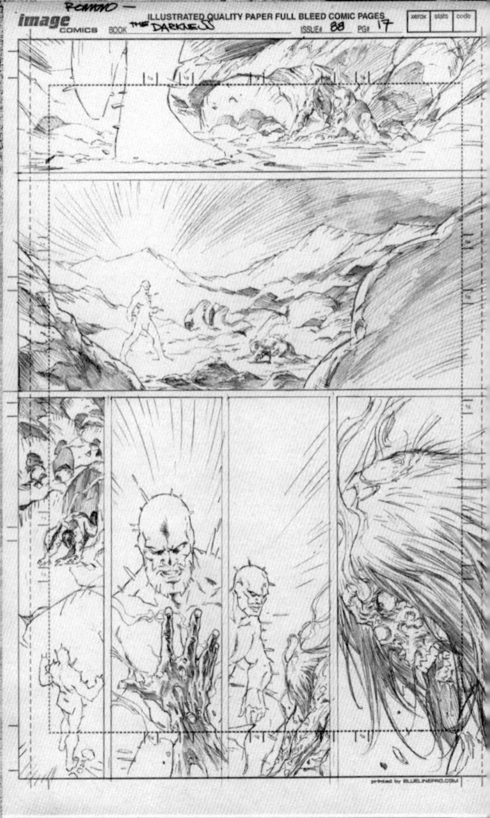

image COMICS
ILLUSTRATED QUALITY PAPER FULL BLEED COMIC PAGES
BOOK THE DARKNESS
ISSUE# 88 PG# 17
xerox stats code

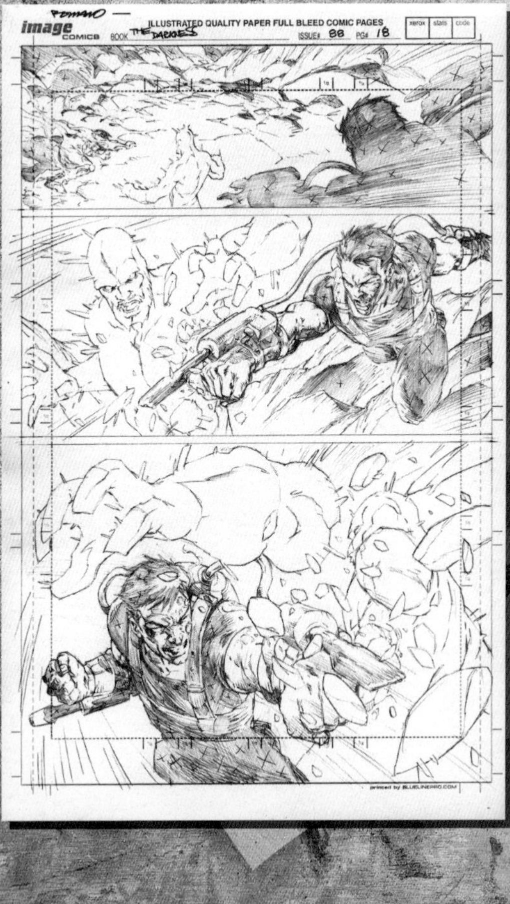

image COMICS
ILLUSTRATED QUALITY PAPER FULL BLEED COMIC PAGES
BOOK THE DARKNESS
ISSUE# 88 PG# 18
xerox stats code

DARKNESS #88 PAGE 18
As Sov gloats, Kim appears with a pneumatic hammer and starts blasting away at the Sov's clay-like flesh.

SOVEREIGN: This has become too piteous to witness, even for me.

SOVEREIGN: Let us end this.

KIM: Yeah...

KIM: Let's.

SFX: K-thudd!

DARKNESS #88 PAGE 19
Although the radiation roasts him, as well, Kim keeps hammering away on The Sov until he's just a puddle of glowing clay.

KIM: You had me, you know? That spell with all the treasure.

KIM: I would have soaked that shit up forever. Slept on piles of gold until I withered and died.

SFX; K-thudd!

SOVEREIGN: You fool! This form will burn you as well.

SOVEREIGN: Your humanity is no protection!

SFX: K-thudd!

KIM: Humanity. That's where you fucked up.

SFX: K-thudd!

KIM: There was no one in the dream to share it with.

SOVEREIGN: No. It cannot be...

SOVEREIGN: My end cannot come in such an undignified mann-

SFX: Splutch.

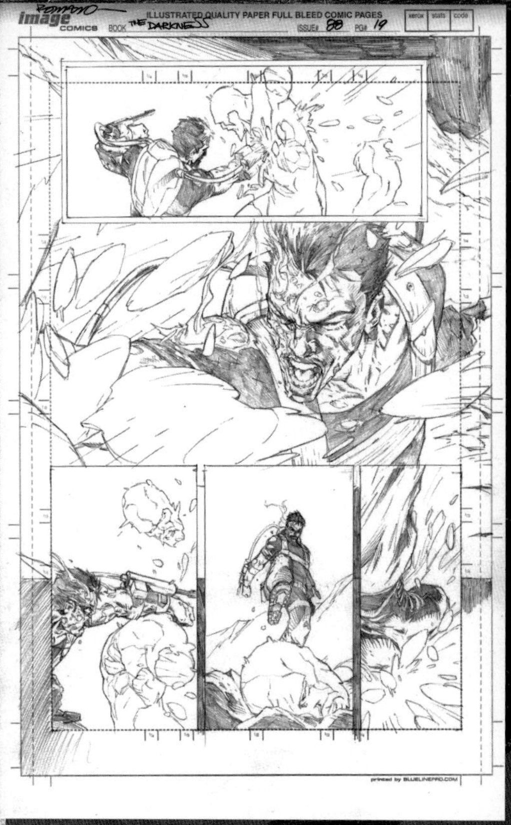
image COMICS
ILLUSTRATED QUALITY PAPER FULL BLEED COMIC PAGES
BOOK THE DARKNESS
ISSUE# 88 PG# 19
xerox stats code
printed by BLUELINEPRO.COM

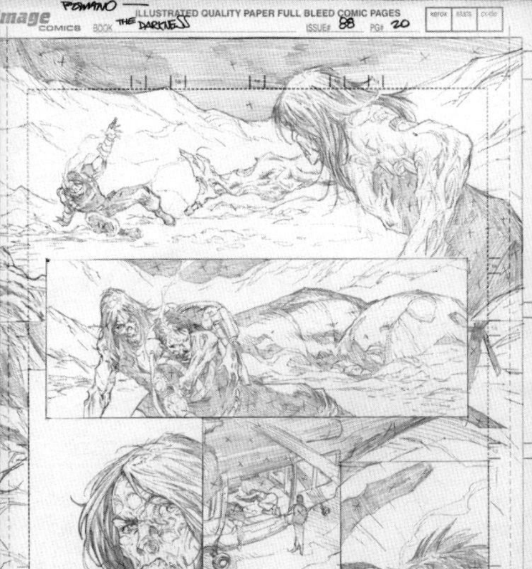
image COMICS
ILLUSTRATED QUALITY PAPER FULL BLEED COMIC PAGES
BOOK THE DARKNESS
ISSUE# 88 PG# 20
xerox stats code
printed by BLUELINEPRO.COM

DARKNESS #88 PAGE 20
The radiation overcomes Kim, who Jackie just manages to drag away. Jackie's armor reforms as he crouches over a dying Kim.

KIM: Uhh!

TYNE: He saved your life.

JACKIE: D- Don't remind me.

SFX: Thrappp!

SFX: Kroom!

JACKIE: Kim, what the hell were you thinking?

KIM (weak): Back when we- when we first met...

KIM (weak): You had me dead to rights, working for the Sovereign. You could have killed me.

KIM (weak): Hell, you should have.

KIM (weak): W- We're square now.

KIM (weak): Besides, two- two million bucks...

KIM (weak): Is two million bucks.

JACKIE: Let me help you, Kim. Maybe I can fix-

KIM: No!

KIM (weak): No offense, boss, but I don't want that shit in me... not even a little.

DARKNESS #88 PAGE 21
Kim dies. Vike and Kash come to, unaware of their friend's sacrifice.

JACKIE: I can't blame you.

KIM (weak): Make sure my little girl– make sure she gets my share.

KIM (weak): The whole thing, you understand?

JACKIE: Forget about that now.

KIM (weak): No. Gotta provide... Never been a decent father. Not for a fucking second.

KIM (weak): But at least...

KIM (weak): At least now I can provide.

KIM (weak): For Miriam.

KASH: What the hell just happened here?

VIKE: Got the mother of all hangovers somehow.

TYNE: Stay back, please. For your safety.

VIKE: What's the big deal, Tyne? The fight's over.

TYNE: Not entirely, Vike.

TYNE: Just the one you can see.

image COMICS
ILLUSTRATED QUALITY PAPER FULL BLEED COMIC PAGES
BOOK THE DARKNESS
ISSUE# 88 PG# 21
xerox stats code
printed by BLUELINEPRO.COM

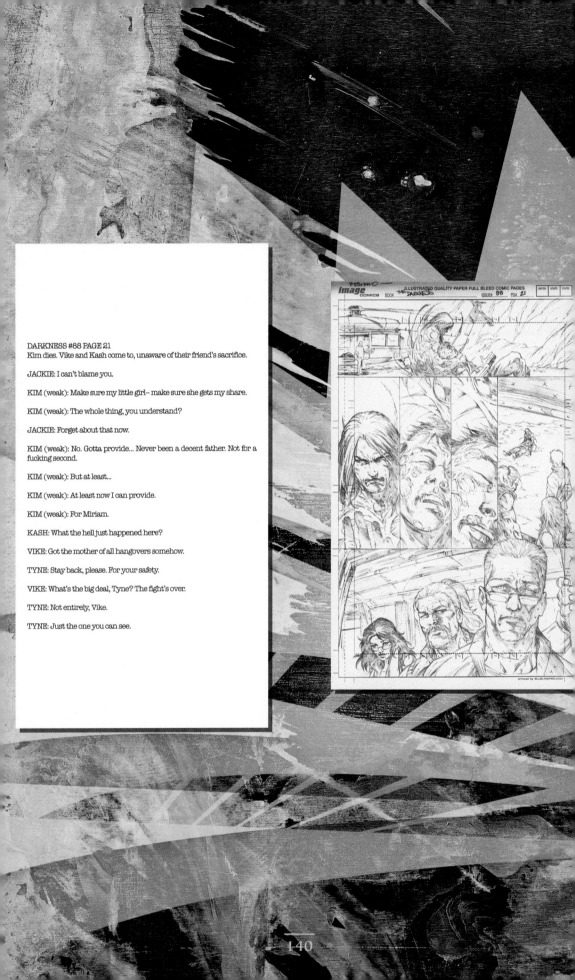

Join the Top Cow Universe with The Darkness!

The Darkness
Accursed vol. 1

written by:
Phil Hester

pencils by:
Michael Broussard

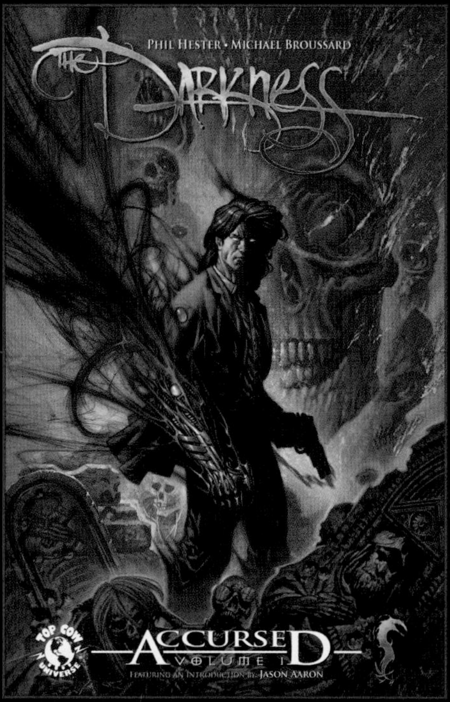
PHIL HESTER • MICHAEL BROUSSARD
The Darkness
ACCURSED
VOLUME 1
FEATURING AN INTRODUCTION BY JASON AARON

Mafia hitman Jackie Estacado was both blessed and cursed on his 21st birthday when he became the bearer of The Darkness, an elemental force that allows those who wield it access to an otherwordly dimension and control over the demons who dwell there. Forces for good in the world rise up to face Jackie and the evil his gift represents, but there is one small problem. In this story... they are the bad guys.

Now's your chance to read "Empire," the first storyline by the new creative team of Phil Hester (Firebreather, Green Arrow) and Michael Broussard (Unholy Union) that marked the shocking return of The Darkness to the Top Cow Universe!

Book Market Edtion
ISBN 13: 978-1-58240-958-0
$9.99

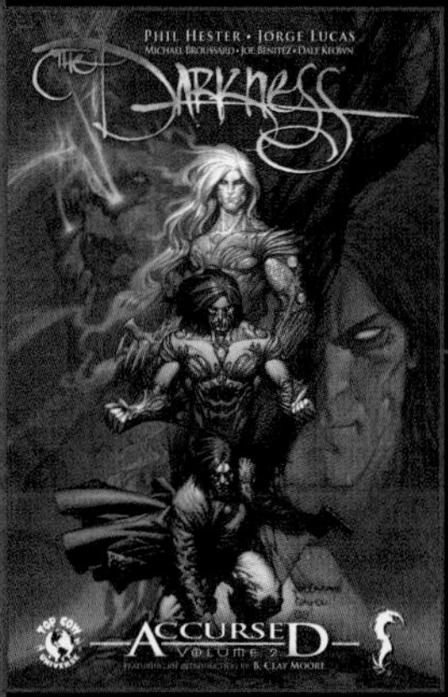
PHIL HESTER • JORGE LUCAS
The Darkness
ACCURSED
VOLUME 2

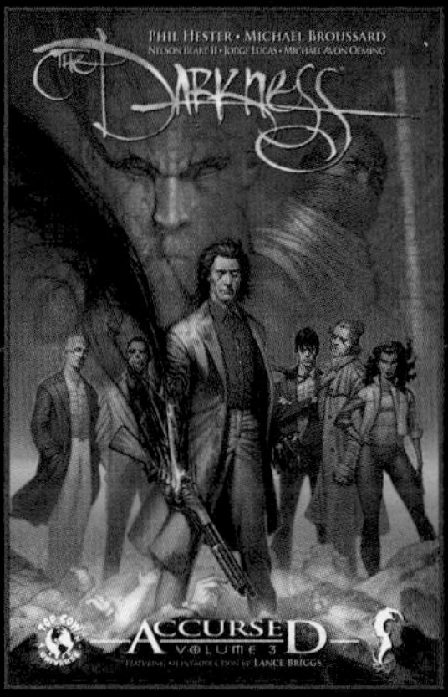
PHIL HESTER • MICHAEL BROUSSARD
The Darkness
ACCURSED
VOLUME 3

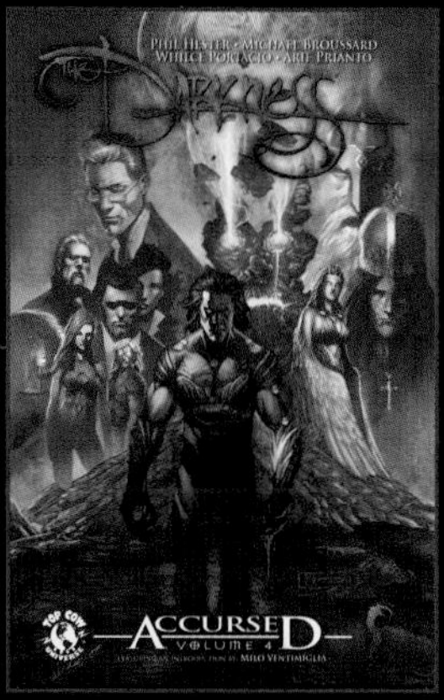
The Darkness
ACCURSED
VOLUME 4

The Darkness
Accursed vol.2
978-1-60706-0-444
$9.99

The Darkness
Accursed vol.3
978-1-60706-1-007
$12.99

The Darkness
Accursed vol.4
978-1-60706-1-946
$14.99

Ready for more? Jump into the Top Cow Universe with *Witchblade*!

Witchblade
volume 1 - volume 8

written by:
Ron Marz
art by:
Mike Choi, Stephen Sadowski, Keu Cha, Chris Bachalo, Stjepan Sejic and more!

Get in on the ground floor of Top Cow's flagship title with these affordable trade paperback collections from Ron Marz's series-redefining run on *Witchblade*! Each volume collects a key story arc in the continuing adventures of Sara Pezzini and the Witchblade, culminating in the epic 'War of the Witchblades' storyline!

Book Market Edtion, volume 1
collects issues #80-#85
(ISBN: 978-1-58240-906-1) $9.99

volume 2
collects issues #86-#92
(ISBN: 978-1-58240-886-6)
U.S.D. $14.99

volume 3
collects issues #93-#100
(ISBN: 978-1-58240-887-3)
U.S.D. $14.99

volume 4
collects issues #101-109
(ISBN: 978-1-58240-898-9)
U.S.D. $17.99

volume
collects issues #110-
First Born issues
(ISBN: 978-1-58240-89
U.S.D. $1

volume 6
collects issues #116-#120
(ISBN: 978-1-60706-041-3)
U.S.D. $14.99

volume 7
collects issues #121-#124 &
Witchblade Annual #1
(ISBN: 978-1-60706-058-1)
U.S.D. $14.99

volume 8
collects issues #125-#130
(ISBN: 978-1-60706-102-1)
U.S.D. $14.99

Explore more of the Top Cow Universe!

Ron Marz • Michael Broussard
ARTIFACTS
volume 1
FEATURING AN INTRODUCTION BY
MARC SILVESTRI

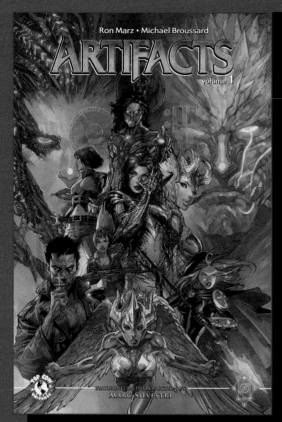

Artifacts
Volume 1

written by:
Ron Marz
pencils by:
Michael Broussard &
Stjepan Sejic

When a mysterious antagonist kidnaps Hope, the daughter of Sara Pezzini and Jackie Estacado, Armageddon is set in motion. Featuring virtually every character in the Top Cow Universe, Artifacts is an epic story for longtime fans and new readers alike.

Collects issues #0-4

(ISBN 978-1-60706-201-1)

From the pages of Witchblade
RON MARZ • STJEPAN SEJIC
ANGELUS
volume 1
FEATURING AN INTRODUCTION BY
ANGELA ROBINSON

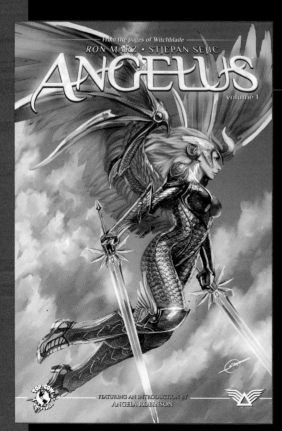

Angelus
Volume 1

written by:
Ron Marz
art by:
Stjepan Sejic

Like so many other twenty-somethings, Danielle Baptiste is trying to find her place in the world. But for Dani, that also means bearing up under the burden of acting as host for one of the Universe's primal forces - The Angelus! Returning to her hometown of New Orleans with her friend and romantic interest Finch, Dani must face an attack from her ancient enemy, the Darkness, as well as betrayal by the very warriors who pledged to serve her.

Collects issues #1-6

(ISBN 978-1-60706-198-4)

Join the Top Cow Universe with The Magdalena!

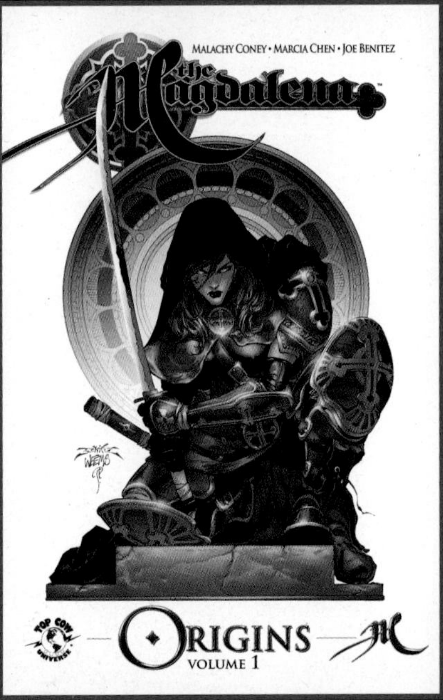
MALACHY CONEY • MARCIA CHEN • JOE BENITEZ
the Magdalena
ORIGINS
VOLUME 1

Magdalena: Origins
Volume 1

written by:
Malachey Coney
art by:
Joe Benitez & Marcia Chen

Discover the Origin of the Magdalena! Patience was not the first Magdalena. Not even the first to make her presence known in the modern Top Cow Universe. Go back and rediscover the origins of the Order of the Magdalena in this first of two "Origin" trade paperback volumes. This collected edition includes the first appearance of the Magdalena by Malachy Coney and superstar Joe Benitez when she came to slay Jackie Estacado in The Darkness Vol. 1 #15-#18. Also collected in this edition is the first three issue limited series starring the Magdalena by Marcia Chen (Wriathborn) and Joe Benitez.

(ISBN: 978-1-60706-2-059) $14.99

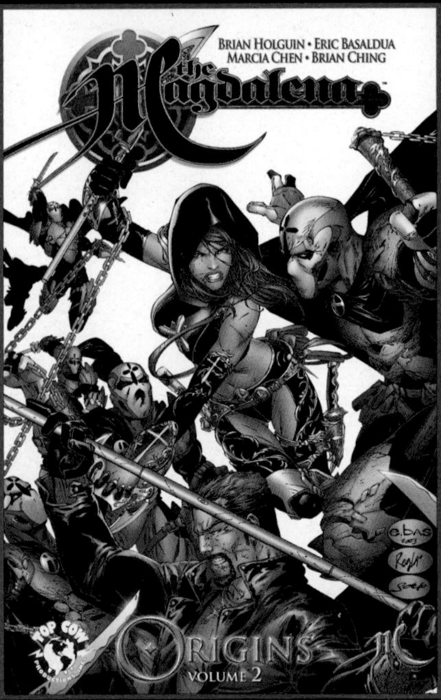
BRIAN HOLGUIN • ERIC BASALDUA
MARCIA CHEN • BRIAN CHING
the Magdalena
ORIGINS
VOLUME 2

Magdalena: Origins
Volume 2

written by:
Malachey Coney
art by:
Joe Benitez & Marcia Chen

Go back and rediscover the origins of the Order of the Magdalena in this second of two "Origin" trade paperback volumes. This collected edition includes Magdalena's first encounter with The Angelus by Marcia Chen and classic Top Cow artist Brian Ching in Magdalena/Angelus #1/2. Also collected is the second four-issue limited series starring the Magdalena by Brian Holguin and Eric "ebas" Basaludua.

(ISBN: 978-1-60706-2-127) $16.99